Greed, Rage, and Love Gone Wrong

Greed, Rage, and Love Gone Wrong

Murder in Minnesota

Bruce Rubenstein

University of Minnesota Press

Minneapolis • London

Four lines of Isabella Gardner's poem "That Was Then" are reprinted from *The Collected Poems of Isabella Gardner* (Rochester: BOA Editions, 1990). Copyright 1990 by the Estate of Isabella Gardner. Reprinted with the permission of BOA Editions, Ltd.

Published by the University of Minnesota Press
111 Third Avenue South, Suite 290
Minneapolis, MN 55401-2520
http://www.upress.umn.edu

Library of Congress Cataloging-in-Publication Data

Rubenstein, Bruce, 1938-
   Greed, rage, and love gone wrong : murder in Minnesota / Bruce Rubenstein.
      p. cm.
   ISBN 0-8166-4337-7 (hc/j : alk. paper)
   1. Murder—Minnesota—Case studies. 2. Murderers—Minnesota—Biography. I. Title.

HV6533.M6R83 2004
364.152′3′09776—dc22

                                             2004009075

Printed in the United States of America on acid-free paper

The University of Minnesota is an equal-opportunity educator and employer.

12 11 10 09 08 07 06 05 04   10 9 8 7 6 5 4 3 2 1

Contents

Preface

There are no good reasons to commit murder, but there are many bad ones. That truism didn't dawn on me until I decided to make a career of writing and started poking around for something to write about. Since then, I've done stories on numerous other topics—the farm crisis, big-ticket litigation, WWF wrestling, financial fraud, politics—but none of them possesses the innate and faintly illicit fascination of murder.

Truman Capote's *In Cold Blood* (1966) and *The Executioner's Song* (1979) by Norman Mailer are the classics of the true murder genre. Those books inspired many writers, but something that occurred between their publication dates had more practical significance. The federal Freedom of Information Act was passed in 1974, and most states followed suit with their own open records laws. As a result millions of documents that once were closed are open for scrutiny, and legions of lawyers and law officers have clammed up for fear that something in the files will contradict them. That second phenomenon has been less remarked on than the first but is just as important, and together they go a long way toward explaining the explosion of investigative journalism and the "gotcha" mentality that pervades it.

It's hard to top the thrill of catching a public servant in a lie, but the records themselves are the really intriguing items in criminal cases. It can be hard work wading through all the extraneous information that official filings seem to require, not to mention deciphering the acronyms, abbreviations, and misspellings, but it is usually worth it. They are full of the kind of baffling, enigmatic, and sometimes poetic details that make a story come alive. They often identify people of interest to investigators who prove to be peripheral to the case but can provide revelations about the context of a crime that never show up in daily journalism.

For example, in 1982 I wrote about the murder of a teenage prostitute for a Twin Cities weekly. She had been found dead in the front seat of a car that sat in a St. Paul alley with its motor running for most of a winter night before someone called the cops. The killer shot her in the back of the head, and then he and the driver fled the scene on foot. The papers described it as a gang-related slaying, but the files revealed that it was more like Romeo and Juliet, with Crips and Bloods feuding instead of Montagues and Capulets. The file noted that a brand-new crucifix hung around the dead girl's neck, and a beeper on the dashboard paged her continuously while investigators searched the car for clues. The noise proved so distracting that they finally had to turn it off.

Their report noted that the girl's street name was Ree, and she had recently dropped out of a suburban high school. The crucifix was a gift from a school friend who had hoped she would come back to the church. The woman who had been paging her, presumably to arrange tricks, was known as "Madam Nhu." The report gave the madam's phone number, so I called and inquired after Ree, assuming I would be talking to a remorseless bitch. Instead a woman with a tiny voice said, "Oh, sir, something terrible has happened to Miss Ree," and she burst into tears.

"The Crucifix and the Beeper" didn't make it into this collection, but ten other stories of murder in Minnesota did. The perpetrators are driven by an array of manias—nympho, pyro, klepto, dipso. Five or six of them (depending on the standard one employs) are cold-blooded killers, and at least three are hybrids who carried out methodically planned homicides for some of the most irrational motives you can imagine. It's no exaggeration to say that they are worthy of fiction. The creepy thing is, they're real.

I have worked with many editors and argued with them all. Even the worst of them prevented me from making some bad mistakes and the best did more than that. I want to especially acknowledge Chuck Carman, a demanding editor who insists that good writing is valuable and a publisher who puts his money where his mouth is.

The Family That Couldn't Sleep at Night

The region near St. Cloud, Minnesota, is blessed with an abundance of high-quality granite, both pink and gray, that can be quarried, slabbed, and sold for a variety of purposes. Granite makes a stately staircase or a handsome gravestone, and it was once the material of choice for prison construction. Slabbed granite is not especially serviceable as a grinding agent, but in a pinch it will do; witness the innumerable weapons that have been fashioned by rubbing pieces of metal against the gray walls of the St. Cloud prison. In fact, the same qualities that make St. Cloud Gray so highly favored for mausoleums and prisons—density, impenetrability, mass—make it useful for sharpening blades.

There are problems, though, practical matters that must be recognized and addressed. Chief among them is the presence of scratches on the grinding surface, something guards are always looking for. If cell walls were made of diamonds, there wouldn't be any scratches to hide (a possibility that prisoners daydream about), but if dreams came true, prisons would be empty, so the inmates make do with what they have, then cover the marred surface with a carefully placed footlocker, a picture of mom, any old thing.

There is no record of what inmate No. 22121 used to hide the scratches on his cell wall during the first half of September 1958. The 22,120 inmates who had preceded him had developed a substantial body of knowledge regarding knives, so it could not have been much of a problem. All we know for sure is that sometime in early September, while the junior guards walked the dog shift and insomnia-plagued prisoners turned things over in their minds, No. 22121 took to rubbing a table knife with a round end against the wall of his cell.

Approximately ten hours of work are required to produce a proper point, and sleep eventually overwhelms even the most troubled mind, so his task must have consumed the better part of two weeks. He probably lay on his side, face to the wall, footlocker pulled slightly askew, and scraped. He used only a downward stroke because an up-and-down motion will produce vibrations, even through granite, and those vibrations might reach the ear of a guard. So it was down down down on one side, then down down down on the other.

By the second week the point was no longer blunt to the touch. Now the blade had to be ground at an angle, requiring either a circular or a back and forth motion. Two or three passes and a pause. Two or three more. No vibrations.

By the morning of September 15, No. 22121 had managed to fashion a deadly weapon out of a standard institutional table knife. He told the guard on duty that morning that he was feeling sick and didn't want to go to his job in the tailor shop.

As soon as the guard left, he pulled his blanket over his head, plunged the knife into his stomach, drew it out, and stabbed himself again. Neither wound was immediately fatal. At that point it may have crossed his mind to go for his heart, but he would have resisted the impulse, remembering the time a year ago almost to the day when he hid in a thicket near the bodies of his dead brothers and turned his pistol on himself. The bullet nicked his heart, leaving him alive but permanently weakened.

So James O'Kasick, twenty, the last survivor of the infamous O'Kasick gang, pushed the crudely fashioned knife into his stomach for the third time, curled up around the hilt, and slipped into unconsciousness. He died half an hour later in an ambulance speeding toward St. Cloud Hospital, while attendants, for reasons that wouldn't have made any sense to him, tried to save his life.

Dad

Everett Warren Allen was walking down Franklin Avenue one winter night when the snow came whipping in on a bitter west wind, and the dog shit on the sidewalk was frozen hard enough to stub your toe. He didn't have anything but a pint of wine, four dollars, a wrist watch, and a pocket knife to scare the muggers away. He stopped at the corner, snuck a hit of wine, then capped the bottle again with numb fingers, all the while peeking furtively down the side street to see if anyone was watching. Somebody was. Hold on there, partner, he heard the guy say.

Maybe the arc light swinging in the wind cast a feral glint off Michael O'Kasick's lazy eye. It certainly shed enough light for Everett to recognize one of the meanest drunks on the Avenue heading his way.

That you Mike? Everett said, as Mike drew near.

Mike didn't answer. He just stood there, glaring. A gust of wind stung the back of Everett's bare neck. He pushed his hands into his pockets and felt for his knife. There it was, under the Zippo. He knew right then he didn't have the guts to use it.

Wouldn't have a few bucks to spare? Mike asked. Naw, I ain't got nothing, Everett replied. Yeah, you do, you've got that watch, Mike said. I seen that before you put your hands in your pockets.

Can't give you that, Mike.

You son of a bitch, Mike said, let's just see what you've got. He grabbed Everett Warren Allen by the arm, pulled him down the side street, and tried to trip him.

Everett was a lot bigger than Mike (everybody was bigger than Mike), so he didn't fall. He kept his balance and started to walk away.

Mike grabbed him again. Just a damn minute, he said, and he pulled a toy gun out of his pocket.

Now what is this crazy bastard up to? Everett thought. Am I supposed to pretend he's fooling me with that thing?

See what this is? This here is a gun!

Yeah, yeah, Everett said, and he started to walk away again.

Mike ran up and punched him on the back of the head. He leaped on him and pulled him to the ground. This is a gun, you son of a bitch, DID'JA HEAR ME? A GUN! He kicked Everett in the ribs.

Everett gave Mike everything he had so he wouldn't get beat up any more, even gave him what was left of the wine. Mike stuffed the bills, the knife, the watch, and the toy gun into his pockets, kicked Everett one more time just for the hell of it, then walked off up the Avenue. He paused and took a long swig from the bottle. He drained it and laughed.

YOU BASTARD, Everett heard himself yelling after Mike, and he lowered his voice abruptly—I'll get you for this, he muttered.

Mike just shot him a dirty look and flung the empty bottle back in his direction. It skidded past him on the crusty snow.

An hour later Mike was bellied up to the bar at the Brite Spot, with one foot on the rail, and Everett's last buck tucked under an empty glass in front of him. He had a nice glow on, and he was trying to get the bartender's attention, when all of a sudden the joint hushed up, literally went silent, behind him. He turned around. There was Everett Warren Allen in the doorway with a cop.

That's him, officer, Mike O'Kasick! He done it. Watch out! He's got a gun!

Now wait a minute, Mike started to say, but the cop drew his pistol, and yelled FREEZE!

Mike froze.

3/18/50–Michael O'Kasick sentenced to two to fifteen years in Stillwater prison for robbery from one Everett Warren Allen, cash and items of value in the amount of $11.52: cash, $4.44; ballpoint pen, 98 cents; pocketknife, $1; watch, $5.

The Family

A probation officer once described Mrs. Florence O'Kasick as "passive, run down, beaten." A friend of the family told a *St. Paul Dispatch* reporter, "The old man would get drunk and beat her and the kids up. She developed a nervous disorder, and just fell apart and died one day, back in '52."

"None of us can forget mother," Doris O'Kasick told a reporter after her brothers were killed. "She just couldn't keep up with it. She died of a broken heart."

Roger O'Kasick was the smartest one in the family, a bookworm who shut himself up in his rented room and read books from the library. He was a rebel and a scofflaw, but he never had an overdue library book. It was a matter of pride with him. When he wasn't reading, he hung around bars and pool halls, and showed off by carrying a gun.

His sister Joyce called him the bitter one, the quiet one, who would pick a fight for no reason at all. The family's poverty just gnawed at him, she said. According to a social worker at Phillips Junior High, he had sadistic tendencies. He was sent to Red Wing Reformatory for burglarizing a safe at Phillips when he was seventeen, and joined the army to get an early release.

For a few weeks after he was discharged, he treated his sister Doris like a girlfriend. He took her out to movies, bought her flowers, held her hand when they walked down Franklin Avenue. Doris told a reporter that she thought it was curious the way he acted. The neighbors had always gossiped about incest in the O'Kasick home. The oldest brother, Richard, later verified that Michael O'Kasick sexually assaulted his own daughters.

As a child Roger was shy and ashamed of his threadbare clothes, but by 1957, when he was twenty-six, the police described him as a flashy barroom tough who dressed in straw hats, single-breasted black sport coats, and cream-colored, draped pants that cut his patent leather shoes just so, about an inch above the heel. They said he bolstered his courage with liquor and was prone to sudden, destructive rages.

Roger's little brother Ronnie was driving around in a stolen car one night in November 1951 with a buddy of his from Franklin Avenue. A cold sleet that sometimes turned to snow was falling. Mom was dead.

Ronnie wanted to get some money so he could go to California and get

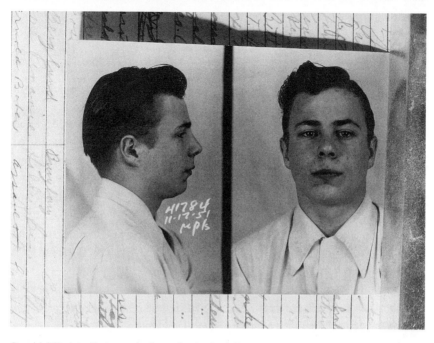

Ronald O'Kasick. Photographs from the St. Paul Dispatch-Pioneer Press News Negative Collection. Courtesy of the Minnesota Historical Society.

Roger O'Kasick. Photographs from the St. Paul Dispatch-Pioneer Press News Negative Collection. Courtesy of the Minnesota Historical Society.

warm. The fuel company had cut them off, and there was no heat in the house. He'd been cold for days.

They drove slowly by the Maddox Grocery on Twenty-sixth Avenue SE. This is called casing the joint, Ronnie told his pal.

It looked like an easy heist, a breeze, even with a toy gun, which was all they had. Ronnie went in while his friend waited in the car. He pointed the gun at the store owner. This is a stickup, mister, he said. Hand over all your money!

The grocer came over the counter, grabbed him by the shirt, and threw him through the storefront window. He and his buddy escaped in the stolen car, ditched it a few blocks away, and started walking back to the Avenue. The sidewalks were ankle deep in icy slush. Ronnie's hand was badly cut, and they made a few lame jokes about the trail of blood they were leaving.

Later that night Ronnie was arrested. He pleaded guilty to attempted robbery and was sentenced to the St. Cloud prison in January 1952. He was eighteen.

He got out a year later and married soon after. He had two children by the time he was twenty-one. He often told his wife about his early home life, how his mother had died when he and his brothers and sisters were kids. He said they didn't have much money and were hungry many times. They lived in a tiny house right across the street from Phillips Junior High, so their pitiful life was on permanent display for their classmates. Sometimes the old man would get drunk on the Avenue and stagger home, but fail to make it through the door. Instead he'd pass out and spend the night in the front yard.

People seemed to agree that Ronnie was a likable guy. He had many friends around Minneapolis, good friends, according to a pal of his, who talked to a reporter in September 1957. The interview took place in a graveyard. His friends had gotten some money together to give Ronnie a little funeral, and the press showed up, as they inevitably did at any venue that might produce some tidbit about the O'Kasick gang.

Ronnie's buddies got drunk and extolled the virtues of their deceased friend. Gusts of wind sent showers of golden leaves falling on the casket. The gravediggers stood around eyeing the mourners and the reporters, wishing it would end, wishing they could fill the hole and go get drunk themselves. It was their first celebrity funeral.

Even the *Minneapolis Star* had something good to say about Ronnie after he was buried. It said that of the three brothers, Ronnie had the least to answer for. "He shot no one, and may have been an unwilling accomplice," according to the paper.

It was probably true. He was a mope and a sad sack, not a killer. His wife had divorced him by the time he started using a real gun to rob stores, and he spent most of his loot in a vain attempt to win her back. She called him a little guy who always wanted to be big. He was five feet three and weighed 127 pounds. He talked about buying elevator shoes all the time but never got around to it.

Jimmy was the youngest of the three, a brawler, more like Roger, whom he idolized, than Ronnie, whom he protected. Jimmy liked to throw hands. He reveled in duking it out, win, lose, or draw. He approached a fistfight with such gleeful abandon that bigger kids feared him. He once knocked his father down for beating his sister Joyce. He was engaged briefly in 1954, but the girl broke it off when Jimmy beat her up.

Jimmy made his debut in the annals of the criminal justice system in June 1938. He was the "squalling infant" in the arms of his mother, a "distraught, disheveled woman, with missing teeth and a downcast demeanor," according to a report filed by the probation officer, who had come by to see her husband, Mike.

Little Jimmy's face and arms were blotched with angry red welts. He squirmed and yowled so vigorously that the officer inquired about his distress. "We don't have much in the way of screens, and the mosquitoes bite us," Mrs. O'Kasick explained. "We can't sleep at night."

Dress Rehearsals

Jimmy told a social worker at Phillips that he dreamed of quitting school when he was sixteen, and he didn't go one day longer. Neither did Roger or Ronnie. They hung around Fourth and Franklin until all hours of the night. They bought beer at the back door of the Shamrock Bar until they were old enough to walk in the front door. They hung out on the roof of the Tremont Apartments on Eighteenth and Park, where they drank bottles of beer laced with vodka and threw the empties down at passing cars. Here comes another dead soldier! they yelled. Their records show numerous arrests "for investigation."

By 1956 Jimmy was in the Marines. His dad was on parole from Stillwater, working as a bellboy in the Hotel Duluth. The oldest brother, Richard, was the head of the household. Richard found Jesus at the Paul Rader chapel on Lake Street, and he was holding down two jobs to keep the family together in a house on Thirty-eighth Avenue S.

"Either six or seven of them lived there," according to Geraldine Donneley, who lived across the street at the time. "We always called their place 'the renters house' because everybody else on the block owned their homes. Other than that they didn't stand out in any way. The girls were kind of shy as I recall. You never saw much of the men."

The house had two tiny bedrooms, a scale-model living room, and a second-floor bathroom the size of a broom closet. Richard and Ronnie slept in the parlor so they wouldn't disturb the girls when they came home. Both of them stayed out late because of the nature of their work. Richard had a job as a cook at an all-night diner. Ronnie was hanging out with Roger, who had rented a room of his own in south Minneapolis. They were painting houses during the day and sticking up drugstores at night.

Roger had a real gift for casing the joint. Investigators who pieced together the O'Kasicks' career after the first big shoot-out realized that their robberies were planned meticulously. They wore odd but effective disguises and never asked where the money was. They knew. According to the victims, the leader was polite but insistent, assuring them that no one would get hurt unless they did something foolish, in which case they'd be shot. He was the only one who spoke. He kept the discourse to a minimum and used a high, unnatural voice that the victims agreed was false.

Ashley Morse, the pharmacist at Zipp's on Thirty-fifth Avenue S., was preparing to close on a Sunday night in July 1956, when two masked men entered the store. They were "sporting rubber skull masks atop natty blue suits," according to the *Minneapolis Star*, and they held the three customers at bay with "a pair of matching .38s." Morse's wife and his two teenage daughters arrived to take him home while the robbery was in progress. "Hands up," the leader squeaked. They stood with their hands in the air while the pharmacist emptied all four cash registers. He didn't volunteer to open the safe in the back room, but the leader gestured in that direction with his gun and told him to make it snappy. The robbers left with $1,800 cash.

That night police chased a vehicle answering the description of the car used in the holdup but lost it.

A few weeks later, on a warm August evening, Roger Lillemoe was watching TV in his living room. He happened to glance out the open window and saw two men wearing gas masks and carrying canvas bags enter Harold's Pharmacy on Forty-first and Cedar. Lillemoe didn't have a phone, so he ran to a nearby fire station. He tried to get the firemen to interrupt the robbery, but they declined and called the police instead.

Meanwhile, two pistol-toting young men were holding a clerk and the pharmacist at gunpoint. The leader issued a muffled command through his gas mask, and the pharmacist emptied the cash register into one canvas bag, and the safe into another. One of the bandits appeared nervous and anxious. As they exited through the back door, he dropped a bag full of cash in the alley. It contained $274, but they still managed to get away with approximately $1,000. By the time the police arrived, they had sped off in a blue car.

Gunmen with the same MO—masks, car stashed in the alley, previous knowledge of where the money was kept—robbed a pharmacy on Thirty-third and Nicollet a few weeks later. An alarm was sounded, and the police arrived just as the gunmen were pulling away. They headed south on Nicollet with the police in hot pursuit. Shots were exchanged. The squad car overheated so badly the engine seized. It was towed into the police garage, where the repair man discovered two bullet holes through the radiator.

Jimmy O'Kasick must have received a letter from Roger describing this incident. He was stationed in Japan when it took place, but he was able to describe it in detail during his long, rambling, semicomatose confession in General Hospital a year later. He pinpointed it as the incident that prompted his brothers to buy three thick metal plates in a junkyard on Washington Avenue. They would be used to stop bullets in case of another shootout, something Roger fully expected, and apparently looked forward to with relish. Jimmy was discharged from the Marines in April 1957.

According to the *Minneapolis Tribune*, on June 28, 1957, "Three stocky gunmen wearing grotesque rubber monkey masks held up a north Minneapolis drug store, and escaped with about $1,200 after holding nine persons at bay in the store. One of them had a .45, the other two had .38s. They were all wearing dark suits and carrying cloth bags. Marlene Fennig, seventeen, thought she recognized one of the gunmen as a fellow employee playing a joke. She said 'Take off the mask, Leroy.' The bandit poked her with his gun. The leader made Arthur Knight, the store owner, go in back and open his safe. After taking the money, they fled in a blue Oldsmobile. Knight said the bandits appeared young and nervous."

The Minneapolis police knew that a gang of stickup men were robbing pharmacies during the summers of 1956 and 1957. The robberies usually occurred around closing time. At least seven holdups occurred with the same MO—masks, pistols, locations where a large sum of cash was available, and precise knowledge of where it could be found. At first there were two gunmen, but the robbery of Knight's Pharmacy on the north side, and then of the Pennhurst Pharmacy on Fifty-first and Penn Avenue S. in July 1957, involved three men. No one ever saw their faces, but the victims noticed they were of the same smallish stature. At Knight's Pharmacy they appeared to be stocky, but the police decided that was the result of padding.

The gunmen planned their crimes carefully. On several robberies, they used cars that had been stolen that day but with license plates that had been taken off other vehicles months before. They had been chased on two occasions by the police and had shot at and disabled a squad car during one of these chases.

Despite the meticulous planning that could be inferred from their method of operation, they were nervous and anxious during the robberies.

Duel at Apache Wells

During the 1956 Christmas season Ronnie charged $400 worth of merchandise at department stores, sold it in the bars for about $200, and used the cash to buy presents. When the bills came, it was the last straw as far as his wife was concerned. She took the kids and split.

Ronnie bought himself a blue Oldsmobile for three times what it was worth, just to ease the pain in his heart. A few months later Jimmy was discharged from the Marines. He bought a 1941 Cadillac with his mustering-out pay.

So Ronnie and Jimmy had a couple of cool cars to drive around in, and that's what they did that summer of 1957. They drove down Lake Street, one arm out the window and a pack of cigarettes rolled up in the sleeve of their T-shirts. They played the radio so loud—BE-BOP-A-LULA—YOU AIN'T NOTHIN' BUT A HOUND DOG—that adults standing at stoplights plugged their ears, then they revved up and laid rubber when the light changed. They tried drag racing too, but neither car had any guts. Ronnie's transmission slipped, and Jimmy's Caddy V-8 hit on about five cylinders.

Most nights they drove over to the Chat 'N Nibble on Twenty-eighth Street to hustle the carhops. The girls thought they were cute. They always had a few bucks to spend.

One night Ronnie and Jimmy took two carhops to the Hilltop Drive-In Theater to see *Duel at Apache Wells*. They made out a little, sipped vodka from a bottle, and watched while the townsfolk slowly got fed up with the way the outlaws lorded it over the decent people.

The desperados rode through town whooping, hollering, and shooting their six-guns in the air. They got into a brawl at the saloon, then galloped off before the sheriff could put a posse together. A few days later they held up the stage, and when they got away with that, they thought they could get away with anything. Cattle began disappearing from nearby ranches. Half-starved calves wandered the range, bawling for their mamas. Law-abiding citizens were subjected to outrageous indignities whenever the bandits came to town. They drank rotgut by the quart and refused to pay the bar bill. They cheated at cards. They made a lewd pass at the schoolmarm, then beat the bejesus out of her fiancé when he came to her defense.

Jimmy went to the refreshment stand for popcorn and orange drinks.

Ronnie spiked the drinks. They passed the popcorn around. The girls straightened their hair, smoothed their blouses, and put on more lipstick.

One of the girls dropped her barrette. They searched for it in the dim glow of the interior light, among the lipstick-stained popcorn kernels. Jimmy found it behind an iron plate that was leaning against the front seat. What's that thing for anyway? his date asked. Nothing, he said. Ronnie turned out the light, and they watched the movie again.

Emboldened by the inability of upstanding people to cope with their viciousness, the robbers shot the old prospector down like a dog and stole all his gold dust. They descended on the Travis ranch and wrecked that once-proud spread. They burned the bunkhouse, stampeded the horses, and rustled the cattle. They spat in old man Travis's face, punched him in the stomach so hard he puked, and laughed at his wife as she stood in the ranch house door, tears of disbelief in her eyes. How could they be so low-down? How long could the reign of terror last?

In fact, it was just about over. The sheriff and some men he deputized for the occasion caught up with the outlaws at Apache Wells. There was a shootout, in which a few good guys and a number of bad guys bit the dust. True to their code, the survivors vowed they'd never be taken alive. Then I'm coming to git'cha, said the sheriff, and by god he did. It wasn't pretty.

After the movie they stopped at the Sunset Drive-In on Central Avenue for french fries and cherry cokes. The girls got a bang out of having carhops wait on them. It was a busman's holiday.

Shootout

An ex-convict who had met Ronnie in the St. Cloud prison gave the following account to the *Minneapolis Star*: "I told Ronnie I'd meet up with him when I got out, and I did. It was the spring of '57. We went into business together, painting houses. He had a beat-up Oldsmobile that wasn't worth $200, but he owed 450 bucks on it. They used to take it to drive-ins, and I guess they used it for their getaway. I'd see those iron plates in it, but when I asked Ronnie what they were for he said 'nothing.' I never saw much of Roger—nobody really knew Roger. I do know he hated cops, just despised them. Ronnie and Jimmy drank two bottles of vodka the day before the cop shooting. They seemed in a big hurry to go someplace. That's the last I saw of them. They disappeared."

On the afternoon of Friday, August 16, 1957, Ronnie and Jimmy met up with their brother Roger. The three of them stole a green Chrysler from a parking lot on Tenth and LaSalle, and drove to a wooded lot near a cemetery on Forty-second Street and Fourth Avenue S. They put the steel plates in place. They loaded a bag with friction tape, water, purifying tablets, roofing nails to spread behind them in case of a chase, and surgical bandages.

Roger kept the guns between holdups and was in charge of buying bullets. While he was off fetching the arsenal, Ronnie and Jimmy fastened a pair of license plates they had stolen several months ago over the Chrysler's plates.

They thought the police were no longer looking for the stolen plates, but they were wrong. The numbers were on a list taped to the dash of every patrol car in town.

Early Saturday evening, August 17, the O'Kasicks picked up the Chrysler where they had ditched it the day before, and set out to rob the Red Owl Super Market on Hennepin and Twenty-fourth. Ronnie and Jimmy were hung over, and all three of them were more nervous than usual before a holdup. There was more was at stake. The Red Owl promised to be a big score, maybe $10,000.

It was a warm evening with plenty of shoppers and lots of traffic. Ronnie was at the wheel. Roger sat next to him with a loaded pistol on his lap and bandoliers of ammunition crisscrossed under his suit coat. Jimmy was in back with a 30-30 rifle. A seventy-pound metal plate was propped up on the seat behind him. They wore white ties, black shirts, and straw hats.

They cruised slowly west on Lake Street, waiting for dark, which was still twenty minutes away. It was a measure of their anxiety that they were on the street so early and so well armed, and it may have been a measure of something else as well. Roger called the shots, and according to many who knew him, he had an irrational hatred of policemen. He was spoiling for a fight. His behavior during the two violent episodes that would soon occur stamped him as a person with an utter disdain for death. He might well have welcomed death, as long as he could take a cop or two with him.

Officers Robert Fossum and Ward Canfield were in a squad car driving west on Lake when they spotted the Chrysler a few cars ahead. Within moments they had identified the plates as stolen. The Chrysler was hot, and they soon identified it as well. They may have connected the elements of a recently stolen car combined with old stolen plates to the MO of the stickup men who had robbed Knight's Pharmacy less than three weeks before.

Ronnie spotted the squad car in the rear view mirror. Uh-oh, cops, he said. Roger took one look and ordered him to make a U-turn fast, and that's what he did. He swung a two-wheeler across Lake Street, narrowly missed an oncoming car, and peeled away, weaving in and out of traffic. The cops duplicated the maneuver, lights flashing, siren howling.

Here they come, Jimmy yelled. He was crouched in back of the steel plate with the rifle across his knees, peeking over the top of the seat.

Take a right, Roger said calmly.

They sped south on Blaisdell, with Roger leaning out the door shooting at the cops, and the cops shooting at them. The back window flew to pieces, just disintegrated. Jimmy managed to get the rifle up and fire a few wild shots. They were doing sixty-five miles an hour as they approached the intersection of Thirty-ninth and Blaisdell, where the street doglegged.

Gene Reagan was watching TV when he heard something that might have been gunshots. He ran out to his front lawn just in time to see the Chrysler careen past, try to make the turn, and smash into a parked car. Moments later the police skidded against the curb and almost flipped over before coming to a stop.

Reagan hit the dirt. He saw two cops emerge from the squad car into a hail of gunfire from two nattily dressed gunmen, who had come charging out of the Chrysler. There were dozens of shots. Bullets embedded themselves in Reagan's lawn, 350 feet away. One officer clutched at his stomach and went down almost immediately. The other tried to get off a shot with a riot gun, but it misfired. Then he too fell to the ground.

According to eyewitnesses, one of the gunmen walked calmly over to the second fallen officer, who was frantically cranking the lever of his gun, and executed him with a single shot to the head.

The gunmen ran back to the Chrysler and joined a third man, who was behind the wheel. They tried to leave the scene, but their front fender was tangled up with the parked car they had smashed into. The driver backed up, attempting to pull loose, and in the process ran over the surviving officer, who was trying to crawl away. They dragged him backward about twenty feet, then abandoned the Chrysler for the car it was hooked to (which presumably had the keys in it) and managed to free that car.

Reagan watched as they drove one block to a gas station, jumped out of the car they had just taken, pulled a woman out of her car, and took off at high speed, east on Thirty-ninth.

Mrs. Stanley McGovern had been hiding under her kitchen table. Now she came out with towels to aid the fallen policemen. She found officer Robert Fossum dead, the victim of an armor-piercing .38-caliber slug through the head. Officer Ward Canfield was crumpled in the street behind the abandoned Chrysler. He had a .45-caliber slug in his stomach, two broken collarbones, a crushed chest, a fractured pelvis, a broken knee, and a dislocated hip.

Mrs. McGovern didn't know what to do. She tried to clean up the carnage a little with her towels. She could hear the sound of sirens, getting closer.

Less than three minutes had passed since the police monitored a call from officers Fossum and Canfield, saying that they were chasing a stolen car

Onlookers at the scene shortly after Officer Robert Fossum was killed and Officer Ward Canfield was wounded. Photograph from the St. Paul Dispatch-Pioneer Press News Negative Collection. Courtesy of the Minnesota Historical Society.

south on Blaisdell. Then the radio had gone dead. Moments later phone reports about the gunfight began coming in. Now squad cars and ambulances were converging on the scene from all directions.

Think Think Think

They could hear sirens from Lake Street, and more coming from the east. Roger ordered Jimmy to lie down in back because the police would be looking for three men. We'd better get a woman, he said. Look for a woman.

They spotted Mr. and Mrs. Alvin Anderson driving on First Avenue S. and ran them to the curb. Roger stepped out of the car waving his pistol. Get the hell out of here and get out fast, he told Mr. Anderson. You're coming with us, sister, he said to Mrs. Anderson. They got in the car and left.

As soon as they turned the corner, Alvin Anderson ran to a phone booth and called the police.

Jimmy got on the floor in back, while Mrs. Anderson sat between Ronnie and Roger in front. Roger blindfolded her with her hanky and told Jimmy to reach up and plug her ears with his fingers.

He didn't do a very good job. She heard the leader order them to "think, think, think!" She heard the one in back referred to as "Jim," and heard the driver say, "Forty-second and Second." Sometimes they seemed to be driving fast, other times not so fast. They smelled of liquor. About fifteen minutes after they kidnapped her, they ordered her out, guided her into another automobile, and drove away.

A few minutes later they stopped. She heard the door open. You can leave now, the leader told her.

She heard a scraping sound as their car pulled away, but by the time she dared take the blindfold off, they were gone, leaving only a smear of blue paint on the wooden garage behind 3325 Columbus Avenue S.

A Brave and Fearless Man

Ward Canfield's brother Neil, a park policeman, was one of the first officers to arrive at the scene. He heard the downed officer whisper, "I can't breathe," before losing consciousness.

In the abandoned Chrysler police found a 30-30 Savage rifle, a paper bag containing a hundred bullets, a receipt from the Chat 'N Nibble Drive-In, a box of armor-piercing .38 shells, three metal plates weighing more than seventy pounds each, a bag of roofing tacks, a roll of friction tape, three ticket stubs from the Hilltop Drive-In Theater, some surgical bandages, a box of water-purifying tablets, and a canteen of water.

A straw hat with a white band was left at the scene.

After examining those clues and listening to eyewitness descriptions, they told the press that they were looking for three smallish, flashy barroom toughs in their early twenties who bolstered their courage with liquor. They said the gunmen were part of an element in town that dressed in a certain style featuring straw hats, black shirts, white ties, and dark suits with pegged pants. They considered the gunmen to be the prime suspects in the holdup of Knight's Pharmacy on West Broadway two weeks before, and it was possible that they had been involved in other holdups as well.

They did not publicize the fact that they were looking for someone named Jim, or that they had identified the blue paint on the garage as being off a 1951 or 1952 Oldsmobile.

Robert Fossum was the best kind of police officer, the *Minneapolis Star* reported on August 19, a brave and fearless man who had loved his work. He had three children, said the article, but only one of them was old enough to understand that daddy wasn't coming home anymore.

Fossum had recently purchased a new home for his family. His wife had a police radio set up in the basement that she often monitored to keep track of Bob, but the night of the murder she wasn't listening to it. She was watching TV with the kids, a Western. A news flash broke in, and that is how she found out her husband had been shot to death.

Canfield was brought to Hennepin County General after the shootout and placed under twenty-four-hour-a-day armed guard. The police feared the killers would try to finish the job so he couldn't identify them.

Twelve days later, he suddenly sat up in his hospital bed, a look of confusion on his face. He had been conscious off and on, but this would be the first time he spoke. What happened? he asked officer James Funder. Why are you guarding me? I didn't do anything wrong!

Funder assured him he hadn't. I guess I've been in an accident then, Canfield said. It must have been an awful one. He spied a nurse standing in the doorway. How long have I been here? he asked. Almost two weeks, she replied. You and Mr. Fossum were chasing three boys, about twenty-six years old, and you were shot.

Yes, and they killed Bob! said Canfield. They didn't have to do that. Then he broke down and wept. By the time he regained his composure, a doctor and another nurse had been summoned. They ran over me, he told them. They ran over me with two cars. Bob is better off than me, he said, before losing consciousness again.

"Ward was a big, powerful man, a physical specimen," says William C. Rieman, retired, formerly a detective with the Minneapolis police. "That was what saved him. Otherwise he'd have never survived. He made medical history, had something like fourteen operations. They had to amputate his leg. He even went back to work for awhile, up at the jail, but he was never the same."

Two days after the shootings the police were certain the gunmen were still in town because of the massive dragnet that had been put in place. Charles Wetherille, chief of detectives, told the *Star* that they were "holed up in the city or the suburbs."

The dragnet consisted of every police car in Minneapolis, two cars on loan from St. Paul, the entire state highway patrol, and several roadblocks, where hundreds of people were stopped.

Two days after the shootout, the O'Kasick brothers cashed $60 worth of bum checks at neighborhood drugstores. That afternoon they told their sister they were taking a construction job out of town. The next morning they got into Ronnie's blue Oldsmobile, slipped unnoticed through the massive dragnet, and headed for northern Minnesota.

The Eight-Hooter

Transcript of interrogation of James O'Kasick, Anoka County District Court:

Q: Now Jim, calling your attention to the day of August 19, 1957, what were you doing?

A: I and my two brothers, Ronald and Roger, were together. Leaving Minneapolis.

Q: What kind of car did you have?

A: A 1952 blue Oldsmobile.

Q: When did you leave?

A: About seven or eight in the morning.

Q: Where did you go?

A: First we stopped in a swampy area near Forest Lake, then we went to Superior National Forest that same day.

Q: What did you do when you got there?

A: Echo Trail had a lot of camping spots and so forth. We would go out on the side road where people didn't camp. We picked up groceries and a newspaper on the way. We camped and slept in the car for about a week.

One night it got chilly, down in the low forties. Ronnie was sleeping behind the wheel. He woke up shivering, and started the car to get some heat going. Jimmy was passed out next to him with a bellyful of vodka. He didn't stir, but Roger did. Roger had insomnia. He leaned up in the front seat with his pistol in his hand and asked Ronnie what was happening. I'm cold, Ronnie told him.

When the three of them talked, their conversation centered on questions of will. Would anyone believe they hadn't run over officer Canfield on purpose? Would anyone believe they hadn't set out deliberately to kill a policeman? That it had just happened?

They'd stopped talking about whether or not Roger had stood over Robert Fossum and deliberately shot him to death after Fossum's gun jammed. Eyewitness reports in the newspaper described a cold-blooded murder, but Roger denied it at first. Then he'd begun to equivocate. Maybe he did shoot the cop execution-style. What did it matter? He was dead, either way.

It mattered to Jimmy. A month later in General Hospital he asked Minneapolis police officer Buzz Winslow for the definitive answer. There is no record of Winslow's reply, but Rieman, who was an investigator on the case, says: "I'll tell you what kind of guy this one dink was, this Roger. Our officer Fossum looked him right in the eye, and said, 'please don't shoot me,' but he shot him in the head—bam. Just like that."

Six days after they arrived on the Echo Trail, the O'Kasicks headed south again. They left on a Sunday night for a swampy area about forty miles north of the Twin Cities, where they had first stopped when they left Minneapolis. An investigator later asked Jimmy what they planned to do. He indicated that they were broke, hungry, and had vague plans to pull another stickup.

Maybe they read the Minneapolis papers and were relieved to find that they had gone from front-page headlines to oblivion—that it was no longer possible to read eyewitness accounts of the shootout, details of the investigation, lists of clues. They drove to a phone and called their younger sister, who wanted to know where they were. They just said they'd be home in a week or so.

According to Jimmy, they spent many hours discussing "this Minneapolis thing, this shooting." They talked about surrendering but decided nobody would believe they didn't mean to do it. They wanted to go home, at least Ronnie and Jimmy did, but they couldn't, so they decided to stay put by the swamp.

They slept in the car.

The sounds they heard were of cattle lowing in the distance, leaves scraping as they blew across the gravel road, poplars rattling in the wind. The dry, waist-high grass rustled when they walked through it. Mosquitoes bit them. Horseflies buzzed their ears. At first the sound of gunshots startled them, but they got used to it. It was just the farmers hunting grouse.

At night they heard the eerie cry of the bard owl, known locally as the eight-hooter, and other mysterious noises that might have been raccoons prowling their fire pit. The sounds made Jimmy wakeful. He spent many a long hour dwelling on the fate of the two policemen. Whenever he glanced at Roger, he noticed his eyes were wide open. "I don't think he ever slept," he later told investigators.

It was damp and cool in the morning. Dew had condensed on the car windows, and they got wet to the knees going out in the grass for a morning piss. Roger had them sleeping fully armed with bandoliers of ammunition under their brown leather Ike jackets, and they had to straighten them to get comfortable.

The maple leaves were turning scarlet and orange. Blue meadow aster, purple thistle, goldenrod, and giant ragweed were in full bloom, but the weeds of high summer had already gone to seed, leaving lots of thorns and spiked pods that stuck to their pants.

The three of them talked about this Minneapolis thing constantly. They had made up their minds not to surrender. If they were found, yes, there would be shooting. But even if there was, they would only shoot to wound. At least Ronnie and Jimmy would only shoot to wound. Roger wasn't so sure. He might aim for the head so no one would recognize them, like he had done in Minneapolis.

Later on, Roger made another decision. I'll never be taken alive, he said.

He had some advice for Ronnie and Jimmy. If you can get away with it, just shoot to injure. But if we have to shoot our way through, shoot to kill. If you have a good chance to aim, shoot for the head.

Jimmy said, if we shoot to kill, then I'll have to be on my own. I just have to go it alone. I don't want to kill anybody else.

Shoot to kill, and stick together. That's my advice, Roger exhorted them. They just sort of left it at that.

On Friday, September 7, they were down to less than a quarter tank of gas. They searched under the seats for change and found nine cents. As dusk approached, they began looking for a place to spend the night, when they came upon a little beer joint on a gravel road, right there in the middle of nowhere. Stop, said Roger.

He strolled into the bar with a pistol in his hand and came out a few minutes later with $40 and some change.

I didn't hear any shots, said Jimmy, hopefully.

I didn't have to shoot anybody, Roger replied.

They headed south and spent the night in the woods near Stillwater. The next day they stopped at a hardware store, bought some gray primer, drove into a wooded area on the bluffs outside Red Wing, and painted the car.

"We stayed around there for a few days, then drove up to Eaton's Ranch by Minneapolis, another wooded area," said Jimmy. "Many times we spent hours looking for a wooded area to hide in. On Friday, the thirteenth of September, we headed back toward Forest Lake. Back to the swamp."

Chance Medley

Minneapolis Tribune: "An Anoka area ranch woman said that a friendly look and a gallon of gas could have changed the whole course of events in Saturday's death chase. Mrs. George Pantsar, Coon Creek Ranch, said a young man who would later be identified as Ronald O'Kasick walked into her yard about 5 p.m. Saturday, and asked for gas.

"'I told him we didn't have any,' she said, 'although I really could have given him a gallon or two. I didn't like the way he looked at me. He asked several times if I was sure we didn't have any. I finally convinced him, and he left. I guess it might have changed everything if I'd given him some gas. It haunts me.'"

The O'Kasicks were down to their last few dollars again. They were twenty miles north of the Twin Cities, heading east on Constance Road in Anoka County, looking for a store to rob, when their car ran out of gas. They rolled to a stop at an angle to the curb.

Ronnie walked down to Highway 6 and tried to bum some gas from a woman in a farmyard, but she refused, so he started hitchhiking. Mrs. Kenneth Sunderlin picked him up.

Ronnie had a disarming smile, but at the same time there was something suspicious about him. Mrs. Sunderlin said she was reminded "of those drawings in the *Tribune*, of those killers." She dropped Ronnie off in the tiny village of Coon Rapids, then drove to the police station to tell Chief Al Bomberger about her suspicions.

Ronnie bought about a gallon of gas in a lard bucket he had picked up from a trash barrel, and started walking out of town. Anoka County Sheriff's Deputies James Sampson and Vernon Gottwald happened along. They offered to give him a lift to his car.

Ronnie had no choice. He thanked them and got in.

About that time, Mrs. Marion Lindgren and her daughter Patty, thirteen, were returning to their home on Constance Road. Patty's father had given her $10 to buy a blouse. He had closed his paint store early so he could watch the two younger kids while Patty and her mom went shopping.

Mrs. Lindgren noticed the unfamiliar gray car with its rear end protruding into the road but didn't give it much thought. She let her daughter off in front, then continued down the long driveway to the garage.

Patty ran inside to show her dad the blouse, but before she could unwrap it, Eugene Lindgren said he had a better idea. He would go out in back and work on a fence he was building, while Patty put her new blouse on. In a few minutes he would come back in to see how it looked on her.

The Lindgren's collie, Twinky, was tied up in the front yard, barking.

Jimmy took his turn hiding in the backseat and tried to get some sleep. It was useless. Some dog kept him up with its endless barking, he later told police.

Roger turned on the radio and found a pop music station. Jimmy would later tell investigators that the songs reminded him of summer days driving up and down Lake Street—days when they had money to spend but hadn't murdered anybody yet. So much had happened in such a short time. Everything had changed. He finally dozed a bit.

Meanwhile, Coon Rapids Police Chief Al Bomberger and Mrs. Sunderlin were looking around for Ronnie. Mrs. Sunderlin wanted to point him out so the chief could see firsthand how suspicious he looked, but Ronnie was gone. A filling station attendant said he had sold him nineteen cents' worth of gas just minutes ago, and he had disappeared.

Deputies Sampson and Gottwald, who had picked Ronnie up, were getting suspicious too. They turned off Highway 6 onto Constance Road, and Ronnie pointed to a parked car about a hundred yards from the gray Oldsmobile and said it was his. They pulled over and let him out.

Ronnie walked to the car, slopping gas out of the bucket. He started to mess around with the gas cap, hoping the deputies would leave. They didn't, and while they were sitting there, Bernard Bass, the owner of the car, yelled from his yard, "Hey! What are you doing, that's my car."

The deputies suspected they were dealing with a car thief. They got out and grabbed Ronnie. They put handcuffs on him and opened the back door. Get in, Gottwald said.

They had spotted the Oldsmobile parked at an odd angle down Constance Road. Now they drove up to it. Roger was sitting in the front. The officers got out of their car and approached to question him.

Jimmy was half asleep, listening to the music. He heard Roger say, "Get your gun ready, Jim," and then he heard shots.

"Roger came at those deputies like a madman, swearing and shooting— it was like he was crazy," says Rieman. A newspaper account has Roger coming at the deputies screaming and cursing and filling the air with bullets, a .38 in one hand, a .45 in the other.

Sampson was hit in the foot, but he and Gottwald both managed to reach cover around the side of a nearby house. They saw Ronnie, still handcuffed, jump out of their squad car and join Roger.

Jimmy fired two low shots from the Oldsmobile to keep the cops from shooting at Roger and Ronnie. As soon as he shot, he ran over near the squad car so the three of them were together. The deputies fired at them. Roger fired back. They ran behind a nearby house looking for a car, but there was none to be found, so they went around front again, and ran next door to the Lindgren home.

Jimmy saw what appeared to be two women inside. He tried the door, but it was locked. Roger headed toward the back.

As soon as Eugene Lindgren saw the gunmen in his front yard, he ran to the garage, where he kept his rifle. Lindgren was a hunter. His rifle was cleaned and ready for use, but it wasn't loaded. He got down on the floor and began crawling toward a cabinet where the bullets were kept.

Coon Rapids Police Chief Al Bomberger and Mrs. Sunderlin were still looking for Ronnie when a message from Deputy Gottwald came over the radio. He and Deputy Sampson had been involved in a gunfight on Constance Road, and Sampson was wounded. Bomberger sent out an urgent bulletin to all law enforcement personnel in the area and headed for the scene.

Jimmy was still trying to get in the Lindgrens' front door, when he over-heard Roger back by the garage, saying, Give me the keys, we need your car! He ran around the house and saw a man lying on the garage floor next to a rifle. Jimmy picked the rifle up, realized it was empty, and put it aside.

Lindgren's red and white Cadillac was still warm. Roger told Lindgren to get in, drive, and do exactly what he was told. He sat in the front seat next to Lindgren and held his .45 to the hostage's head. Ronnie and Jimmy got in back. Ronnie was still handcuffed.

They backed out of the driveway and headed east on Constance Road, toward the Carlos Avery Game Farm.

Gottwald and Sampson didn't shoot, nor did they follow. They sent out a radio report that included a description of the gunmen, the color, make, and year of the Lindgrens' car, and the direction it was traveling.

Moments later Chief Bomberger screeched to a stop in front of the Lindgren home. Marion Lindgren was out in front. "My husband is in that car," she shouted.

"The look of terror on that woman's face was pitiful," Bomberger told reporters.

The radio was still playing in the Oldsmobile.

Fugue

Minneapolis Tribune, September 16, 1957: "Joyce O'Kasick had a dream. She was 22 and in Shakopee prison at the time. In her dream she saw her dead mother with Ronnie. 'I woke up scared. I knew something terrible would happen,' she said.

"The next day, Saturday, about four in the afternoon, she began writing a letter to Jimmy. Then, instead of finishing it she walked over to the prison laundry, sneaked out the back door, and ran across a field before the guard could spot her. She had escaped. She had to find her brothers."

At that moment her brothers were going ninety-five miles an hour down a gravel road in a stolen Cadillac, with a hostage at the wheel.

Rocks smacked the underside of the car and rattled off the oil pan. Jimmy retreated to the farthest side of the backseat and plugged his ears. Roger leaned over from the front, put the muzzle of his gun to the links of Ronnie's handcuffs, and blew them apart. BAM! The Cadillac filled with gun smoke.

The hostage was plenty scared. He told Roger to be careful. Just drive, Roger said, and drive fast. Roger was very cool and calm. He told the hostage that he was riding with the cop-killers from Minneapolis, and he'd better do what he was told if he wanted to survive.

I've got a wife and kids, the hostage said.

Me too, Ronnie told him, I've got a wife and kids.

Roger gave Ronnie his .45 because they had left Ronnie's pistol in the Oldsmobile. There were four rounds gone, so Ronnie dumped the magazine and reloaded. They had plenty of ammunition.

They saw a police car ahead on the left side of the road, and two policemen with rifles standing behind it. Get down, Roger ordered, but there wasn't any room on the floor, and they were approaching fast, so Jimmy and Ronnie had to sit up.

Tell the cops not to shoot, roll down your window! Roger said to the hostage.

They roared right by with Lindgren yelling, HOSTAGE! DON'T SHOOT!

If he looked low under the dust plume they were raising, Jimmy could see a police car behind them, red lights flashing. They saw a road going south and took it. That was a mistake. It led directly to the little village of Forest Lake. They sped three blocks down the main street, then doubled back, somehow losing the police car in the process. They got on the gravel road again and took off in the direction they had just come from. Roger saw a plane overhead.

Keep going, step on it, he told the hostage.

About a minute later the car sputtered to a stop. Get it moving, Roger ordered.

It wouldn't start. The hostage tried pumping the accelerator and pulling the choke. Nothing. They got out and looked at the plane circling overhead.

Roger said they should make a run for some trees about a hundred yards down the road on their right. He grabbed the hostage by the arm and stayed in the rear. Jimmy led the way. When they glanced over their shoulders, they could see dust rising on the road behind them, and they knew what was coming.

Highway patrolmen James Crawford and Kenneth Cziok (pronounced Chuck) had been in separate cars when the report about the incident on Constance Road came over the wire. Crawford almost caught up to the Cadillac in Forest Lake, but his brakes failed when he tried to double back. Moments later Cziok arrived, and Crawford got in his car. The pictures that appeared in newspapers the next day created the impression that a massive posse was involved in the chase, but that was a misconception.

"There were two cars at first, then we had the one car," Crawford explains. "All those people you see in the pictures arrived after the shooting was over. Kenny Cziok and I chased them, with the help of the airplane."

Minutes after Crawford jumped into Cziok's car, the pilot told them that the Cadillac had stopped in a ditch on the Carlos Avery Game Farm. "He told us that four people got out," says Crawford. "He said two of them were close together near the car, and the others had run down the road. We pulled up right behind the car, and I saw two individuals in the road. One of them had a gun to the head of the other one. Kenny took his pistol and jumped out the driver's side. I left mine on the seat and grabbed the shotgun.

"I advanced, they backed off, and we went maybe twenty-five yards down the road that way."

The Sheriff

The O'Kasicks were stickup men and killers who committed at least fifteen armed robberies, stole more than $20,000, and gathered an arsenal of deadly weapons that they used with reckless disregard in three shoot-outs with the police. They dressed in the gangster style of their day to signify the status they craved, and their crimes, though carefully planned, were increasingly brazen. They wanted to be outlaws, and outlaws they were, but when they met James Crawford, they met the Sheriff. The movie was over.

Roger and the hostage had made it nearly to the thicket, with Ronnie and Jimmy about fifty feet ahead, when the patrol car pulled up behind them. They saw two officers jump out, one holding a shotgun. A pistol shot zinged over their heads.

Don't turn around, Roger told his brothers calmly. Just run to the swamp on the other side of that brush as quick as you can.

Crawford advanced to within ten feet of Roger and the hostage. Ronnie and Jimmy crouched half hidden in the bushes. Their guns were drawn.

It was a standoff.

Roger had positioned the hostage facing him, with his back to the shotgun. He held Lindgren by the collar behind the neck with his left hand, shoved the barrel of his pistol up under his chin with his right hand, and made a move toward the patrolman.

Crawford didn't flinch. "HOSTAGE, FALL DOWN!" he commanded.

"Stand still," said Roger quietly. "Do what I say."

Lindgren looked back over his shoulder at the officer, then at Roger. He didn't know what to do. There was a pistol crack, then a thunderous blast.

"The gunman tripped, or maybe the hostage tripped, but both of them went down," says Crawford. "There was a shot, then the one with the gun got up. I fired at him, he dropped in the brush, and I fired again where he'd fallen because his gun was still going off."

Roger O'Kasick had checked out the way he would have scripted it—an automatic weapon jerking his dead hand, finger squeezed on the trigger, blazing away at a cop. A bullet went through Crawford's pants leg.

"I saw the other two individuals rising up from where they'd ducked," says Crawford. "One of them pointed his weapon at me, and I shot him too."

Jimmy hugged the ground, momentarily deafened by the blasts. He caught a glimpse of Roger's buckshot-riddled Ike jacket down in the weeds, smoke rising from the ragged holes. Ronnie was nearby, choking and coughing up blood.

He bolted toward Ronnie, wondering as he ran why nobody shot him. Ronnie's eyelids fluttered. He tried to say something. Then his eyes rolled back. Jimmy thought he should die too, that they should all die together. He saw a patch of high weeds and ran for it so he could have a few moments to think.

The first thing he did was open his .38 and let two empty casings fall out, along with the live ammunition. Then he reloaded carefully. He didn't want the gun to jam when he killed himself. He was concerned about the hostage, he later told police. He wondered where Lindgren was.

Lindgren was dead. Roger shot him through the neck as they fell.

Jimmy crouched in the weeds. He was just about ready to charge out and go down trying to avenge his dead brothers. Then it occurred to him; there was nothing to avenge. His brothers were dead because they were ready to die, because they preferred death to surrender.

He didn't know what he preferred. He saw the plane circling and knew the pilot must be able to see him. It wasn't dark yet, but the crickets had begun to chirp. They were down so low they thought it was night.

Hours passed before he heard car doors slamming and the sound of voices all around, as if an army were gathering and coming closer.

Roger O'Kasick, right where he fell at the final shoot-out. Photograph from the St. Paul Dispatch–Pioneer Press News Negative Collection. Courtesy of the Minnesota Historical Society.

He put the gun to his head, but he couldn't bring himself to pull the trigger. They were just a few feet away. He held the gun to where he thought his heart was and fired. Someone said, "There he is, he shot himself." Another voice said, "Fill him full of holes."

He felt a foot on his back, and someone ordered him to slide the gun out from under himself. Then he was in an ambulance.

Postmortems

Eugene Lindgren was born in the Anoka area and lived there all his life. He had a wife, three children, a thriving business, a red and white Cadillac, and a new home on Constance Road. He was thirty years old when the O'Kasicks happened to him.

Marion Lindgren was in a state of paralyzing grief and shock for a few days after her husband's death. Patty did most of the talking. "Dad saved our lives," she said. "They would have broken down the door and taken us if he hadn't run for the gun."

According to psychological tests administered when he was in the St. Cloud prison, Ronnie had an inferiority complex, probably due to his size, and a speech defect that he covered by mumbling. He thought most people were "two-faced." He hated his father and looked to his older brother Roger for guidance.

A week before the murder of officer Robert Fossum, Ronnie had visited his ex-wife and two children. He promised to come back in a few days, but they never saw him again.

His ex-wife told the *Tribune* that everything seemed OK in their relationship until Roger came around. "He would just start something between us, and take Ronnie away for the rest of the night. As soon as Roger arrived everything got all hush-hush, and secret."

Ronnie was twenty-four when he was killed.

Roger was bitter with life, according to his sister Joyce. "I've never seen a guy with so much misery in him," she said. "He never hung around with other guys. He liked girls, but he only had a couple dates in his life, and he was good looking too. My girlfriends thought so. I remember when I told him how Jerry's (her fiancé's) friend had been shot and paralyzed by the cops, he had tears in his eyes, and he swore at the cops. Over someone he didn't even know. He was smart in school, he was a lot smarter than the rest of us. He hated to go to school though, because he didn't have the right clothes and other kids laughed at him. He hated people. He'd think too much. I guess you could say he had an inferiority complex or something."

Roger had worked in factories a few weeks at a time for a total of less than six months. Those were the only jobs he ever held. What he liked to do best was sit in his rented room and read library books. He was killed at the age of twenty-six.

Around midnight September 14, hours after news reports of the Anoka County shoot-out began coming in, and twenty minutes after the first pictures of the three dead bodies appeared on Twin Cities television screens, the police received a tip that Joyce, who had escaped from the Shakopee prison that afternoon, could be found at the Dugout Bar in downtown Minneapolis.

When the police arrived, Joyce ran out the back door into the parking lot. She tried to hide in a car. The officers approached cautiously, guns drawn, and threw the doors open.

Joyce was in the backseat, sobbing. "Why don't you kill me like you killed my brothers, you dirty coppers," she said.

Jimmy had nicked his heart when he shot himself. His lung collapsed, and a tracheotomy tube was inserted down his throat in the ambulance. By the time he reached General Hospital in Minneapolis he seemed to be in stable condition, but a few hours later he turned blue from the waist up and went into shock. An emergency heart operation was performed. Ten stitches were sewn in one of the major heart muscles.

Shortly after the operation, while he was still groggy, the police began taking statements from him and continued doing so for the next three weeks. He confessed to shooting officer Ward Canfield in the stomach at point blank range, and said Roger, who was "criminally insane, someone I never knew," murdered officer Robert Fossum. He said that running over Canfield and shooting Eugene Lindgren were both accidents. He told of armed robberies he had participated in since being discharged from the Marines, and was able to provide details of his brothers' career as holdup men for the two previous years.

Jimmy's interest in life waxed and waned during his confinement. He and his brother Richard became convinced that the hostage was shot by Crawford rather than Roger, and both of them expended a lot of energy trying to convince others of their theory.

Jimmy was quickly convicted of second-degree murder in Hennepin County, then of first-degree murder in Anoka County. The Anoka conviction threw him into a permanent state of depression. The sentences were imposed consecutively, which left him no hope of ever getting out of prison. Testimony in the Anoka case contradicted his contention that Crawford shot Lindgren.

Jerry Roy, a friend of his from his Franklin Avenue days, says he attempted suicide several times at St. Cloud. "That last time they just did him a favor

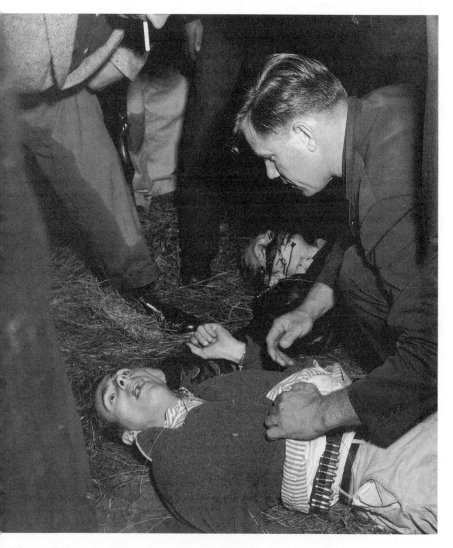

Police pulled the dead O'Kasick brothers out of the weeds so the press could photograph them. Photograph from the St. Paul Dispatch-Pioneer Press News Negative Collection. Courtesy of the Minnesota Historical Society.

and let him bleed for a while before they called the ambulance," Roy says. "He wanted to die real bad."

James Crawford had a long and varied career after he shot the O'Kasicks. He headed the state highway patrol, served as state registrar, and then went to Saudi Arabia, where he set up a system of outposts and surveillance in that country's remote borderlands. After he returned, he was elected mayor of Forest Lake. September 14, 1957, was surely one of the pivotal points of his life, but when he recalls that day now, he doesn't think so much of the danger he faced, or the adrenalin-pumping drama. The texture of the moments as they passed is what sticks with him—the way the ankle-deep water in the grass squished in his shoes, the eerie quiet that descended after the shooting was over, how cold his feet got as dusk settled in, and he and his partner waited behind their car for backup. "We'd been ordered not to go in after that third guy until help arrived, but it took a long time," he says.

Highway patrolmen, police from nearby jurisdictions, and local farmers who just grabbed their rifles and joined the posse had been quickly organized, but they were confused about where to go.

"They'd been told to look for the airplane," Crawford explains. "Our plane was circling over the area, but one of the sheriffs sent up another plane that he had flying for him. As soon as it got to the scene our pilot told him to get out of there because he was busy watching the ground, and he didn't want to worry about crashing into him. So the second plane went and circled over Coon Lake, and that's where all the backup went. It took a long time to straighten that out."

Queried if there was any way the hostage might have been saved, Crawford says, maybe. "If I'd have shot before the two of them fell I might have managed to hit the O'Kasick kid without harming that poor fellow. But it seemed like an awful chance to take."

Postscript

Decades after their crimes, the O'Kasicks' trail is marked by missing files and blank stares. One of the few cops who agreed to talk about them was Rieman.

"The nurses at General Hospital treated that kid pretty special," he said of Jimmy. "They babied him. Of course he was a celebrity."

According to newspaper accounts, investigators interrogated Jimmy for more than twenty hours during his three-week hospital stay, but quotes in the newspapers and a few pages of transcript labeled "Dying Declaration-James O'Kasick" are all that survive. The rest, more than one hundred pages, have disappeared. Rieman hinted that they were deliberately destroyed.

"Kid made excuses," he said, "whined about his rotten life, claimed they were always broke and hungry, said the old man had them boosting car parts and selling them down at the junkyards when they were ten years old." He sighed, as if to say that there is no end to human gullibility. His attitude implied a question: Why are you writing about them?

"Remember anything else about the O'Kasick case?" I asked, hoping he would say, no, and the interview would be over.

He corrected my query. "You mean the Fossum-Canfield case. The murder of Minneapolis police officer Robert Fossum, and the attempted murder of officer Ward Canfield." Just stating those facts was an emotional effort for him. His face was flushed, but he continued.

"They shot the handcuffs off that one kid while they were going ninety-five miles an hour on a dirt road. Do you know how crazy that is? Put a hole right through the gas tank, that's why the car quit on them. They were murderers, vicious little dinks, but I'll tell you something. They didn't kill that hostage on purpose."

Rieman has deduced this as follows: "There was no postmortem. Usually there is, you know, but it should have been done in Anoka, and instead they sent the bodies to Hennepin County because nobody knew what to do out there." He shook his head. "God, it was a mess. Anyway, my partner and I had to view the bodies at the morgue, and this Roger O'Kasick's finger on his left hand, his index finger, was taped together at the knuckle. It had been shot in half. . . . Stand up here once," he said.

Rieman came out from behind the desk.

"Now Roger had the hostage like this," he looped his left hand behind my head and jerked me toward him. "And he was leading him along, stepping backwards with his pistol shoved up under the hostage's chin, like this." He jabbed a finger into my neck.

"Now Roger, he must have stumbled as he stepped backwards in the weeds, and his gun fired, shot the hostage through the neck, and blew his own finger off. And then, of course, that highway patrolman shot him. Shot him dead."

Rieman sat back in his swivel chair and nodded, folding his hands in front of him—big powerful hands, with fingers the size of midget bananas, one of which was missing at the middle knuckle. He smiled an enigmatic little smile. "Now what was that patrolman's name? Crawford, I think."

Happenstance

The victims of the gory murders that took place behind a Minneapolis bar the night of July 26, 1998, were nice guys, but they had some perilous habits. They met frequently at the saloon where they had their last drink, and rarely left sober. According to friends, they were trusting souls, willing to gab with anyone they encountered in their cups, including the kind of mean bastards they'd have done better to avoid. They pulled crumpled wads of small bills out of their pockets to pay for a round, dropped a few on the bar, and maybe one or two on the floor. One of them routinely drove home drunk in his pickup truck, while the other wobbled off on his bike in the same condition. They had gone to the parking lot to smoke a joint when they met their demise.

In short, Don Pyle and Jim Brandby were reckless fellows, poised for misadventure. Yet, they had somehow managed to survive until the ages of thirty-eight and forty-six, respectively. Then they ran into Robert Jackson and Frank Mendoza.

Jackson and Mendoza are drifters whose paths crossed by chance. "I met Robert in Kansas City, near a spot where the trains all crisscross, kind of a hangout for the homeless," says Mendoza. "I was sitting under a bridge with my pet timber wolf when I saw him chasing some white guy down the tracks with a two-by-four. Dude called him a nigger, I guess. I just laughed and laughed, it looked so comical. I said to him, 'Come on over here, bro! Get yourself a drink!' So that's how Robert and me got to traveling together. We shared a little jug of my favorite libation, the cherry bomb—cherry juice mixed with Everclear, about half and half."

A few cherry bombs later they spotted a slow train coming and caught it. It was the kind of spur-of-the-moment decision that gives rootless alcoholics the illusion of freedom. Someone watching from a safe distance would have seen two tough-looking men with big, loopy grins on their faces hoisting their four-legged pal aboard a flatcar for the journey to wherever. Bombs away!

Fourteen hours later they jolted to a stop in Little Rock, train weary and hungover. Jackson had the dry heaves.

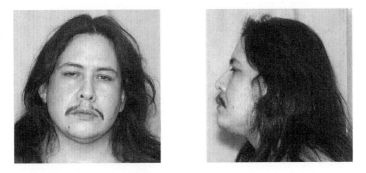

Frank Mendoza. Photographs courtesy of the Minnesota Department of Corrections.

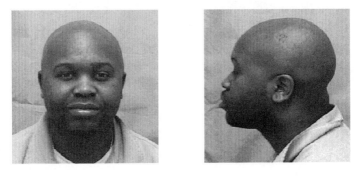

Robert Jackson. Photographs courtesy of the Minnesota Department of Corrections.

"Robert decided to steal us a car," Mendoza says. "He went away, and maybe an hour later, here he comes, driving a blue van. That's what Robert is about—stealing vehicles. If it's got wheels, he'll steal it."

Jackson's version of how their highway odyssey begins is identical in all particulars but one, but that one is crucial. According to him, Mendoza disappeared for awhile, and he stole the van.

"I never did ask him where he got it," Jackson says. "I didn't care. It was better than a train."

That's how their story goes. They agree on everything except which one is the perpetrator, a question that keeps coming up. They are both in prison now, but even the prosecutor admits he can't say exactly who did what that summer day, when the two of them, along with an ex-con from Mexico and a mysterious man known only as Mike, went on a bloody rampage. By the time it was over, a woman had been robbed and terrorized, their Mexican buddy was in the hospital with multiple stab wounds, and Don Pyle and Jim Brandby lay dead in the parking lot behind Arone's Bar.

"I come from everywhere and nowhere," says Mendoza. "Most of my history is a blank. I know that I'm part Choctaw, part Cherokee, and part Irish. No wonder I'm a drunk, eh?" He laughs a short, mirthless laugh, alarming because of his size and the situation. Mendoza is six feet three, three-hundred-plus pounds. The two of us are locked in a conference room behind the visiting lounge at Oak Park Heights, Minnesota's maximum security prison. A guard is visible through a wall made of the kind of thick glass that gorillas are exhibited behind, but he has his back to us, and the glass is soundproof.

Mendoza was born on a reservation in Washington and raised in South Central Los Angeles. "I was adopted by the Mendozas," he explains. "My mom was in the habit of traveling, like me. I had a brother named Johnny, and I'm told the state of Washington wanted us to stay together because we were the only ones in the family with the same mother and father, but I've never seen him since the day they took me to L.A. I was about two at the time. I'm either thirty-nine or forty now."

He spent his adolescence gangbanging with the East Side Wemas, a Cholo term meaning tough guys. "I really wasn't that tight with them, because I'm Indian," he says. "The Latinos called me Tonto, but not to my face. Not after I started to grow. I was about fourteen when I filled out."

He hit the road soon after. "Sometimes I hitchhike, sometimes I hop a freight, but I never stay in one place long unless I'm incarcerated," he says. "In L.A. I learned to take care of myself. I learned Spanish, and proper English. I already knew Cherokee. That's what I took with me when I left."

He also took his weapon of choice, a dagger about fifteen inches long with a serrated edge. "I keep it inside my boot or up my sleeve," he says. "There are gangs riding the trains. You've got to be ready."

Mendoza's road handle is Boogie-Man, because he is rarely seen during the day. The sun makes him break out in a rash. "I'm a late-night guy anyway," he says. "I like to party." He hasn't done drugs since 1979, but he drinks quite a bit and tends to black out when he gets drunk. Queried what it means to black out, he replies, "I'm on my feet, but unconscious, usually for forty-five minutes or an hour. I continue to function, but I have no memory of what I did, or what happened to me."

He has been arrested many times, often during a blackout, which means he enters the fugue state a free man and wakes up in the slammer, where the god-awful cherry bomb hangover and the depressing circumstances tend to put him in an ugly mood. He did hard time in Oklahoma for an incident that began as a jailhouse beef and escalated. He was in the drunk tank of a county jail and claims that a man, in the presence of four deputies, said he was going to kill an Indian.

"I guess they thought he should kill me, because they put me in the bull pen with him," he says.

According to the record, when the fight was over, one Eugene Watson was pretty close to dead, and Mendoza had been charged with assault and battery with intent to kill. "I assaulted him alright, but if I'd intended to kill him I surely would have," he says. "I did ten years flat for that."

He also did time in Nebraska, for robbery. "I learned to speak Lakota in the Nebraska prison," he says. "It's good to learn different languages. If you don't know what people are saying, they'll talk shit about you."

Robert Quarry Jackson, twenty-nine, was raised in St. Louis. He has a common-law wife in Overland, Missouri, but his weakness for booze and bumming around screwed that up. "I was just running," he told police, "like traveling, you know, sleeping under a bridge, drinking on the street."

A cop who was trying to draw him out said he envied Jackson's lifestyle. "I love your traveling, man," he said, "the way you move around so free and easy."

"Yeah, well, it gets dangerous," Jackson replied. "Frank and me, we watched each other to survive."

He told them about life-threatening situations he had faced, including run-ins with racist gangs, and the dread "thumper," in which two freight cars bang together, the loads shift, and a man on the bum alone can be buried alive in commercial cargo. It is wise to travel in pairs, he explained, and especially prudent to travel with a man like Mendoza, who is known on the rails as a quick-tempered brawler.

Jackson came across as quite a gentleman at his trial. The judge was impressed. So was one of the jurors, Mary Diercks, a case worker for a private social service agency. Diercks voted to convict and wrote a letter to the judge, an old friend of hers, begging for mercy on Jackson's behalf. She has since taken over his affairs. He referred requests for an interview to her.

Diercks was immediately suspicious. She inquired about my motives for writing this story. I never know how to answer that question, but she does. "I can see what you're up to," she said, and she nixed any contact with Jackson.

Once Mendoza and Jackson acquired the van, they became "rubber tramps," driving from city to city, working temporary labor for booze and gas money, crashing for the night on riverbanks, under bridges, or in the no-man's-land near the railroad tracks—the kind of alienated spaces where stray dogs run in packs, and broken glass is forever crunching underfoot. Their moods cycled from drunken excitement to a sullen rage provoked by all the indignities, real and imagined, that the homeless are forced to swallow.

They meandered through Oklahoma City, St. Louis, Chicago, and Milwaukee, spending a few days in each place, then drove to the Twin Cities on a whim. They had gotten lost on the way to Green Bay, and by the time they realized they were on I-94 heading west, they had decided they'd reached the point of no return.

"Frank, he knows some people in St. Paul," Jackson told the police. "We thought we'd get together with them, but they didn't want nothing to do with us, so we slept by some barges, near the river. Then we went to that Salvation Army place to clean up."

The Harbor Light shelter, operated by the Salvation Army, is on the edge of downtown Minneapolis. It is situated between a freeway and the Target Center, home to the Minnesota Timberwolves basketball team. The area is a magnet for transients because of its proximity to the tracks and the bus depot, but the shelter and a few pawnshops are all that remain of a skid row that practically vanished when pro basketball came to town.

Mendoza and Jackson arrived at Harbor Light around 9:30 a.m. on Friday, July 26, 1998, a day that dawned hot and oppressively humid, with the threat of rain hanging in the air. They parked, took showers, and then went looking for a liquor store on foot. On the way they ran into Juan Esquivel, twenty-six, a tiny, hard-drinking Mexican national.

"I saw him sitting by the bus station, sipping from a jug in a paper sack," says Mendoza. "He looked homeless, so I said, 'hey man, what's up?'"

Esquivel had been discharged from a Florida prison a few days before. He was supposed to be heading for Mexico. Why he was in Minneapolis with a bus ticket to Chicago in his possession is anyone's guess, but it might have had something to do with alcohol. Almost everyone involved in this story—perpetrators, witnesses, three of the four victims—were stone drunk when the events transpired. Several, including Esquivel, had blood alcohol levels high enough to kill the average person.

Jackson later told investigators that he didn't know why Esquivel joined them. "When Frank gets to talking to his own kind, he changes languages," he explained. "Dude just came with us."

By the time they returned to the shelter, their ragged band had grown to include several more transients, among them Mike, a black man in his mid to late twenties. All except Mendoza got in the van and drove off. "They were smoking crack," Mendoza explains. "I don't do crack, so I just sat around outside the shelter with some people. They were trippin' off my wolf—'That's a beautiful dog, where'd you get it?'—Like that. My codefendant and his friends came back about four in the afternoon."

A few minutes later the van left again, with Jackson at the wheel and

Mendoza, Esquivel, Mike, and the wolf inside. They proceeded in the general direction of the University of Minnesota, passing joints and drinking beer, and soon became snarled in a traffic jam. The university hockey team was playing a preseason exhibition game, and thousands of people were scrambling for parking places.

The conversation in the van had been evolving along a drunken tangent. "We were telling Juan about our escapades," says Mendoza, "you know, stealing vehicles and having fun, and he's saying, 'I'm a good thief too, I can steal,' and we said, yeah yeah, whatever. He took that to mean we didn't believe him, that we were dissing him."

The talk became heated. Esquivel slurred something about being a bold crook and an all-around hard-ass, which caused Mendoza to break into peals of laughter. Jackson and Mike didn't need a translator to get the drift. They laughed too, and Esquivel began to sulk.

Fat drops of rain were falling on the van's windshield as they inched their way down Fourth Street SE. Jackson, frustrated by the bumper-to-bumper traffic, saw an opening and turned onto a bus transit way that runs between the university's Minneapolis and St. Paul campuses, ignoring the sign that warns private vehicles to stay off.

He saw a woman on a bicycle pedaling furiously and said to Esquivel: "Here's your chance, Chico. Show us what kind of thief you are. Go on!"

More than two years have passed, but Judith Sims still gets agitated when she talks about her run-in with that van full of drunks. "It seemed almost comic at the time," she says, "but in retrospect it was really creepy."

Sims is a television producer who lives near the university's St. Paul campus. She is middle-aged, with long, straight ash-blonde hair and glasses. She had biked to the library in Minneapolis that afternoon to do some research. It was 4:30 when she decided to go home.

"As soon as I stepped outside, I could see it was about to storm," she says. "Normally I'd bike home on the side streets, but I wanted to make some time before the downpour, so I headed for the transit way."

The transit way is a limited-access road. Bicycles and buses can use it, but private vehicles are prohibited. By the time Sims reached the entry point, raindrops were falling. "I began pedaling as fast as I could," she says. "I was really concentrating, keeping my eyes on the pavement in front of me, but pretty soon I became aware that this blue van had pulled alongside me. I knew it didn't belong there. I glanced over and saw arms flailing around inside, and heard people talking in loud, excited voices—maybe in Spanish. Somehow I knew I was in trouble."

The van cut her off, forcing her to stop abruptly. She jumped from her bike and started retreating.

"After that I only recall images," she says. "I remember this little Hispanic man who stumbled out of the back and grabbed my bike. A dog jumped out too, probably a German shepherd, but gray like a wolf. Then there was this Native American–looking fellow who got out the front door. He was really big, with a huge upper body and long hair down his back."

The nearby parking lots were full of people, but no one seemed to be paying any attention. "I let out a shriek, hoping somebody would help," she says, "but nobody even turned their head. Then I noticed another van had pulled up behind me, and I thought, 'Oh no, now I'm really hosed.'"

But the second van was her salvation. Ben Richards, a detective from the Red Lake Indian Reservation in northern Minnesota, was behind the wheel.

"It was a complete coincidence that I was there," says Richards. "My wife and I had taken my grandson to Minneapolis for the hockey game, and to tell you the truth, I was lost. I was following the blue van because I thought he might be heading for a parking lot, then I saw what was going on."

Sims got into Richards's vehicle. Richards whipped out his notebook and began jotting down descriptions. "We watched as this unreal, kind of comic scene slowly unfolded," says Sims.

The thief, who reeked of beer and was having a hard time keeping his balance, slipped trying to load the bike into the van. He fell, and the bike landed on top of him. He cast a sheepish look back toward Sims, as if to apologize to her for the indignity of being robbed by such a clumsy thief. He managed to push the bike into the van from a prone position and crawled in behind it.

Meanwhile, the wolf was determined to play. It barked and crouched and wagged its tail, while the big Native American did everything in his power to lure it back into the van, which was rocking on its springs due to some commotion going on inside. Finally, dog and man jumped back in the van.

The van lurched forward, banged over a curb into a closed parking lot, and sped to the other side. But there was no exit. It squealed to a stop at a barrier.

"One of them opened the door," says Sims. "He stood up on the running board, peered around, ducked in again, and back they came my way, peeling rubber. They jumped the curb, got on the transit way, and roared off."

Sims tried to report the crime on Richards's cell phone. 911 connected them with the Minneapolis police. "I told them the thieves were getting away as we spoke," says Sims, "but they insisted on switching us over to the university police. That took awhile, then the university police kept asking us what we were doing on the transit way."

Finally, an officer arrived. Sims reported her bike stolen. Richards turned over his notes, which included good descriptions and the number of the blue van's Arkansas license plates.

"I was shaken, but not terribly," says Sims. "Mr. Richards looked grim though. He told me he had the feeling that something very bad had almost happened, and when you think about what occurred later, maybe he was right."

About the time Sims was reporting her bike stolen, Don Pyle, a cook at a downtown Minneapolis restaurant, got on his bike and began pedaling to Arone's Bar on East Hennepin Avenue. He was bound for his usual Friday afternoon rendezvous with his friend Jim Brandby.

"Jim worked at a sheet metal fabricating shop a few blocks from Arone's," says Howard Brandby, Jim's father. "He and Don drank beer and played darts there. They were the best of friends."

"They were ordinary working guys," says a bartender at Arone's. "Nice fellows. They usually came for happy hour, maybe stayed a little later on a Friday."

While Brandby and Pyle were getting settled in at the bar, Mendoza was busy trying to convert Sims's bicycle into cash. First he offered it around to the crowd in front of Harbor Light shelter. When nobody bit, he hocked it at a nearby pawnshop, for sixty-five dollars. The swag was divided as follows: Esquivel got some weed from Mike for his bold theft, about enough for two joints. Mendoza pocketed half the money. Jackson bought crack from Mike with the rest, and he and Mike proceeded to smoke it.

The four of them drove around for awhile, consuming their drugs of choice. They considered going back to the shelter for the night, but feeling flush and in need of more drink, decided instead to drive to a liquor store. Mendoza handed Esquivel his end of the loot and directed him to buy beer, lots of it.

"We waited for him, but he never came back," says Mendoza, with a rueful smile. "Pretty soon we realized he'd just ducked out the side door and took off."

Time has mellowed Mendoza's view of that incident, but he admits to being enraged when it happened. He scoffs at the notion that Esquivel considered the money his since he had swiped the bike. No, it was a rip-off, Mendoza insists, and it cried out for revenge.

"Where I come from, if a man steals from you, you take something from him," he explains. "You take his dignity, you maybe take his finger off at the knuckle. You don't take his life, but you take something serious."

Such were his thoughts as they left the liquor store empty-handed. The fun was over, supplanted by a mood of seething anger. Jackson dropped Mike at the shelter, and he and Mendoza dealt with adversity in true rubber tramp fashion. They hit the road.

According to Jackson, they were a good twenty miles south of town on I-35 when Mendoza announced that they had to go back and square accounts with Esquivel. Jackson told the investigators he did everything in his power to dissuade him, but Mendoza was adamant.

Mendoza has a different story. "I told Robert to let me out because I didn't want to go south. I'd decided to hitchhike up to Canada and see some people I knew on a reservation. I said he could keep the van, we would just part ways right there, but he wanted to stay with me. He insisted."

However the decision was made, it was crucial. Once Jackson and Mendoza turned around, Brandby and Pyle were living on borrowed time.

Happy hour had faded to evening by the time they parked the blue van near the Harbor Light shelter once again. Mike was among the crowd of transients standing on the sidewalk, trying to decide whether to get sober and go inside for the night, or stay drunk and sleep out in the rain. Jackson and Mendoza joined him, and their conversation turned to finding Esquivel. A witness later told police he overheard Jackson say, "We're going to get that little wetback Mexican and beat his ass."

"We figured Juan had to be in the area because he had a bus ticket," says Mendoza. "We were about to go look by the depot when here comes Juan, walking down the street."

Jackson whistled to get his attention. "Hey, Chico, where's our money?" he shouted.

Before Esquivel could reply, Mendoza approached him. "I told him, 'You been to la pida [the tomb, the rock, the penitentiary], man. You know what's got to happen.'"

Witnesses say that he appeared to punch Esquivel in the midsection several times as he spoke, but when the Mexican turned and bolted toward a nearby alley, his shirt was bloody.

"Yeah, I stabbed him," says Mendoza. "I stuck him in the ribs—two, maybe three times. I wasn't trying to kill him. If you want to kill a man, you stick him in the chest or the throat. I wanted to hurt him."

The wolf thought it was time to play again. He leaped out of the van as Jackson opened the door to get in. Mendoza calmly collected his animal. Then he tucked his knife in his boot, got in the van, followed by Mike, and the three of them drove away. The witnesses were struck by Mendoza's cool, unhurried demeanor.

"There was nothing to be excited about," he explains. "The man ripped me off. I did what I had to do. It was over as far as I was concerned."

Esquivel hovered near death in Hennepin County Medical Center for several days, but one medical dilemma resolved itself within a few hours.

According to the physicians who did blood tests, had he died soon after his arrival, it would have been a toss-up whether to list the cause as alcohol poisoning or wounds inflicted with a knife.

Eventually Esquivel recovered, made a plea bargain in return for a statement concerning the bike theft and the stabbing, and left for parts unknown.

According to Mendoza, Mike and Jackson were pumped after the stabbing. They drove around high-fiving, laughing, and passing the pipe. Mendoza claims he didn't join the celebration. The booze was catching up to him, he explains.

Back at the shelter, the police had responded to a 911 call. Investigators soon gathered descriptions of the assailant, his companions, the vehicle, and its out-of-state plates. They also connected the van to the bike theft on the university transit way. Because there were so many witnesses to the stabbing, several officers stayed on the scene to take statements after the first bulletins were sent out.

The blue van pulled into Arone's parking lot about 10 p.m. According to Jackson, Mike had suggested going to Arone's for some down-home southern cooking. Why he thought they would find it there is a mystery. The neighborhood where the bar is located has changed in recent years, but Arone's is a throwback to an earlier era, when the kitchens featured meat and potatoes, and the bars were lily-white.

"I was at Arone's that night for a friend's retirement party," says Randy Nordling. "The three of them, two black guys and a big, Spanish-looking guy came in. Altogether I'd say they were in the bar for about ten minutes."

Jackson and Mike went into the dining room, where they were told that the kitchen had closed. They made no attempt to hide their displeasure at that development as they headed back to the bar area to find Mendoza. He was in the men's room, where he asked a friend of Nordling's for twenty dollars. The man declined politely and left. Mendoza joined the others.

"They walked around the bar for a few minutes, looking things over and acting obnoxious," says Nordling. Pressed for details, he says they didn't look sociable and kept bumping into people. "Maybe it was because they were drunk," he says. "After a bit they went over by the pool table. Jimmy Brandby and Don Pyle were playing pool, but I don't think they hassled them at that point."

Nordling saw Brandby and Pyle leave. He cannot say for sure whether Jackson, Mendoza, and Mike followed them out the door or had preceded them.

Mendoza claims he was asleep in the backseat of the van when the trouble began. Actually, he claims he was never in the bar, but several witnesses, including Nordling, place him there. However, Charles Carpenter, a witness who was just pulling into the parking lot, corroborates Mendoza's version of his role in the violence that followed.

"I was asleep in the backseat when I heard a big commotion outside," says Mendoza. "It woke me up, so I got out to take a look."

Brandby and Pyle had been seated in Brandby's pickup truck. Mike and Jackson had approached them, and an angry confrontation had erupted. Police would later characterize the incident as an attempted robbery.

By the time Mendoza heard the noise and emerged from the van, Mike was leaning through the window, stabbing Brandby. Pyle flung the passenger door open and fled in the direction of the blue van.

Witness Carpenter was just pulling into the parking lot. He had to swerve to avoid running into Mendoza, who was heading toward Brandby's truck. Carpenter watched as Mendoza collided with the fleeing Pyle, then punched him.

"He said something to me I couldn't quite hear, but it didn't sound friendly, so I hit him," says Mendoza. "I punched him in the forehead."

Carpenter saw Pyle fall to the ground. He saw a black man pounce on him and begin beating him.

"Chuck Carpenter came in hollering about a fight in the parking lot," says Nordling. "My brother and I were the first ones out there. I walked up on Jimmy, then I told my brother to stay back. I didn't want him to look at it."

A steady, warm rain fell on the grisly scene. Rivulets of bloody water snaked across the parking lot toward a storm sewer. The perpetrators were nowhere to be seen. Brandby, who had thirty-six knife wounds, including one that nearly severed his head, had somehow managed to open the door of his truck and stumble a few steps before he collapsed. He was sprawled in a puddle. Pyle, stabbed twelve times, had crawled back toward the truck and died with his head propped against the rear wheel.

The police were called. The descriptions of the killers matched those of the men involved in the earlier stabbing outside the Harbor Light shelter.

The ferocity and swiftness of the crime left the people who were at Arone's when it happened shaking their heads. Several remarked on the fact that Brandby and Pyle had been shooting pool and laughing five minutes before they were killed. "They were here and then they were gone," says one.

"My son Jim had a head full of ideas," says Howard Brandby. "I'm an inventor with patents on many sporting goods items, and he helped me out with almost all of them. We hunted and fished together all his life. We were very close." Brandby had been divorced for four years when he was murdered. His son Mitchell was five.

Pyle was by all accounts a sweet-tempered, generous man. A few weeks before he was murdered a storm had wiped out the electricity on the block where he lived. Pyle purchased a generator and invited his neighbors to hook up.

"Don loved to talk," says Nordling, "loved to tell stories. He was good to people. I guess maybe he drank a little too much, but he didn't have a mean bone in his body."

According to Jackson, Mike rifled Pyle's wallet as they sped away from the scene. "He told us they threw it in the river, probably off the Third Avenue bridge," says Sergeant Rick Zimmerman.

They drove to within a block of the shelter and pulled over on a side street. "Robert and Mike smoked some weed, then Mike got out and walked toward the shelter," Mendoza says. "That's the last we saw of him. We drove around front, looking for a place to park."

The police were still there, taking statements about the Esquivel stabbing. Sara Mingo, who had just finished talking to one of the officers, saw the blue van. "That's them!" she said. "That's the van!"

The officers approached, guns drawn, and ordered Mendoza and Jackson to get out. Jackson did as he was told, but Mendoza attempted to run and fought back when they caught him. It took several officers to subdue him, and he suffered a cut lip and a bloody nose in the process. He claimed that the bloody shirt later used in evidence against him came as a result of the beating he took when he was arrested.

Witnesses from Arone's were quickly shuttled to the scene by investigators. They identified both men. A search for Mike was unsuccessful. Witnesses say that he had walked in the front door of the shelter before the ruckus ensued, and exited out the back door when he heard what was happening. In the following weeks investigators followed many leads looking for him, but ultimately they gave up.

Jackson denied any role in the stabbings. He said he was sitting in the van when the murders occurred. Mendoza claimed he stabbed no one.

"Our witnesses put Jackson in the thick of it," says Robert Streitz, who prosecuted both men for Hennepin County. "I told the jury that in all the chaos, what the witness Carpenter perceived as a black man beating Pyle was actually a stabbing. It was probably Jackson who stabbed Pyle, and he may have stabbed Brandby as well, although the third man, this Mike, could have been the main culprit there. I believe Mendoza used his knife too, but whether he stabbed anybody or not is really immaterial. He aided and abetted murder."

Mendoza's sentences for two second-degree murders and a second-degree assault add up to 112 years. With good time, his anticipated release date is

2044. Jackson is doing less time for the same crimes. He could be out in 2036. The discrepancy rankles Mendoza. According to Streitz, it is because of Mendoza's record. Jackson had been arrested only once before.

"I should be doing about twelve years for stabbing Juan," Mendoza says. "I have that coming. I should not be doing time for murder."

He says that after he knocked Pyle down, he saw a black man, whom he will not identify, stab Pyle to death. He claims he has no idea who killed Brandby, nor does he know what precipitated the murders. He vaguely recalls Jackson and Mike talking to two men who were playing pool in the bar but doesn't think anything unusual transpired between them.

Streitz says it is possible that the perpetrators overheard the victims talking about going out to smoke a joint. He thinks the trouble might have begun when Jackson and Mike followed them and demanded marijuana.

"Maybe that's how it came down," says Mendoza with a shrug. "What does it matter? Nothing they did made any difference."

In his view, curiosity about random misfortune is fruitless, a flophouse on the road to paranoia. There is no fateful characteristic that distinguishes the victim from the rest of the human race—the ones whose luck hasn't run out.

"You can't avoid something like that," he says. "It all depends on who you run into, and what the circumstances are. I've been around enough violence to know that it happens fast. If you don't see it coming, you're dead."

Judith Sims has had years to reflect on what she now considers a near-death experience when she ran into Brandby and Pyle's killers. "Later I recalled something," she says, "the look of surprise on one of their faces. I can't remember which one, and I can't be certain what surprised him, but from behind they could have easily mistaken me for a college girl. I was wearing jeans, I'm skinny, I have long hair, we were near the university. Then, when they pulled around and cut me off, they were confronted by a middle-aged woman. I think somehow that threw them, and maybe it saved me."

According to Mendoza, Sims never was in danger. At least not from him.

"I got out of the van because the wolf jumped out, and I'm the only one who can control him," he says. "I didn't have any intention of hurting her, and Juan, he just wanted the bike. I don't know what Robert and that other asshole would've done if she got in their face. Probably nothing, although they were pretty drunk. Who knows?"

Queried if he has any regrets about the deaths, Mendoza replies, "Yes, I'm sorry that my stupidity inflamed the ignorance of another man." He says that his companions' moods changed noticeably after he stabbed Esquivel, and the punch he threw at Pyle might have further aroused them. "Other than that, I didn't murder those men, I didn't know them, and I can't say that their deaths make much difference to me. I've seen so many people die. I've seen drive-bys, fatal beatings, stabbings, I've watched people get shot to death. I was sitting in a Burger King in L.A. when someone came in and executed a man at the next table. I just finished my hamburger."

A pair of drifters heading for Green Bay take a wrong turn and wind up in Minneapolis. A woman gets on her bicycle to pedal home and encounters a trio of thieving murderers, but she is saved by an off-duty cop who is in the vicinity because he is lost. Two guys out for drinks on a Friday night are stabbed to death for no apparent reason by complete strangers. Fate and how free will or happenstance might alter it will always be a mystery. Mendoza claims he has come to terms with that.

"I know I'll spend the rest of my life in prison," he says. "This prison, probably, but if I ever get out of here, the state of Oregon wants to try me for another serious crime. So I will certainly die behind bars. I just don't know when. Or how."

Miss Abyss

Anna Marie Vanderford was a heartbreaker in her youth. The kind of beauty she possessed doesn't stop traffic in Paris or Bangkok, but it did in Minnesota, and that was where she grew up, a lotus flower among the snow queens. Her loveliness set her apart, and so did certain childhood experiences she had.

When she was in the third grade her family lived in suburban Rosemount, a place where dark-skinned people were scarce, but Anna's exotic looks and her brains tended to mitigate whatever problems that might have created. If anything, she was viewed as special by teachers and classmates alike.

Her father thought she was special, too. According to Anna, she would often be watching television with her brother and sister when her father would pick her up and ask, "How is my number-one girl today?" Then he would carry her off for some exclusive attention. On one occasion that she described in detail years later, he took her behind a shed in the backyard, removed her clothes, and licked her over her entire body. He often would rub his privates against her until he ejaculated. She says he tried to penetrate her sexually but was unable to do so because she was so tiny. The incest began when she was five.

"It went in spurts, sometimes once or twice a week, sometimes every night," she says. "At first I was confused and afraid, not really having full knowledge of what was going on. Later I was still afraid, feeling like nobody knew or cared what was happening. I became invisible. My brothers and sisters never seemed to know that I'd disappear for an hour or two, and it developed into a really resentful and just a violated feeling. There was always the fear."

When she got a little older, she began protesting to her father, but to no avail. He warned her never to say anything, and she complied. "He was the biggest one in the house, over six feet. Nobody argued with him," she says. "It remained a secret."

One April evening in 1976, after the family had finished dinner, eight-year-old Anna found herself the last one at the table with her father. She remembers that distinctly, she says, because she always tried to avoid being alone with him. She excused herself quickly and went to her room. He followed her, but for a change, he didn't have incest on his mind. Instead, he handed her a note. Then he took his 12-gauge shotgun out of the closet, walked out the back door, put the barrel in his mouth, and blew his head off.

The contents of the note remain a secret. Just before the police arrived, Anna gave it to her mother, who screamed, tore it to pieces, and swallowed it.

Writing emotionally charged notes that were forever falling into the wrong hands would become a pattern for Anna. In a sense, her life ever since her father's suicide can be viewed as an effort to get that first note disgorged and out into the open.

By age nineteen Anna was a professional model and a beauty pageant winner, the former Miss Faces of Tampa, Florida. She had had one marriage—"a disaster," according to her—and innumerable affairs. She had wrecked the careers of several men (with their eager complicity) and left a trail of lurid notes and broken homes behind her.

Ahead lay the most important appearance of her life: not an audition or a "shoot" but a trial on the charge of first-degree murder. Her ability to sway

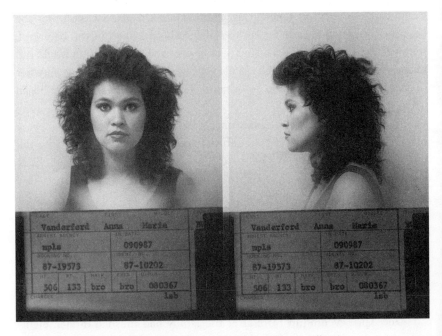

Anna Marie Vanderford's mug shot. Photographs from author's collection.

the jurors, to convince them that she too was a victim and remorseful about what she had done, would determine the course of her life for years to come. Anna's preparations were as unorthodox as they were rigorous. She prepared a list of twenty cosmetics and items of jewelry to be readied for her use each day, including translucent powder, earrings, lip liner, eyeliner, eye shadow, blusher, mascara, mousse, and eyebrow brush. She chose what she used every morning on the basis of her intuition about the peculiar chemistry of the moment. By then she was a person who reinvented herself daily, an artist who was her own most important creation, and a pathological liar.

A cosmetologist did Anna's hair. She came with firm instructions from Anna's lawyer about how she should look—"china-doll bangs, kind of prim and innocent"—but Anna was having none of that. She instructed the cosmetologist to do her hair the way it had always been done—sexy.

The persona Anna contrived made a striking, if somewhat spooky, impression on the jurors. They listened with rapt attention and a certain amount of sympathy to the tale she told, but in the end they decided against her. They found her guilty of first-degree murder, and on December 20, 1987, she was sentenced to life in prison.

"We kept expecting a psychologist to take the stand and explain some things to us," says the foreman of the jury, "but it never happened. Frankly, I was surprised."

Anna's relationship with her father and its violent conclusion seem to have left a permanent scar on her character. The police reports corroborate her story about Flloyd Franklin Vanderford's suicide. Officer Lyle Knutsen, who was the first investigator on the scene, has some observations to add.

"The wife was hysterical, in shock," he recalls, "and she didn't speak very good English. We couldn't get much out of her." Most of the information in Knutsen's reports came from eight-year-old Anna.

"There must have been some sort of domestic dispute, that's all I can think of," he says. "The father got the gun out of the closet, and the mother gathered the kids together and ran out the front door with them. She didn't know what he intended to do with that gun, that would be my guess. She must have been in fear for her life, and the lives of her children. They looped around the house the opposite way from where the father had gone. Then they heard a shot, continued around, and found him lying there."

Friends and family of the young man Anna later murdered question whether she was ever sexually abused by her father at all. They wonder if the incest tale was not just the first in what would prove to be a long string of lies.

"She lies about everything, you know," says one of them. "She lies about crucial matters, she lies about trivial things. She lies practically at random. I think the fact that she says something is true is good reason to doubt its validity." (Many people were glad to be sources for this story once they were assured their identities would not be revealed. They live in fear that Anna will either be released or escape from prison and kill them. "She is evil incarnate," says one.)

Nevertheless, an objective observer can find good reason to believe Anna's story. Her recollection of her father's suicide, accurate according to police reports, indicates that there was more to the relationship between them than met the casual eye. Furthermore, her description of him ("He was the biggest one in the house . . . . Nobody argued with him") and other details of her family life are telling. A 1981 study by Harvard Medical School psychiatrist Dr. Judith Herman concluded that the most striking similarities between incestuous families were the father's tendency to tyrannize and the mother's fear of questioning his authority. This kind of family structure is said to be a deliberate device to ensure that "the secret" will remain hidden.

Most telling of all is Anna's bizarre personal history. A clinical psychologist hired by her attorney diagnosed her as having a "Narcissistic Personality Disorder characterized by pathological lying, grossly delusional behavior and thinking, grandiosity, and an inability to cope with any form of real or perceived rejection."

Anna, however, did not become the kind of eternal victim many abused girls become. "She is supremely intelligent," says another person who ran afoul of Anna. "Others may have been taken by her beauty, but I was more impressed with her mind. She might be the most intelligent person I have ever met. She always knew exactly what she was doing."

The record reveals that Anna, cruelly victimized from age five to age eight, then further traumatized by her father's suicide, became a victimizer, not a victim. She took what nature gave her and set out to destroy men's lives with it.

The record of the Vanderford family's wanderings from 1976 to 1981 is sketchy. "The mother is really strange," says Hennepin County prosecutor Stephen Redding, who handled the case against Anna. "She would pack those kids up and move them all around the country like they were pieces of baggage. Sometimes she wouldn't even take them, she'd leave them with relatives and other people."

The Vanderfords spent some time in the Tampa area, where they became involved with a woman named Kelsey Hoffman. Anna refers to Hoffman interchangeably as her grandmother and her godmother, but she is not a blood relative. Hoffman put up $100,000 in cash to bail Anna out after her arrest for murder.

At age fifteen Anna was enrolled at the Temple Baptist Church School in St. Paul. She was a cheerleader and a participant in the TV ministry, a program that included videotaping of students. An assistant pastor who coached the basketball team was in charge of making the videotapes. He was forty years old, married, with two children. He drove the basketball team and cheerleaders to games as part of his duties. He and Anna had an affair. He denies having sexual relations with her but admits to some hugging and touching, which he claims took place at her instigation.

"She made herself available in every way," he says.

"We had sexual relations," says Anna. "It started out in the church, then we went to various places, hotels, his home. Once we had sex in his office, off to the side of the altar."

The two of them also exchanged notes of an explicit nature. Anna persuaded the assistant pastor to take her to his home and deliberately left some of those notes where his wife would find them. The wife blew the whistle, precipitating a rancorous counseling session between the head pastor, the assistant pastor, and Anna's mother.

"I was forced to leave the school," admits the former assistant pastor of Temple Baptist, who now lives and teaches in another state.

Anna had to leave, too. She went to Richfield High School, near Minneapolis, where she excelled in the sciences and became part of a program for gifted and talented students during her junior year.

"Anatomy, physiology, and biology were my fortes," she says. She was one of fifteen students picked to go to various area colleges for special science days. Her biology teacher at Richfield was in charge of transporting the gifted students, and that was how her affair with him began. He was forty-two, married, and had two children.

"We had sex in a locked classroom," she says, "at his office, in hotels."

A former student at Richfield High says that sixteen-year-old Anna had a reputation for promiscuity. She says Anna often bragged of her affair with the biology teacher, saying she would deliberately smear lipstick on his collar in an attempt to get him in trouble. According to her, Anna was seeing another teacher at the same time and was having affairs with other older men as well. One of them, a University of Minnesota tennis coach, was blackmailed by Anna.

In a deposition taken in connection with her 1986 divorce, Anna admits to affairs with two Richfield teachers.

On the afternoon of May 16, 1984, Anna and the biology teacher drove to Hidden Falls, in St. Paul, and parked. According to the police report of the incident that followed, two officers patrolling the area saw a car that appeared to be empty. When they approached, they observed movement in the front seat and saw a male with his trousers off on top of a girl whose skirt was hoisted and whose blouse was open, exposing her breasts. The officers could not tell for certain if sexual intercourse was taking place.

Anna and the teacher became aware that the police were watching and pulled themselves together hurriedly. The teacher asked Anna to claim she was his wife, but she immediately told the police she was his student. The teacher denied that they were having intercourse.

An officer took Anna aside and questioned her.

"How long has this been going on?" he asked.

"Since last December," she replied.

"How did it begin?"

"We started out just holding hands, and I would write notes to him."

"What were you doing just now?"

"Hugging, kissing."

"Were you ever together down here before?"

"Yes, we came here yesterday."

"Has he ever made you touch him?"

"No, but I've done it on my own. On the way over here today I touched him, and he really got hot. I thought he was going to explode."

"But you've never had sex?"

"No, but when I found out we were coming here today, I didn't wear panties."

"Do you have a regular boyfriend?"

"Yes."

"How old is he?"

"He's twenty-four."

Anna produced an ID indicating that she was sixteen. One of the officers read the teacher his rights off a Miranda card. "Can't we just forget this?" asked the teacher. "My life will be ruined."

The teacher was booked but never charged. He left his wife and children and later pursued Anna across the country in hopes of marrying her. He no longer teaches for a living.

Anna and her family moved to Sanibel, Florida, where she spent her senior year in high school.

Anna graduated with honors from Cypress Lake High School in Sanibel. After graduation she moved to the Tampa area, where she lived with Hoffman, the woman she calls her grandmother or godmother. While she was living with Hoffman and modeling part-time, she met a man named Vernon Blitch.

"We dated one month, and I married him," says Anna. "On the record it lasted five months. Realistically it lasted about three. There were very hard feelings on both sides, for good reasons."

The reasons were especially good from her ex-husband's point of view. "He caught her screwing other guys," says prosecutor Stephen Redding, who characterizes Blitch as "a real nice, real naive guy who thought he'd died and gone to heaven when this beautiful girl came along and blew his socks off in the sack. It was every schoolboy's dream."

But the dream soured when Blitch discovered a diary detailing a visit from the Richfield teacher and Anna's continuing sexual activities with him, as well as with other men. According to Blitch, she also contracted genital herpes from a male prostitute she visited, and gave it to him. During the bitter arguments that followed, Anna threatened Blitch verbally, assaulted him physically, and made a serious attempt to stab him with a knife.

Blitch readily admitted that he was deeply involved with Anna on an emotional and sexual level, but he was also square enough to demand fidelity. Anna has never talked about the reasons for her hard feelings toward him or about where all of her rage came from, but some clues emerge from a close reading of the court records. Blitch's determination to end their relationship was clearly a new experience for Anna, who preferred men cast in the mold of the Richfield teacher—willing to end their careers, break up their homes, and chase her halfway across the continent. The fact that Blitch rejected her did not sit well with Anna Vanderford.

Blitch is a sportsman who owns several guns. "He was so scared of her that he took his guns, disassembled them, and hid the parts in different places," says prosecutor Redding. "He was just absolutely terrified that she was going to kill him and feels lucky that she didn't."

Within weeks of breaking up with Blitch, Anna had moved in with three other men and was making plans to marry one of them, John Emmanuelson. According to the divorce records, Emmanuelson contracted genital herpes from her. She dated several other men, including a photographer who was helping her assemble a portfolio.

At the same time, Anna's modeling career was taking off, and by late 1986 she had won two Tampa-area beauty pageants, the Miss Faces contest and one sponsored by a Tampa department store. The Miss Faces victory earned her a trip for two to the Bahamas. Shortly before Christmas, she and Hoffman took the trip, during which Anna had a brief fling with a man named David Spence.

Anna's family had moved back to the Twin Cities, but they joined her and Hoffman for Christmas in Tampa, and it was then that Anna made up her mind to return to Minneapolis. "We had spent a wonderful Christmas together," says Anna, "and I guess I got persuaded to come back. I just wanted to spend some time with my family."

Subsequent events—and a note she left explaining those events—suggest another explanation for her departure: Anna had suffered a setback in the field of sexual relationships, her rejection by Blitch. She was withdrawing from the scene, full of bottled-up rage.

"I am sure after the shock and hatred wear off you will have a vague understanding of what happened," she would write to Dr. and Mrs. Thomas Wittkopp, the day before she murdered their son, Edward. "No one else knew I was going to do this, but a lot of things entered into it. . . . I had several reasons. All I can offer you is my sincere apologies, and my guilt in this premeditated state. I am sorry for the embarrassment in your community, the loss in your family and your hearts, and that it had to be this way; that it was Ed, and not some other teen, that intervened in my life."

"It was as if there was a script all written," says Mrs. Nadine Wittkopp, "and Ed happened to be the guy who walked in the door."

Anna moved in with her mother, who was employed at the Sawatdee Thai Restaurant in Minneapolis. Her mother got Anna a job as a hostess at Sawatdee. Among her duties was taking applications, and one of the first she took came from Edward Wittkopp, who was looking for work as a bartender. "I handle these things," Anna told him, "and you're going to get the job."

Ed was a twenty-year-old boy who had recently dropped out of the University of Minnesota and gone to bartending school. "He was looking around for some new experiences for a while," says one of his friends. "He probably would have gone back to the U. He was kind of math-oriented."

Ed was a Minnesota Twins fan. He liked the Grateful Dead. He liked gardening and held several jobs at garden centers during his brief life. He especially liked roses. "How would I describe Ed?" says Jeff Wyman, who lived with him. "Mellow, easygoing, never upset. He was a very happy, very positive guy."

His mother remembers a day in March 1987 when Ed told her that he had met a really stunning girl at work, and she seemed quite interested in him. "I'd had lunch at Sawatdee," says Mrs. Wittkopp, "and I knew who he was talking about. I agreed that she was quite beautiful. He seemed flattered but at the same time confused."

His confusion seems to have stemmed from the fact that this was a new experience for him. Although he had had girlfriends, he was not the kind of guy that girls fell all over, and furthermore, this was no ordinary flirtation. Anna came on like a Mack truck from the moment she laid eyes on him. Later she would tell him, "You know why I like you, Ed? Because you look like my father."

She also told him that her attraction was based on the fact that he came from a good home in Edina. "I always wanted to come from a good home," she explained.

By the time she had known Ed for two days, she was sending him steamy notes. "We wrote notes back and forth all the time," says Anna. "I mean we wrote a lot. My mom, being in a managing position [at Sawatdee], was very concerned with us showing that there was a relationship going on. We had to pass notes through waiters."

Ed mentioned the tone, if not the content, of these notes to his family. He told his parents Anna had written that she wanted to be Mrs. Wittkopp. What's the rush? they asked. His father, a psychiatrist, also took note of a troubling fact.

"There is no question Ed changed the moment he met Anna," says Dr. Wittkopp. "He was such an outgoing kid, and his interests were so varied, but as soon as he met Anna, he became subdued. There was little enthusiasm for the kinds of things he used to enjoy. His interests centered on her, exclusively. He wouldn't talk about himself anymore. It became 'Anna and I.'"

After Anna and Ed had been going together for a few weeks, the Wittkopps invited them to dinner. It was Ed's idea. He wanted his parents and his sister Emily to meet her.

Anna and Ed showed up more than an hour late and announced that they had already eaten. While the Wittkopps ate, Anna kept up a steady line of chatter, completely dominating the conversation. Ed, who was usually verbal, was quiet and withdrawn. His dress and appearance, marginally acceptable in the manner of a normal twenty-year-old, made a stark contrast with Anna, who was bejeweled, and wearing layers of thick makeup. She punctuated her nonstop talking with intimate little gestures, grabbing Ed's hand and referring to him as if he were not in the room. "I think she called him 'the white boy,'" recalls Mrs. Wittkopp.

Within a few minutes Anna had discovered that seventeen-year-old Emily was soon to go to her junior/senior prom. Anna proceeded to give Emily elaborate instructions on how the evening should go. "Surely you don't allow your boyfriend to pick out his own tux," she said. "You pick it out for him and make sure it complements what you wear." She said she was knowledgeable about proms, having been a member of the royal court at the Richfield High prom. "Later we found out that was not true," says Mrs. Wittkopp.

All in all, the Wittkopps found Anna to be unpleasant and strangely disquieting.

So did Ed's friends and roommates: Paul Teien, Jeff Wyman, and Tod Sigler. Teien, who has since moved to Colorado, was the bluntest of the three. Less than half an hour after he met Anna, he took Ed aside.

"Want my advice?" he said. "Get rid of her."

Ed did not heed his friend's advice. He and Anna began to discuss marriage seriously. They spent all of their time together and continued writing long, sexually explicit notes to each other. Also, Anna was pregnant—although the question of how pregnant and by whom would later arise.

"So much happened that it seems like it must have taken a long time," says Wyman, "but it didn't. It took a very short time. Afterwards we figured it out. They met March ninth. They were heavily into it by mid-March, and then he broke it off with her by the middle of May."

It was eerie while it lasted. In his roommates' words: "Anna cut him off from everybody." This was not merely a figure of speech. It was a physical fact. The two of them spent long hours in Ed's bedroom together, and when they emerged, Ed was an oddly diminished figure.

"Even if we were in the same room," says Sigler, "she not only dominated his attention—his eye contact and conversational attention—but she dominated his body. I mean by constantly being on top of him, or touching him, doing all her clingy, seductive things. Not that it was so overtly sexual. It was more like she wanted to keep him from relating to us in any way. She had phenomenal social skills that way, you know, with body language. I mean she would literally sit in front of him to block our view of him. I can still see him slumped back in this saggy old couch we had, and Anna leaning forward, between us and Ed."

"If you asked Ed a question," says Wyman, "Anna answered. And it would upset her if he did anything with anyone else. I was seeing a girl at that time, and the four of us made a plan to do something together one evening. I had to work, so my girlfriend drove my car, picked up Ed, and then the two of them came to get me. That meant Ed and my girlfriend were together in the car for about ten minutes, and when we went to get Anna, she was really upset. She insinuated that Ed was cheating on her, and she refused to do anything that night."

The next day she and Ed made up, but Anna told him she never wanted to do anything with his friends again.

Despite Anna's possessiveness, she was still carrying on with other men.

She slept with another bartender at Sawatdee, and she continued to write Spence, the man she had met in the Bahamas a few months earlier.

By late April, Anna's hold on Ed was slipping. She had insisted on moving into the house he shared with his roommates, a situation they found intolerable. "She was just this terrible, negative presence," says Sigler. "I avoided the house."

Ed and Anna's sex life had been so hot and heavy for awhile that the bloom was coming off that rose, so Anna resorted to courtesan-like ploys to revive Ed's interest. She made up little coupons, each worth a different sexual "favor," and told Ed he could earn these favors by performing various time-dominating tasks for her.

When sex didn't work, she tried something else. "She would just rage at him," says Wyman. "I can still picture her with her nose about an inch from his, screaming at the top of her lungs."

Anna's version of events differs from that of Ed's roommates. She claims they were a bad influence on him, urged him to smoke pot, and never liked her. "We were picnicking in the backyard once, and they threw water on us," she says. "It seemed like a small thing at the time, but then they started leaving girls' numbers in Ed's room and sending girls around to his door at night." She says she had to take care of Ed's finances because he was so slipshod about practical matters, and that led to charges that she was domineering.

In early May, Anna and Ed had a messy quarrel. That was when Ed began to be truly frightened. He told his parents that Anna was sitting behind the wheel of the car while they argued, and he was in the passenger seat. She suddenly took off and headed straight for a nearby retaining wall at high speed. She veered at the last moment, but Ed got the distinct impression that she had come close to smashing into the wall. He jumped out of the car and ran the three miles to his house.

By May 5 Ed was telling his roommates that he now saw Anna in a different light. He said he wanted to stay home with them that evening. Generally speaking, he had begun allotting more time for friends and less for Anna. She had been demanding that they go shopping for maternity clothes, an odd request in view of the fact that she was either less than two months pregnant or pregnant by someone else. She finally took a check from Ed and called her brother to take her shopping.

On May 13 Ed told Anna that their relationship was over. She left their house late that night in tears and returned the next day to get her clothes. She called Ed's mother and told her, "I can't believe Ed broke up with me." She confessed that her attraction to him had always been partially based on the good home he came from and on the fact that he was from Edina.

"She also said she had gotten pregnant in February," says Mrs. Wittkopp, "and I questioned her carefully on that, because it did not correlate with the starting point of their relationship at all. She very specifically said she expected to have the child around Thanksgiving, which does put the date of conception in February." Anna aborted the pregnancy after her arrest.

A few days later, Ed and his father had a long talk about Ed's responsibilities. "We agreed that he should get a blood test done to see if it really was his child," says Dr. Wittkopp, "and we also agreed that if it was, then he was duty bound to shoulder half the responsibility—for the delivery, the care and raising, all of it. It could have been an unpleasant conversation, but it was not. I remember he was more like himself than he'd been for a long time. He made a little joke about how I'd just given him two free hours of psychotherapy, and we laughed about that, and, well, I never saw him alive again."

The events of that week included a visit by Anna to the welfare office to apply for benefits and several stops at Ed's house. During one of these, she says, she and Ed argued. He asked her to leave. She started to cry and pointed out that she was still technically a resident of the house, although without keys, since the two of them had shared a set when they were together. Ed glared at her and walked upstairs, at which point she spied some keys lying on a chair and quickly picked them up. Then she followed Ed to his room, where they continued to argue.

He asked her to get a blood test. "Fine, no problem," she said, sobbing, "but how can you even think it isn't yours?"

"Get out," he said. "Now."

Anna claims she spent the next few days in a funk on her mother's couch, alternately crying and sleeping. "I didn't comb my hair, brush my teeth, wash, nothing. If I made it to the bathroom, I was lucky."

She testified in court, however, that she did go out a few times—for pizza and to go horseback riding.

Meanwhile, Ed was sharing certain fears with his friends. He and Sigler were watching television together when he told Sigler, "I'm afraid she could get a gun and kill me." He also confided this fear to Teien. He and Teien discussed going to Colorado together.

Unfortunately, Ed failed to act on his premonition. Anna did purchase a weapon, a 12-gauge shotgun, on May 20. Then she stopped at a Taco Bell for something to eat and went horseback riding again. Sometime during that day she wrote three letters—one to Ed's parents, one to her brother and sister, and one to her mother. In these letters she declared her intention to murder Ed, along with unspecified others, and to commit suicide.

She and her brother went to a movie that evening, and she dropped him off at home. About 12:30 a.m., Anna took the car and drove to nearby River-side Park. She says she sat and pondered suicide for a while.

She drove to the house where Ed was sleeping, parked, and loaded the shotgun. Her story, which the jury did not believe, was that she called out Ed's name until he woke up and let her in. Then she went up to his bedroom with him, shotgun in hand, and they talked. She said their conversation quickly became an argument, then a physical confrontation, during which he shoved her to the floor and turned his back on her. Thereupon, she seized the loaded gun "and it went off."

Ed's roommates say it would have been physically impossible for her to do what she described without waking them. They say she used the keys she had taken to let herself in, tiptoed up to Ed's bedroom, and shot him in the back as he slept.

The blast awakened Ed's sleeping roommates. Anna told Wyman, "I've shot Ed." She held onto the gun when he tried to take it away from her.

"Don't go in there," she told him when he looked toward Ed's room. "You'll have nightmares the rest of your life."

She told Wyman to call the police but asked him to "please give me time to kill myself first." Wyman says he doubts if she meant it, and Anna ulti-mately handed him the gun without much of a struggle. The police discov-ered the letters she had written when they searched her car.

Another person familiar with Anna says, "Anna kill herself? That's a joke. She may have envisioned suicide as fitting in nicely with the production she was staging, but when it came down to it, it would be impossible for her. Narcissists never take their own lives, and Anna is the ultimate narcissist."

The statement she made to police when they arrived was suppressed at her trial. She told them, "I'm relieved that there is no capital punishment in this state. I had to kill him, you know. He was really irresponsible."

In a letter written from her prison cell, she bemoans the fact that she cannot express her real feelings to the media. Those feelings, she wrote, are: "No regrets, because Ed was such a loquacious asshole."

Anna made the news again when she flew to Thailand while she was free on a $100,000 cash bond. She called her lawyer, Thomas Bauer, from Bangkok and told him she had fled with the intention of avoiding prosecution. He replied that he was duty bound to tell the police her whereabouts unless she promised to return. She said she would, adding that she had already made the decision to come back before she called.

"She told me it was too dull in Bangkok," says Bauer. "No VCRs, no color TV, no nice restaurants. I was relieved that she was planning to return, but I had to wonder what was going on in her head. I mean, I'd already told her we had a very tough case, and the prosecution was not willing to accept any kind of plea bargain. I told her that in my opinion an acquittal was impossible, and we'd be damned lucky to get a second-degree [murder] verdict, yet here she was comparing life in Bangkok to life in Minneapolis. If she was facing reality, she would have been drawing comparisons between Bangkok and Shakopee prison."

Anna's bond was revoked when she returned, and she has been behind bars ever since. She is scheduled for release in 2004.

While she was awaiting trial, she wrote as many as ten letters a day—to her lawyer, friends and family, and prison pen pals whose names she picked up from newspaper stories. "She seemed to have a compulsion to write," says a deputy who was on duty at the county jail at the time. The testimony about the lurid notes she and Ed exchanged garnered some publicity at her trial, as did an occasion when the courtroom was full of Ed's friends, all wearing roses in their lapels.

"We did it because Ed loved roses," says Sigler. "It was a gesture, something in his memory."

Anna was convicted of first-degree murder. "Her story included twelve separate unlikelihoods," says the foreman of the jury. "It did not ring true." Although the jury members discussed the case for quite a while, they were unanimous the first time they were polled.

"We were grasping at straws, trying to find some way to show her a little mercy," says the foreman, "but her story didn't do the trick. We could have found her guilty of a lesser crime if we decided she committed murder in the heat of passion, but the evidence of premeditation was overwhelming. Sure, it was a crime of passion; you can say that of any violent act. But 'the heat of passion'? No."

The jury concluded that Anna had entered the house surreptitiously and murdered Ed in cold blood.

Anna's new lawyer, Ron Meshbesher, filed a motion for retrial, alleging that the judge erred in not allowing a psychologist to testify and that Anna's former lawyer, Bauer, had compromised the case by having sexual relations with Anna while she was out on bond and while he was conferring with her in the Hennepin County jail.

Bauer calls those accusations "common lies."

"There were some due process issues involved, too," says Meshbesher. "The state of Minnesota does not allow a finding of 'diminished capacity,' which would effectively make it possible to find Anna guilty of second- rather than first-degree murder, and I think that is wrong. Juries are not allowed to consider something like a history of abuse or the effect of profound depression on behavior. My client is a very sick lady. I think she is just now coming to terms with how sick she is."

Anna apparently agrees. "I consider myself to be the classic incest victim," she said in a phone interview.

Bauer vehemently denies ever having sexual relations with Anna. "It would be unethical," he says. He also points to the fact that he was in possession of divorce records indicating she was suffering from various venereal diseases. During the time she was being held in jail (where she alleges that she and Bauer had intercourse in a tiny conference room that a deputy walked past frequently), Bauer had to facilitate her treatment for outbreaks of genital herpes. He says her accusations began immediately after her trial, when he told her he would no longer represent her. In his opinion, the way she lashed out at him was consistent with her reaction to other rejections.

Meshbesher's motion alleges that Anna was unable to fire Bauer when she thought she was being inadequately represented because of the emotional bond between them. Bauer counters that the record of certain proceedings that took place in the judge's chambers proves otherwise.

On December 2, 1987, during the trial, there was a conference between Anna, Bauer, and Judge Isabel Gomez, in which the judge asked Anna if she was satisfied with her representation. She answered that she was. The judge took note of how active Anna had been in her own defense.

Anna later would berate Bauer for not asking witnesses questions she suggested. For example, she wanted him to question Ed's mother about her premarital sex life and was angry when Bauer refused.

Defending Anna was also difficult in other ways, according to Bauer. "She lied to me about all the major aspects of the case," he says, "and then at intervals she would tell me the truth. Also, I spent a lot of time telling her how she should present herself, but it had no effect. She dressed exactly the way she wanted to dress. She wanted to wear a rhinestone-studded jumpsuit into the courtroom one day. I had to ask the judge not to allow her to wear it, out of courtesy to me."

Anna did wear a different outfit to the trial every day, favoring tight-fitting wool suits and six-inch spike heels. "It was the Anna Vanderford Show," Wyman says, "there's no doubt about that. She came on like Dragon Lady."

Bauer claims that Anna's answer to his first question when he put her on the stand was somewhat counterproductive. He asked her to identify a picture of herself taken for her modeling portfolio. "That was taken when a couple guys came down from Chicago for a shooting," Anna replied.

"Then," says Bauer, "she turned her head toward the jury with a maniacal grin on her face, like Linda Blair in *The Exorcist*, and said, 'Oh, I guess I shouldn't say things like shooting here,' and she laughed."

"I couldn't believe it," says Bauer.

Anna did go on to explain that "shooting" is a common term for a modeling session with a photographer, but the damage had been done.

Bauer makes no bones about why he refused to handle her case any longer. "I just could not control her," he explains, "and I never really knew what she might say or do. There were times when we would discuss things for hours, go over her version of events meticulously, then at the end of the discussion she would look at me and say, 'About half of what I just told you is a lie. It's up to you to figure out which half.'"

Bauer says Anna gave other professionals involved with her case—private investigators and other lawyers she considered hiring—completely different stories from the one she gave him. She told the first attorney she spoke to that she shot Ed in his sleep, according to Bauer.

"It's a pretty helpless feeling, putting your client on the stand and not knowing what might come out of her mouth," he says. "She lied just for the fun of it. I agree fully with Ron Meshbesher's theory about diminished capacity, by the way. I conducted the trial in a manner that would facilitate an appeal on that basis."

Bauer hired the clinical psychologist who diagnosed Anna as suffering from a narcissistic personality disorder. Her pathology is characterized by an inability to distinguish fact from fantasy, grandiosity, grossly delusional behavior, pathological lying, and hysterical reaction to any real or perceived rejection. This type of disorder is said to be common among career prostitutes, and there is speculation that childhood sexual abuse may be a contributing factor in its development.

Redding, the lawyer who prosecuted Anna Vanderford, opposed the motion for a new trial strenuously. "She is not crazy within the definition of the law," he says. "She knows right from wrong. I'd say that of all the murderers I've prosecuted over the years, and there have been many, she is the most likely to repeat. She scares me. She is a hateful, remorseless, angry, amoral, sociopathic killer. She thinks it was all right to kill that boy. She thinks he deserved it."

Redding agrees that sexual abuse as a child may have been a contributing factor in her later lifestyle, but he sees no reason to excuse her on account of it.

The motion for retrial was denied.

Anna is locked up but far from forgotten. After her trial and its attendant publicity, Spence contacted Bauer and told him he had met Anna in the

Bahamas in late 1986, where they had a brief but memorable affair. He said they corresponded regularly after that, exchanged gifts, and planned to marry, but in May 1987 (around the time of the murder) Anna's letters mysteriously ceased. He felt let down.

"He should count his blessings," says Redding.

Others who were involved with Anna think about her, too. These are the people who spoke only on condition of anonymity. They seem to have an image in their minds of an evil succubus who may yet creep into their beds some night to screw their brains out, steal their souls, and murder them.

Mrs. Nadine Wittkopp has a thought to share about Anna. She reads a paragraph from Samuel Yochelson's seminal work, *The Criminal Personality*, volume 1, in which he describes the classic female criminal: "She regards herself as irresistible. She regards her man as a possession to be managed in line with her own objectives. Her control tactics may be obvious or devious. She demands fidelity and accountability from her partner, and yet expects to come and go as she pleases without question. She expects confirmation of her irresistibility. She does not exchange views, she issues directives and ultimatums. She is intent on conquest, and uses sex as a vehicle for achieving control. Sometimes these women are so intent on maintaining control that they deliberately become pregnant, or pretend to be pregnant when they are not."

"There, does that ring a bell?" asks Mrs. Wittkopp.

She says that the observation and her offering of it are really uncharacteristic of how she and her husband view things now (this story was first written a year after the murder) because it concerns Anna. They think about her far less often than about the young son they lost.

"You don't ever really get past it," says Mrs. Wittkopp. "After a while, you get so you're not physically sick when you think about it."

"I got sick all over again talking to you about it," says her husband. "My stomach was all tied up in knots. I couldn't think about anything else for a while."

Anna's thoughts on the matter are typically egocentric. "I am the classic incest victim," she says.

Self-serving as that statement sounds, it is probably true.

The Courtship of Linda Winbush

Linda Winbush met Leonard Richards in March 1986. A nephew of hers who had done some work for Richards introduced him, but under a different name. "Linda, meet Martin," he said. Richards, a husky, bearded man of thirty-eight, with intense, hypnotic eyes, just nodded.

Richards liked his women credulous. A few days later, after he had taken a good long look at Winbush, he told her he needed a place to stay. He didn't tell her it was because he was one step ahead of an IRS agent. Instead, he concocted a story about allowing a married couple to live with him in his house on Twenty-ninth Avenue S. in Minneapolis. As soon as they had moved in, they had started talking about getting a divorce, he explained. Now he had to get out of his own house to avoid taking sides in a marital dispute.

In fact, a homeless man Richards had befriended was living in his southside home. Richards had agreed to let him stay in return for maintaining the house. There wasn't much maintenance to do, but there was one repetitious chore, and Richards made it harder than it had to be. When his tenant emptied the garbage, which contained paper waste from an office Richards kept in his home, it had to be brought to a dumpster two blocks away. Never empty the garbage in my trash barrel, Richards instructed him.

The house itself was a rarity in Minnesota. It was built on a concrete slab and had no basement.

On March 3, 1986, "Martin" moved into a house that Winbush rented on Dupont Avenue N. He agreed to pay her twenty-five dollars a week but soon began complaining about the noise her sons, ages five and seven, made, and used that as an excuse to withhold the money.

Between his griping and refusal to pay, Winbush didn't think things would work out, but when she told Martin that he might have to move, he said that wouldn't be necessary. On the evening of March 29, a romantic relationship developed between Winbush and her tenant, who revealed his real name in the throes of passion and told her a little bit about himself. He said he was a paralegal and could train her to be one as well.

Winbush's training commenced immediately. She learned to copy documents, shop for office supplies, and run errands.

Just before Thanksgiving 1986, Richards, Winbush, and her children moved into a house on Second Avenue N. Richards set up an office on the second floor, where Winbush observed him doing "different kinds of work for a number of different attorneys." Occasionally she assisted him by delivering documents to people, who either seemed angry or totally baffled upon receiving them.

Shortly after they moved, Winbush's nephew told her that Richards was a suspect in the murder of his own sister. Her nephew was pissed off at Richards when they spoke, because of a dispute over money, so she pretty much dismissed his story. Nevertheless, she told Richards what he had said. Richards denied the accusation.

"I believed him," she would later tell police.

During the first two months of 1987, Richards's work often kept him out until the wee hours of the morning. He racked up dozens of hours on a word processor at a Kinko's copy center in southeast Minneapolis. The charge for using the processor was eight dollars an hour until 1 a.m., when it changed to four dollars an hour. Richards tried to create all his documents for the lower price, hence his strange schedule.

By the latter half of February, Richards was working at a frantic pace. He often sat down behind the processor when the eight-dollar fee was in effect, sometimes as early as 10:30 p.m., and worked until morning. The clerks at Kinko's knew him well because he rarely left without disputing the fees. He would claim that he had spent less time at eight dollars an hour than he was being charged for and try to chisel them out of a few bucks that way.

Late one night a clerk named Jean Preston had an odd, almost scary conversation with him. Preston mentioned that she had been on a jury in which a defendant was found guilty of tax evasion. Richards appeared to be angry that she had voted to convict. He seemed to take it personally, she recalled. He asked her question after question about the case and grilled her about what the conviction hinged upon.

Around the time that Richards's document production was peaking, Winbush's training intensified as well. Richards told her that the basement of their house had to be cleaned and made ready as a reception area because he was expecting some clients on Monday, February 23. He instructed her to put curtains over the basement windows but seemed dissatisfied with the result. He bought a spray can of window frosting and applied it himself. That didn't work either. While Winbush kept busy with a brush and a mop, Richards covered the windows with contact paper. He asked if she owned some tools he might need—an ax, a hacksaw, a sledge hammer. She told him she didn't.

By Sunday afternoon Winbush had done everything a paralegal could to make the place presentable. In her opinion it still looked like a basement, and a dark one at that, despite the bare bulb that cast a pool of wan light on the middle of the reception area but failed to illuminate the walls. A heating duct hung from the ceiling. There was a smelly drain in the middle of the floor. It hardly seemed the place to entertain important clients.

Are you sure you don't want to talk to them upstairs in your office? she inquired. Richards was sure. She asked if he would need refreshments for the meeting. No, he replied.

Richards arrived at Kinko's earlier than usual that night. He had Preston do some copying for him, an affidavit, more than ninety pages long. She noticed that each page had the name "R. T. Stratton" on the upper right-hand corner.

Richards put in his usual stint on the word processor while the copies were made, and paid without disputing the charges, which was unlike him. His mind seemed to be elsewhere, according to Preston. He left just after 2 a.m., Monday morning, February 23.

About 11:00 that morning Richards emerged from the basement, where he had been making final preparations, and drove Winbush and her kids to her friend's home in the suburbs. By the time he dropped her off, he was in a rush because he was expecting his clients at noon. He told her he would have the phone off the hook until 5:00 p.m. or so, and he would call her and pick her up about 5:30.

That afternoon a man who investigators suspect was Patrick Kelly, the tenant at Richards's south-side home, brought a document titled "Affidavit of R. T. Stratton" to a notary public. He signed the name Robert T. Stratton on each page before it was notarized.

Richards didn't arrive to pick up Winbush until almost 11:00 that night, long after he had said he would be there. As soon as he walked in the door, she noticed that the cuffs of his pants were rolled up, and his legs had reddish stains on them. She asked if he had been painting the house. He said he hadn't. She thought little of it at the time, but his behavior over the next twelve hours was so strange that she began to think something was amiss. It began on the way home when he informed her that one of his clients, a master electrician, had started rewiring the basement while they conferred. As a result, there were open electrical boxes all over the place, he said, and neither she nor the children should go down there under any circumstances.

After she put the kids to bed, Winbush sat down and lit a cigarette in the kitchen. Richards sat next to her, and they talked while she smoked, which she found strange. They rarely conversed, and he normally refused to come near a lit cigarette, yet he hovered around and made small talk until she went to bed that night. She couldn't help noticing that he stayed between her and the basement door.

Before she fell asleep, he asked her if she ever got up and wandered around at night. She assured him she didn't.

The next morning she noticed something sticky on the hallway floor, but it was too dark to see what it was. Some furniture had been placed against the basement door, and there was a smell in that area that she later described as "sweet, and sort of like steak or hamburger."

Richards hovered while she dressed, then handed her $100, and told her to take the kids and go shopping. That was so wildly out of character it made her really suspicious. She agreed, but before they left, she managed to blot some of the sticky stuff in the hall onto a square of toilet paper and hide it in her purse.

Richards dropped her at Bank's department store. As soon he drove away, she grabbed the children, ran to the Riverplace shopping center a few blocks away, and called the police.

About 10:00 a.m. on February 24, 1987, Winbush was interviewed at Riverplace. She said she was afraid someone had been murdered in her basement, and her boyfriend had done it. "I love him," she said, "but sometimes I'm afraid there's something wrong with him." She handed over the square of toilet paper. The officer recognized the stain as blood.

Any lingering doubts about her story were dispelled when she uttered the name of the man she suspected of committing the murder. Homicide detectives were well acquainted with Leonard Richards.

Leonard Richards. Photographs courtesy of the Minnesota Department of Corrections.

Richards's half sister, May Wilson, was a registered nurse who spent four years on active duty in Vietnam during the war. She contracted encephalitis in the service, and her health deteriorated badly. Shortly before she was discharged, an Air Force doctor told her she would be hospitalized many times in the future. He advised her to get plenty of health insurance.

When Wilson left Vietnam, Richards was running a storefront church in Keewatin, Minnesota. It was one of six churches he established, with names like Free United Mission Association of Churches, Free United Mission Mother Church, Incorporated, and the Hiawatha Free United Mission Church.

Wilson told her brother about the Air Force doctor's advice. He saw to it that she took it to heart. By 1972 Richards and Wilson were living together in Minneapolis. The record and Richards are mum on whether their relationship was sexual, but it was certainly financial. Wilson had forty different hospitalization policies, most of them tied to certificates of participation in various organizations she had joined because they offered group insurance. Many of the policies paid her cash for lost income during her stays in the hospital. Over a three-year period starting in 1973 Wilson collected more than $700,000 in cash. The entire amount was donated to various churches, charities, and trusts controlled by Richards.

"She was definitely the goose that laid the golden egg as far as Leonard was concerned," said an ex-friend of Richards's. "He set May up in what you might call 'the used insurance business.'"

Richards has several former friends who spoke of him only after a promise of anonymity. "He'll sue at the drop of a hat," one said. Besides their apprehension, they have something else in common. They are attorneys who met Richards through their association with Libertarian or antitax organizations.

The insurance companies that paid money to Wilson eventually became suspicious. Lawsuits against both Richards and Wilson were filed in 1977. Richards showed up for a deposition in conjunction with one of those suits wearing a ski mask and dark glasses. When the lawyer asked him his occupation, Richards replied that the question was an invasion of his religious privacy.

At the time Richards could show only $2,500 in yearly income. He listed his profession as a consultant to gay newspapers.

Eventually the insurers were forced to admit that there was nothing illegal about what Wilson and Richards had done. A settlement was reached in which Wilson was paid a lump sum, and her health coverage was canceled. But there would soon be more insurance taken out—twenty-seven policies in all, millions of dollars' worth of coverage—this time on Wilson's life.

Two charities controlled by Richards were named as beneficiaries. According to a scenario that would be laid out by the insurers' lawyers, Wilson found herself in the uncomfortable position of being worth more to her brother dead than alive.

In January 1982, Richards established a taxi company. Its sole asset was one taxi, which Richards drove. A short time later several policies on Wilson's life were purchased that paid double indemnity for accidental death while in a common carrier such as a plane, train, or taxi. The largest paid $500,000 for accidental death, but $1.5 million if the accident occurred in a common carrier.

On the evening of March 14, 1982, Richards invited his sister out to eat. Dinner was on him, he explained, but he would have to transport her in his cab, and charge her a fare for the service. She agreed, unwisely, since the arrangement made her a passenger in a common carrier.

Richards later told police that he forgot to take his trip sheet when they left for the restaurant, so he pulled his cab into a garage connected to the house in which he and Wilson lived. Then he left the motor running, closed the garage door, and went into the house. He still hadn't returned when a comatose Wilson was rescued by the fire department half an hour later. The exhaust fumes filling the garage had triggered a fire alarm.

Captain Arthur Caple, one of her rescuers, recalled Wilson's words upon awakening: "Do you think my brother is trying to kill me?" she asked.

Two months later a new package of twenty-five insurance policies, with new stipulations, were taken out on Wilson's life, a total of over $3 million coverage. Most of them paid off for death by homicide but not suicide or illness. Five of the policies were good for thirty days only, including May 10 to May 16, 1982, the period in which a medical examiner would later testify Wilson was murdered.

Her body was found in the basement of a storefront building on West Broadway in Minneapolis. It was owned by a corporation called The Administration Center, which was controlled by Richards. Shortly before Wilson's death, Richards had instructed Gerald Gross, an ex-convict he had befriended, to cover the windows of The Administration Center with paper.

The employees of a nearby bank called police when they detected a strange odor in their basement and surmised it was wafting over from the building with the windows covered. Thus, Richards established a pattern with his first murder that would be repeated in the second. He covered the windows before he struck. He lured his victims to a place of his choosing, dispatched them on the first floor, and dragged them into the basement. He prepared for his crimes meticulously, planning them months in advance, but the odor of decomposition gave him away because he failed to formulate an efficient method for disposing of the bodies.

It wasn't for lack of trying. In Wilson's case, Plan A had something to do with boxes, lots of them. Gross told investigators that his duties consisted solely of collecting used boxes.

"Did he ever tell you what kind of business he was going to have at 1028 Broadway?" asked an investigator.

"No," Gross replied, "he just wanted me to get more and more cardboard boxes and put them in the basement. He was never satisfied with how many I'd get. I suggested buying some, but he said we didn't have the money. I'd spend about five hours a day going up and down Broadway getting boxes."

Wilson had been dead for days when the stench became so overpowering that the police entered the premises, forced the locked door to the basement, and encountered Plan B. It consisted of two unused French Ticklers placed near the bloated and badly decomposed body, which was naked except for a pair of panties pulled down to the ankles, and high-heeled shoes. The remnants of Plan A, an eight-foot-high pile of flattened cardboard boxes, were shoved against the wall.

Apparently the police were supposed to overlook $3 million worth of insurance and assume that Wilson had been raped and murdered by a stranger. One of only two keys to the basement door was later discovered lodged in Wilson's vagina. There was blood upstairs, and a puddle of blood under the stairwell. A medical examiner determined that Wilson's throat had been slit.

Gross provided some insight into Richards, his sister, and their sick relationship when investigators interviewed him. Gross explained that when he was an inmate in the North Dakota State Prison, he wrote a letter to a gay newspaper in Minneapolis, seeking a pen pal. Richards answered. Gross joined Richards at his south Minneapolis home shortly after his release, in January 1982. May was living there when he arrived, but Richards threw her out three days later.

Investigators asked him to describe the relationship between Richards and Wilson. "She seemed scared and paranoid," he said. "When Leonard asked her to do some work she wouldn't, but she'd go in her room. He'd get very upset, and tell her 'why are you here? You're just living off me. I wish you would leave.' She'd tell him she was trying, but she was sick and didn't feel good. She was scared of him. He would yell at her. He told me she was nothing but trouble, and he didn't want her in the house. He said she cost everybody money, him and the rest of the family."

There was another reason he didn't want her around. "Leonard and I had sex the first few nights I was there," Gross said. "He wanted me to be very quiet about it. He said he was a homosexual, but May didn't know it."

According to Gross, the day before Wilson left, the three of them went to the Marquette Bank in downtown Minneapolis and withdrew about $2,000 from an account she had there. It was a difficult trip, because Wilson feared crowds and could barely function in public. The next day Gross overheard Richards shouting at Wilson. Among other things, he told her he wished she were dead. He ordered her to leave immediately.

"I never saw her after that, but she'd call all the time," Gross told investigators, "up to twenty times a day. We could hear her through the speaker, but we never answered the phone."

The investigators found evidence that Wilson had made at least one attempt to get out from under her brother's thumb before he reduced her to a state of slavish dependence. They recovered three boxes of her clothing, one of which contained a wedding dress from Dayton's bridal shop. According to the receipt pinned to the sleeve, it had been charged to the account of a James R. Brown, who had a Minneapolis address. A note found with the dress indicated that a wedding date of June 6, 1977, had been set. The dress had never been worn.

Gross told investigators that his residency at Richards's house had come to an abrupt end shortly before Wilson was murdered. Richards woke him up at 2:00 one morning and told him to pack and get out. Gross called the priest at a local parish where he had been worshiping, and arranged to spend the night. Richards offered to drive him there just to be rid of him. He demanded and received Gross's keys, one to the house and one to the storefront on Broadway.

"On the way over he kept hitting me and smashing my head against the window," Gross said. "He called me a faggot. 'Go join the faggot Christians,' he said. 'I hate you, you son of a bitch. You use me just like my sister. I never want to see you again.'"

Wilson's murder quickly became the subject of lurid headlines and extensive television coverage. The insurance scams were revealed bit by bit in newspaper articles, often accompanied by a picture of Richards, his demonic gaze locked on to the reader's eyes. But the fear he inspired was mitigated by the perception that it was an open-and-shut case, and he would soon be locked up for good.

It didn't work out that way though. He was never even arrested. The investigation failed to yield any physical evidence connecting him to the crime.

Meanwhile, Richards did everything in his power to frame Gross. First, he claimed Gross had retained keys to the Broadway building, which Gross denied. Then one of Richards's lawyer friends tried to help him manufacture false evidence. An inmate at Stillwater prison, John Gammell, signed an affidavit in which he described Gross as violent and abusive and "anxious to set up Leonard Richards."

A police investigator talked to Gammell, who quickly admitted that an attorney had paid him $750 in the form of a cashier's check to sign the affidavit. He said that most of the statements in it were false. A check of bank records verified that he had been paid as he claimed.

Nevertheless, a competent defense attorney could have made a credible suspect out of Gross. It was a prospect that haunted Assistant County Attorney John Brink, who was in charge of the case. As months passed, then years, he became thin-skinned over repeated inquiries by insurance company investigators and reporters concerning what, if any, progress he was making.

"It's not my job to meet deadlines for the press or the insurance companies or anyone else," he carped to a *Star Tribune* reporter in 1985. "The more we find the more we find we must find. We may find in six months that it will take ten more years."

The problem Brink described went to the heart of what Richards is all about. The investigation was constantly getting lost in the profusion of entities that Richards created. Much of the evidence against him concerned the profit to be realized from Wilson's death, but to explain that to a jury, they would have to understand how a cash settlement paid to the May V. Wilson Miscellaneous Household Trust could be funneled through the May V. Wilson Conservative Investment Trust to the Free United Mission Mother Church, Inc., thence to Happy Times, Inc., on to The Minneapolis Taxicab Owners Association, and finally into Richards's pocket via the Cerro Gordo Charity Foundation.

By the time he was finally jailed, Richards had set up more than fifty trusts and nonprofit corporations, in Minnesota, Montana, Florida, South Dakota, and Washington DC. They were all designed to route the money he had made off his sister's illnesses into his hands with as few legal and tax consequences as possible.

Richards's Promethean capacity to beget corporations wasn't slowed by the knowledge that the state of Minnesota was trying to put him in prison. If anything, it was goosed. His intention was to beat the murder rap and collect the millions he thought he had coming. He was confident that his agile, albeit one-dimensional, mind was equal to the task before him, but he wasn't a member of the bar, and there were some filings only a lawyer could certify.

"Robert Stratton was a young, impressionable lawyer when they met," says a former friend of Richards's. "Leonard was a bright, articulate, and extremely focused individual, and I believe he bowled Robert over. He saw Leonard as strange and unique, and he also saw that he had plenty of money, and he was in need of legal services."

According to Brink and his investigators, Stratton began to provide those services in 1982, thereby entering a labyrinth from which he would never emerge. Four years later, less than two months before he was murdered, Stratton would tell his friend Jane Bailey that Richards was ruining his career, and he wanted to stop working for him. "This case is killing me," he said.

In 1982, Richards and Stratton set up an entity called the Alango Trust at the Richfield State Bank. The affairs of the Alango Trust followed the same jumbled path as the rest of Richards's business affairs. Stratton was named grantor of the trust, and the Richfield State Bank became the trustee.

In 1983 the Peel Realty Co., purportedly a holding company for real estate, was incorporated, with Richards as president and treasurer. Stratton and Richards were both listed as board members. Stratton purchased a controlling interest in Peel and donated it to the Alango Trust.

Timothy Davis, a lawyer and a trust officer at Richfield State Bank, asked Stratton who the other stockholders in Peel were. Stratton said they were people from Costa Rica who had met Richards through The Humanist Association. He did not tell Davis that The Humanist Association was another Richards-generated entity, with a list of fictitious associates. When Davis pressed for details, he explained that the Costa Rican humanists "owed Leonard some favors."

Davis was suspicious. He was concerned that holding a controlling interest in Peel Realty (as trustee for Alango, the majority owner) exposed the bank to an unacceptable level of liability. On February 9, 1983, Davis informed Stratton and Richards that the bank was resigning as trustee.

Stratton took it stoically; Richards was furious. He said the brevity of the bank's tenure would cast doubt on the legitimacy of the trust. A few days later Stratton was appointed trustee.

The Alango Trust and Peel Realty became the subjects of an IRS investigation in spring 1984. The records of many of the entities that Richards had formed were subpoenaed, and summonses were issued in each of the federal districts where they were located. Stratton represented Richards in those proceedings, alone in Minnesota and with local counsel in other jurisdictions.

During his representation in Minnesota, affidavits supposedly authored by "David Harvey" and "Paul Boe" were filed, along with Stratton's certification of their authenticity. After an investigation revealed that no such parties existed, the shadow of sanctions and possible fraud charges hung over Stratton.

An order that Stratton and Richards pay the government $12,000 in attorney fees and expenses for their "improper activities" was the last straw. Stratton told friends he did not know where he would get the money, and Richards wasn't helping him, either financially or in disproving the charges. He said Richards now disgusted him, and he couldn't believe a word he said. Furthermore, Richards was not as solvent as he used to be. The proceeds of the multiple insurance policies on Wilson's life were the subject of a civil trial in 1985. The jury, operating under the preponderance of evidence standard that civil judgments require, found that Richards had either murdered Wilson or hired someone to do it. As a result, the insurance companies did not have to pay. If the IRS had its way, much of the money Richards had received from Wilson's health insurers would be forfeited as well.

As 1986 drew to a close, Stratton filed a motion for amended findings in the order for payment of fees to the government. In it he wrote of a conflict of interest between providing the court with evidence about his dealings with Richards and the attorney-client privilege requiring confidentiality. He hoped the conflict could be resolved and indicated that he would comply with any order he received.

A month later he received one. Summonses were issued to both Stratton and Richards concerning the IRS case against the Alango Trust and Peel Realty. Richards moved in with Winbush to avoid service, but Stratton wasn't hiding. He agreed to meet with an IRS investigator on February 25, 1987.

It was an appointment he wouldn't keep. During the next few weeks Richards created a false affidavit in Stratton's name, in which Stratton blamed himself for Richards's tax problems and cleared up questions about the Alango Trust and Peel Realty in Richards's favor. Then Richards made preparations to murder Stratton. He never revealed how he lured him to Winbush's house, but it couldn't have been hard. Throughout his career Richards displayed an uncanny ability to bend people to his will.

The jig was up the day after Stratton was killed when Winbush discussed her fears with a police officer. A search warrant was obtained for 1707 Second Avenue N. Winbush gave the officers a key to the back door. They knocked before they opened it. There was no reply, but they heard someone moving around inside.

"IT'S THE POLICE," they shouted.

When no one answered, they opened the door with guns drawn and saw Richards trying to exit through the window. They ordered him to stop. "OK, I'm coming out, don't shoot," he said.

As they marched him to the squad car, Richards told the officers that he hoped they wouldn't draw any "unwarranted conclusions" from what they were about to see.

What they saw was a trail of bloody water that led through the hall and down the stairs. Stratton's body was lying on the basement floor, partially covered with a bloody bedsheet. There was a brand-new ten-pound maul with the price tag still on it standing against the wall a few feet from the body.

"Between this maul and the body was a metal table measuring approximately 2 feet by 3 feet that was cleaned off with only a roll of paper towels on same," according to the incident report, which also lists two other implements that were near to hand—a hatchet and a wire cutter.

Four garbage bags full of blood-soaked bathroom towels were on the floor near the body. A hose had been connected to the washtub sink. Bloody water was running down the floor drain. A postmortem revealed that Stratton had been shot in the head and stabbed numerous times.

The search of the premises and the subsequent search of Richards's house on Twenty-ninth Avenue S. yielded papers and legal documents concerning May Wilson, the Alango Trust, Peel Realty, and other entities, along with the fake Stratton affidavit, and several "plaques and framed documents" pertaining to Wilson and Richards. Many of the items seized were valuable evidence in the Stratton murder, and Brink said that some of the documents would be key evidence in the Wilson case as well.

Richards has been behind bars since his arrest, but justice was not swift in coming. Robert Cragg Jr., an insurance industry lawyer who had battled Richards for more than a decade, predicted that Richards would demand to represent himself, then proceed to tie the legal system in knots. He told the *St. Paul Pioneer Press* that Richards was "ingenious, one of the most intelligent people I've ever encountered. He knows the legal system very well, and he will use it. I don't know how they'll ever get a trial completed. He could take days picking one juror."

Despite the new evidence, which swelled the material amassed in the Wilson case to a total of 130,000 pages, Brink still did not feel confident about bringing Richards to trial for the murder of his sister. The evidence in the second case was better, and in 1989 Richards went to trial for Stratton's murder. He was convicted, after demanding to represent himself and instead having a defense attorney appointed over his objections.

Linda Richards née Winbush was a witness against him, even though she had accepted his proposal of marriage while he was locked up awaiting trial. Her testimony about Richards's behavior before and immediately after the crime was devastating, but it was substantially undercut by the fact that she had married him. "We thought she had a screw loose," one of the jurors said after the trial.

Richards wrote his own appeal in his cell in the county jail, and a year later the Minnesota Supreme Court ruled in his favor, granting him a new trial.

"Leonard is a very assertive guy," explained a former friend of his, "and the judge who presided at the first trial let himself get suckered into a test of wills with him. Even the prosecutors told him that Leonard had satisfied every requirement for handling his own defense, but the judge ruled the other way. That's why he got the second trial."

While he awaited the court's decision, Richards amused himself by running for state treasurer in the 1990 election. He got 33,000 votes.

The jury selection process for the second trial took months. Once it was under way, the defense, conducted by Richards with a standby attorney to advise him, alternated between pure stalling tactics and some good legal strategy. Nevertheless, he was convicted a second time and sentenced to life in prison.

In 1991, after a seven-year investigation, he finally came to trial for the murder of Wilson. He employed the same tactics he had used in the second Stratton trial, with the same result, another life sentence. The evidence included testimony by Dr. James Guerrero, who had treated Richards for an unspecified mental problem in 1979. During therapy Richards told Guerrero that he was in an intense, long-term relationship with his sister in which he was constantly frustrated in his efforts to help her and to manage her financial affairs. Guerrero said he and Richards reached a "therapeutic impasse" when Richards told him that killing his sister might be a way to resolve his frustrations.

Richards currently resides at Minnesota's maximum-security Oak Park Heights Prison. He spends a great deal of time reviewing transcripts and preparing writs. For awhile he delighted in writing screeds that maligned Judge Alan Oliesky, who sentenced him for Wilson's murder:

"Mr. Oliesky has time and again displayed the rankest of ethnic prejudice against Appellant," he wrote in a brief to the Court of Appeals. "Appellant has no doubt whatsoever that Mr. Oliesky is not only ignorant and bigoted, but also in the grip of a severe thought disorder that manifests itself in a broad delusion. That delusion of Mr. Oliesky's is that Mr. Oliesky is 'Semitic.' Far from being Semitic, Mr. Oliesky is an Ashkenazi Jew, as are approximately 98% of all the Jews in the entire world. . . . Coupled with his delusion that he is Semitic is Mr. Oliesky's unfounded belief that his ethnic group is somehow morally superior to the rest of humanity. That false and pernicious notion can be disposed of by a simple list:—THE TWO MOST PROLIFIC MASS MURDERERS

OF ALL TIME ARE—1) Mao Zedong. Han Chinese. Early in life Mao was a Libertarian. Before he died he had murdered more than 20 million Chinese civilians. 2) Lazar Moiseevich Kaganovich. Ashkenazi Jew. Kaganovich murdered at least 10 million Gentiles in the Ukraine."

The argument is pure Richards, an exercise in intellectual masturbation that leaves everyone but him scratching their heads. He lists a few more mass murderers—Stalin, Hitler, Saddam Hussein, and rests his case.

Richards has continued his life's work of forming corporations during his incarceration—among them the Richards for U.S. Senate Volunteer Committee and The Wilson Lectures in American Penology, apparently in memory of his late sister. His marriage is solid, even though his wife voiced some concerns during her testimony that he might get out of prison someday and kill her. She said she loved him nonetheless, and found him to be a "fun guy."

A Marriage of Convenience

This is the story of three misfits whose flaws dovetailed so neatly that they were destined to find each other. Jamie Dennis was bold and manipulative. Michael Gianakos was shy and easily manipulated. Jamie had a history of getting pregnant to control men. Michael wanted children. Jamie viewed her children as an impediment to her social life. Michael made an excellent babysitter. Ann Camp entered the picture later. Ann was so lonely she would do anything for a kind word, a trait that Jamie exploited.

Jamie is a writer, a compulsive scrawler in notebooks, journals, diaries, and sometimes on Michael's bare chest when he was passed out drunk in bed. She writes the story of her life—the real one, fantasy versions, and combinations of the two. They are tales of loneliness, infatuation, unrequited love, love triumphant, imagined weddings, imagined friendships, slights, wrongs, and retributions.

Much of Jamie's writing concerns the experiences of her alter ego, Elizabeth Veronica Devereaux. Liz's and Jamie's autobiographies are identical until adolescence, when Liz blossomed into a world-class beauty, and Jamie became a love-hungry outsider.

Jamie devised elaborate invitations for her wedding to Jonathan Knight, a member of a rock band called The Backstreet Boys—"on this one hundred and nineteenth day of the year xxxx, in the realization that this is the real beginning & now is forever"—but the ravishing Liz had to break Jonathan's heart. Liz explains her decision in a letter she writes to a friend one "rainy and just plain yucky day" when she's stuck at an airport. "I miss him already, but I know I am doing the right thing by leaving him now, before I can't. I've begun to enjoy parts of his lifestyle. But not all of it. I hate the bodyguards & the fans. The total lack of privacy. The fact that we cannot go anywhere.— OK, so I didn't like some of his family members—he never knew that!"

That tale was written when Jamie was a twenty-one-year-old intern at a juvenile lockup in Bemidji, Minnesota, a position she lost when she was caught having quickies with the inmates.

Often, after Jamie had used a pen to scratch graffiti ("butthead," "asshole") on Michael's chest, and he was still dead to the world, she amused herself by putting lipstick and eyeliner on his face. Once he woke up and answered the door, hungover and fully made-up. "I had a tough time explaining that," he says. He claims to be put out about it, but you can tell by the expression on his face that it is one of the few fond memories he has of his marriage.

Ann grew up in Moorhead, Minnesota, mentally ill, overweight, and friendless. "They made me take her out of Head Start because she was so out of control," says Ann's mom, Kathy Forness. "She was so big, and she'd run around like a truck when she got mad. She had a bad temper."

But her sister Lisa, two years younger, remembers Ann's soft side. "Nobody liked her, so me and her were best friends," Lisa says. "When mom and dad would fight, I'd get so scared. She'd lie down by me and rub my back. She was sweet."

By age twelve, when Ann was diagnosed as bipolar, her fate was sealed. Her peers were repelled by her withdrawn demeanor when she was down, and feared her hysterical rampages when she was up. She was a loner for life.

Ann was raped when she was a teenager. Boys took advantage of her generally. By age twenty-one she had a baby daughter and was in a custody struggle with the father, an alleged drug dealer from Fargo named Andy Bedrosian, who beat her. Bedrosian told his girlfriend that he would shoot Ann before he would let her get custody of their daughter.

In some ways things improved for Ann after she reached adulthood. She was on medications that seemed to work. She used her SSI check to rent her own apartment in downtown Fargo, a big step toward independence. The custody fight with Bedrosian caused her some pain, but it also brought an element of drama into her life, which she craved.

Michael wanted to play high school football. At age fifteen he had the kind of build that might have fit into a defensive line, but luck was against him.

"I got hit by a car when I was a freshman," he explains. "It wrecked my knee, so I was unable to play sports. I suppose that's one reason I was a loner, but I was an outsider anyway. I'd always gone to Catholic elementary schools, so I was used to small classes where I knew everybody. Then suddenly I was in this huge public school in Moorhead, where I didn't know anybody."

Over time Michael developed a stress-induced facial tic, which made him the butt of high school ridicule, as did his increasingly rotund appearance. "I was easy prey," he says. "I turned the other cheek."

That statement is typical of Michael, who seems to view his life as if it were an approaching train, and he were tied up on the tracks. Jamie used him like a ball of human Silly Putty, yet she was able to convince two juries that he planned and carried out a cold-blooded execution and dragged her along as an unwitting accomplice. Their pasts alone make that scenario implausible.

Jamie was born in Duluth in 1971 to a single mother who gave her up. After a few months with foster parents, she was adopted by Jody Dennis and her husband, Jeffrey, a lieutenant colonel in the Air Force. Jeffrey died in a plane crash when Jamie was five.

According to a psychiatric report, Jamie was sexually abused by her mom's boyfriend after her father died. "I've never believed that," says her aunt Diane Mellis.

Mellis's brother, Sylvester "Red" Zurn, married Jamie's mother after she left the alleged abuser. According to Mellis, Jamie's mom threatened to accuse Red of abusing Jamie several times. "It's a weapon she uses when questions are raised about her gambling and other habits," says Mellis. "I'd bet that's how it became part of Jamie's story."

Michael Gianakos in Stillwater prison. Photograph by John Abernathy.

But the psychiatrist believed it, and Jamie's behavior suggests something traumatic in her past. Jamie and her mother refused repeated requests for an interview.

Jamie was raised in Callaway, a small town in northwestern Minnesota. Zurn's brothers and sisters live nearby.

"One of the problems we had as a family was Jamie," says Mellis. "If she came to visit, you always had fewer possessions after she left. And the things she took were just senseless. My sister's prescription glasses, for example. Once she spent a day with my son, who was working for his master's degree at North Dakota State. He took her to his lab and later discovered that she'd stolen his lab partner's research notebook. She stole my sister-in-law's embroidered Care Bears. She stole stuff that meant something to other people but nothing to her."

Mellis suggested that Jamie get counseling, but her mother refused. "I think Jody and Jamie are two of a kind," says Mellis. "They are people with no conscience, no sense of consequences."

Troy Hackett met Jamie at a party in Baudette, Minnesota. "I had some friends in juvenile hall in Bemidji who knew her," says Hackett. "She was going to Bemidji State and interning there."

According to Hackett, twenty-one-year-old Jamie's promiscuity was legendary at the hall. Before she was asked to leave, she had allegedly had sex with four resident offenders. She fell in love with a sixteen-year-old and wrote a letter to his father in which she discussed her emotional involvement with his son. She said she understood the problems their age difference created, and was willing to wait until the boy reached eighteen before they married. His father tried to have her arrested.

The disappointment that relationship engendered may have led to one of her several attempts at suicide. She crushed up a bottle of Nytol pills and swallowed them with an alcoholic beverage, but they didn't kill her. They just made her very sleepy.

She and Hackett had an affair. "It was strange," he says. "We never went on a date, never talked on the phone. She'd just show up, and we'd screw. She told me she'd been in trouble for stealing a car, that her dad had died in a plane crash and she'd be rich when the insurance came through. That's all I knew about her."

There was some question about paternity when Jamie got pregnant, but Hackett ultimately accepted responsibility. "In her eighth month she said she was going away to Colorado to put the kid up for adoption," he says. "I didn't hear from her for a long time, then I was living with another gal in Detroit Lakes, and there she was again. She'd, like, follow me around. Then she cornered my girlfriend, and said, 'You know, I've got Troy's kid.' That was the first I knew that Cameron hadn't been adopted. A few weeks later I was in class at tech college, and Jamie walked in. She stood up in front and told everybody she had my kid. It was creepy."

It was not until several years later, during a custody fight, that Hackett found out about Jamie's criminal record. By then it included felony theft of services, receipt of stolen property, and car theft. Cameron, age seven, lives with Jamie's parents.

Jamie was about to give birth to her second child ("The one with the mystery father," says Hackett. "I think it was a guy I went to school with.") when she met Michael.

Michael had a few dates in high school, a few more after he graduated in 1990, but he had never been in a serious relationship. "I'd planned on being a priest, mostly because I had no luck at all with women, and I wanted to belong somewhere," he explains, "but I love kids. I wanted to have kids. So I didn't know what to do. One night in 1996 I went to a bar in Detroit Lakes for karaoke night, and Jamie was singing. It was cool to see her standing there, nine months pregnant." A baby girl, Bailey, was born the next day.

A few months later Jamie was pregnant again, this time with Michael's child. Michael, Jamie, and the newborn moved into Michael's parents' house.

"I guess that's a little strange," says Tracy Lowrance, Michael's sister, "but my parents felt sorry for the baby. Also, this was Michael's first girlfriend, and they knew how much he wanted kids. They wanted it to work out. They liked Jamie, at first."

Their enthusiasm cooled quickly. Jamie spent most of her time in the bedroom, writing and chain-smoking. She routinely blew her AFDC checks on pens, hundreds of them. "She stole pens too," says Michael, "from the doctor, from the store. She must have had a thousand or more pens."

Jamie's odd habits were nothing compared to her legal hassles. She had run up a $600 phone bill under a false name before she met Michael. The calls were traced to her, and she was arrested at the Gianakoses' home. She was sentenced to eight months in jail but released early due to her pregnancy. It was her first stint behind bars, and she didn't like it.

Shortly after the couple's child, Myra, was born, they moved to St. Cloud, Minnesota. "I'd been working at the Holsum Bakery in Moorhead, and they transferred me," says Michael. "We got an apartment in return for caretaking, we had two wonderful kids. Things were going well."

But caretaking proved to be a dubious concept when Jamie had the keys. "One day I got home from work, and she'd been caught red-handed swiping stuff from one of our tenants, so that was the end of that," says Michael. "We headed back to Moorhead. Welfare found us a place."

Michael proposed marriage. Jamie just laughed. She also refused to cut back on her nightlife. "If I complained, or suggested that she stay home with us once in a while, she'd threaten to hurt the kids, or me, or leave," says Michael.

Their life settled into a routine. Michael took care of the kids and drank. Jamie barhopped at night and wrote all day. After a few months, Michael found work as a night clerk at the Super 8 Motel, which left Jamie in a jam. She needed to find a babysitter, preferably one who worked for nothing.

"Jamie and Michael were living across the hall from me," says Kathy Forness. "I met Jamie when she knocked on my door and asked if I'd watch her kids. She met my daughters, Ann and Lisa, through me."

By late 1996 a pattern had emerged. Either Kathy Forness, Lisa Forness, or Ann Camp was caring for Jamie's children most nights, while she toured the bars with whichever of the three wasn't babysitting.

"We went to this place called The Bowler a lot," Lisa says. "She was after this guy Craig who was the bartender."

Money was a perpetual problem for Jamie and Michael. Michael viewed his job at the motel as a dead end, but Jamie saw it as an opportunity. "We never exactly planned it," says Michael about the motel robbery. "Jamie just started talking about it, and a week later we did it. Yes, I was a willing participant."

It was his first stab at crime, and it was a disaster.

On the night of January 27, 1997, Jamie called Ann and asked her to babysit. After Ann arrived, Jamie went to the motel where Michael was clerking, duct-taped his hands behind his back, taped a pillow case over his head, and left with about $1,200 in cash.

Michael claimed strangers had robbed him. The investigators thought it sounded fishy. It took them two days and several interviews to break Michael—less a measure of his fortitude than his fear. "I wanted to confess, but I was afraid of Jamie," he says. Nevertheless, he made a statement implicating her.

They tried to question Jamie, but she was a tougher nut to crack. She refused to talk without a lawyer present. When a public defender was appointed to represent her, she simply stated that she had been home with her children and knew nothing of the robbery.

"She was furious with me for telling on her," says Michael. "She talked about killing herself, killing the kids."

Her fury was soon compounded by something her lawyer discovered. The investigators had interviewed Ann, who had told them that she had babysat the night of the crime, while Jamie went out. She said Jamie came home earlier than usual, with a bag full of cash. They used some of the money to buy pizza, Ann said.

Jamie could almost hear that cell door slamming. She went into action. First, she bullied Michael into changing his story. He told the investigators that he alone had taken the money and taped himself up to make it look as if he had been robbed.

That solved half of Jamie's problem, although she wondered if Michael would stick to his guns under pressure. How could she make sure he wouldn't testify against her?

A few days later, Michael beamed happily as the justice of the peace pronounced him and Jamie man and wife. The bride wore white. She didn't cry. Their marriage took place two weeks after the Super 8 robbery. Jamie later admitted that she had married Michael so he couldn't be forced to testify against her.

John Murack, Michael's only close friend, was not surprised when he was asked to be the best man. Jamie had no old friends, so she chose a new one, Ann, for maid of honor. After the ceremony, the four of them drove to the bar where Michael and Jamie had met. It was karaoke night again. They drank and sang until closing.

Murack recalled riding home with Ann after the celebration. "She seemed like a really nice person to me," he says. "A little slow maybe, but that might have been her medications." He couldn't stand Jamie from the moment he met her. "There was something scary about her," he says.

Two weeks after the wedding Michael and Jamie were charged with the Super 8 robbery. Michael resigned himself to jail with his customary torpor. Jamie tried frantically to figure a way out, but no easy solution presented itself. She began to brood about her prospects.

"She complained that Ann might sink her," says Michael. He claims he just shrugged, and said, "What can you do? It's the truth."

In fact, there wasn't much to be done. Jamie knew that Ann was easy to manipulate and even easier to confuse. Whatever she agreed to, there was no telling what would happen when she took the stand.

Jamie had a lot to ponder. Meanwhile, she went on with her life much as before. She began calling herself Jamie Dennis-Gianakos, but that was her only nod to marriage. A bartender named Craig McShurley remained the center of her attention. McShurley told Clay County Sheriff's Deputy Bryan Green that Jamie came into the bar and flirted with him constantly that spring. After he broke off what he characterized as their "so-called relationship," he said she continued to show up at the bar and make overtly sexual comments. Then she began driving by his Fargo home and harassing him on the phone. He told Green that he felt threatened because Jamie told him she had friends who could take care of anybody she wanted them to.

Michael had gotten acquainted with the owner of a pawnshop near their home, where he was a frequent visitor. On May 1, 1997, he did something unusual there. He bought an item instead of pawning one. He purchased a 12-gauge shotgun. According to him, Jamie asked him to buy it so she could protect the family after he went to jail. Jamie swears the gun was Michael's idea.

About 5:30 p.m. that day Jamie gathered up her children and knocked on Ann's door. She asked if Ann wanted to take a ride in the country.

Jamie says Michael was driving the car. Michael denies it. He says he took advantage of the fact that Jamie had the kids for a change and spent the evening at his parents' home. He claims he had no idea what Jamie was up to.

Whoever accompanied her, the last few hours of Ann's life must have passed as if in a dream. The moment she got in the car, Jamie admits to handing her a bottle of wine cooler laced with twenty or more crushed Nytol pills. By the time Ann had consumed half of it, she was in the "woozy" state Jamie later described to investigators.

The fragrance of an awakening spring must have blended with the cloying smell of the drink and created a candy cocktail of odors as they drove east on the back roads of Clay County. The sounds of frogs singing in the swamps would have come and gone, intermittently rising in intensity until they drowned out the persistent ringing in Ann's ears, one of the symptoms of an overdose of doxylamine.

It was dark when they turned into the long gravel drive that led to the abandoned farmhouse.

Maybe she had just stepped out of the car when it happened. Maybe she staggered over to the house and stumbled into the murky wreckage of the living room first. If so, she was only inside for a few minutes before she stepped out again and took her last breath. The shotgun, fired at point-blank range, tore off most of her face and the top of her skull. Her throat was cut, but it was never ascertained whether that happened when she was dead or alive.

The ear-shattering noise and the bloody aftermath surely traumatized Jamie's children, both less than two years old. According to her, they were a few feet away when the gun was fired.

Ann's body was discovered three days later by a neighboring farmer. She had been dragged behind the house, about fifty feet from where she fell. Investigators assumed that it took two people to move her because she weighed 215 pounds.

A pair of latex gloves was found nearby.

The months following Ann's murder were eventful ones for Michael and Jamie. Michael pleaded guilty to the motel theft and served a sixty-day jail sentence. In January 1998 Jamie stood trial. Michael lied on her behalf. She was convicted anyway, with the help of a policeman's recollections of Ann's statement, and sentenced to nine months in jail. She appealed and remained free on bond.

Investigators may have suspected that Michael and Jamie were involved in Ann's murder, but it didn't translate into an aggressive probe. They soon discovered that Andy Bedrosian, the father of Ann's child, had threatened to kill her. For awhile his arrest seemed imminent, but eventually he was cleared. Jamie was questioned twice, but only about the men Ann was involved with. By mid-1998 the investigation had bogged down. Then, in September of that year, Michael made a frantic call to his parents.

"I think I'm living with a killer," he told his mother, and he described a story he claimed he had read in one of Jamie's notebooks. It told about Ann's murder in the first-person voice of a wife who had committed the crime with the intention of framing her husband.

According to Michael, the writer said she had worn latex gloves so she would leave no prints. She had used sleeping pills in a wine cooler to drug Ann, hoping that would kill her, but she had come prepared to shoot her if necessary.

"There was a lot of gory detail," he says. "The victim was drugged, the wife blew her head off, then used a knife to slit her throat. It was a kitchen knife the wife selected, because it had the husband's prints on it, then it was buried nearby, so he could be implicated if he ever ratted on her. It seemed too real, it scared me, so I called my parents and asked them what I should do."

They told him to call the police, but he didn't. Instead he asked Jamie about the story. He claims she simply replied, "Have you been snooping in my notebooks, Michael?"

Michael's parents and sister told investigators about the story, and on September 10 Michael and Jamie's apartment was searched. The account of Ann's murder was nowhere to be found, but from then on the probe focused on them.

Jamie claims that she never wrote such a tale. For awhile Michael agreed. When he was questioned by police, he denied ever seeing it. "My lawyer told me to," he explains. "He said to deny everything unless I was guaranteed immunity from all charges."

Now he says he did see it, and that the description he gave his parents that night was accurate. Queried why he changed his story so often, he says he lived in fear of Jamie's constant threats to leave him or to harm him and the children. Whenever he summoned the courage to stand up for himself, she would intimidate him with her rage until he backed down. "That was the story of our life," he says.

In March 1999 Jamie was arrested for shoplifting at a bookstore, thus violating her probation for an earlier theft. The violation report noted: "The subject has developed a reputation for being dishonest, manipulative and untrustworthy . . . she has been increasing her sophistication for criminal activity, rather than leaving it behind."

In June 1999 her probation was revoked. She was committed to Shakopee prison for up to a year. That gave investigators a big advantage, and they pressed it. They pressured Jamie to blame Michael and used Michael's family to pressure him to blame his wife. They told Michael that Jamie was about to break, and vice versa.

"They questioned me about Michael twice," says Tracy Lowrance. "The BCA guy, Dave Bjerga, told me, 'They're both guilty, but one of them is going to turn on the other, and get a deal. We don't care which one it is.'"

Bjerga would neither confirm nor deny making the statement.

The investigators told Lowrance to call Michael and try to convince him to tell them everything he knew. It never occurred to her that all her conversations with her brother would be recorded and then edited for use against him. One of his statements would later make jurors wince.

"He kind of lost his temper with me," says Lowrance. "He said he was tired of being harassed by everybody, the police, his own family. I was trying to reason with him. I said, 'That poor girl is dead, and the truth has to come out.' He replied, 'This sort of thing happens all time,' meaning the murder. 'I didn't do it,' he added, but he sounded very calloused about Ann's death, and that didn't go over so well at his trial. His denial kind of got lost because of the tone he employed."

Michael's story of what happened the night of May 1, 1997, has never varied. He claims Jamie left home early in the evening with the shotgun and the two children. "She told me she was going to her mother's place in Callaway to learn how to shoot it, because I'd be going to jail for the motel theft," he says.

He swears he spent most of the evening at his parents' house, and they back him up. When he returned home after midnight, Jamie and the girls were still gone, he says. They soon returned but without the gun. "I asked her where it was, and she told me she'd left it at Red's," he says.

The gun has never been found, nor has the knife used to cut Ann's throat.

On January 14, 2000, Jamie gave investigators a detailed statement. She said the murder was planned and executed by Michael. "I thought he was just gonna like scare her real bad and convince her that what she was telling the police wasn't true," she said. "I didn't even know he had a gun."

Her only role, she claimed, was to entice Ann to accompany them and hand her the drugged wine cooler.

In February 2000, Jamie pleaded guilty to second-degree murder. The plea bargain she made called for a twenty-five-year sentence. Three months later, when Michael went on trial for first-degree murder, she fulfilled the rest of her bargain by testifying against him.

Michael's attorney fought the prosecution's plan to use her as a witness, citing case law that prevents spouses from testifying against each other. The judge ruled that her testimony was admissible. Although the trial took place in state court, he cited a federal law that grants an exception to marital privilege when the marriage is not entered into in good faith.

Michael's trial began on April 28, 2000, and lasted eight days. Clay County prosecutor Chris Meyers described Michael as "a full partner in a husband and wife murder team." Michael's attorney, Charles Chinquist, claimed the evidence pointed to Jamie alone as the killer.

Jamie was an effective witness. She broke down and cried several times and provided some convincing detail. She told the jury that Michael drove the car around aimlessly for awhile before they reached the abandoned farm because he didn't want to arrive before dark. She said she and Ann went into the farmhouse for a few minutes, and both of them used cigarette lighters to see their way around. After a few minutes, Michael called to them to come out. "I saw Michael come from behind the house with a gun," she testified. "I saw Michael walk up behind Ann, I heard the gun go off, and Ann fell. I was just stunned. I didn't do anything. The gun fired, she fell."

She said she was so shaken she could hardly function. Nevertheless, she followed Michael's orders to put on a pair of latex gloves and help move the body. They started to drag Ann's body toward the woods, but her leg caught on a pipe that was protruding from the ground.

"I freaked out," said Jamie. "I thought she was alive. I thought she was fighting us. Michael said there was no way she could be alive because he had blown the back of her head off, and a person couldn't live without the back of her head."

According to Jamie, they soon realized that Ann was too heavy to move, so they rolled her closer to the house, where she wouldn't be readily seen. "Michael said he had a knife in the car and he wanted me to cut her throat with it, but I said 'no,' I couldn't do that. He never said why he wanted me to."

She claimed she watched while Michael stood over Ann's body and shot her a second time. According to Jamie, the children witnessed everything and were crying and screaming as they left. She testified that when they got home they saw that Michael's clothes were bloody, and a piece of Ann's tooth was lodged in his shoe. She said they burned the incriminating clothing.

According to Jamie, Michael returned to the scene alone later that night and dragged Ann's body to where it was discovered. After he returned home again, around 2 a.m., Jamie told the jurors, she took the car and drove back to the scene for another look at Ann's corpse. "I walked toward her, and I could see her mouth hanging open, and I started to get sick to my stomach. I went back to the car and prayed. I don't know why. I just felt I had to."

Jamie's description of Ann's murder was high drama, but it was at odds with the scenario that medical examiner Michael McGee posed for the jury. According to him, Ann had a huge dose of doxylamine in her system, the highest he had ever seen, and may well have been dead of poisoning before she was shot. Her arms were stretched above her head, and there were abrasions on her face and chest, McGee noted, indicating that she had been dragged face down to where she was found. He said she most likely had been shot after she was placed there. He told the jurors that he could find no evidence that she had been shot twice, as Jamie described.

Her throat was probably cut before the shooting, he said, and if the poison hadn't killed her, the knife wound did.

His testimony raised questions beyond the cause of death. How could Ann have left the car under her own power, as Jamie described, lit a cigarette lighter, and maneuvered around a cluttered, abandoned house with so much doxylamine in her system?

In her statements to police and again at trial, Jamie was adamant that she had seen Michael crush up a bottle of Nytol pills to drug Ann. But the manufacturer of Nytol had changed its formula since Jamie's suicide attempts and was using another active ingredient. McGee positively identified doxylamine in Ann's system, so the pills that were crushed had to be another name brand or a generic.

Michael's attorney pointed out that Jamie accused her husband of planning the murder carefully, yet he had purchased the presumed murder weapon on the day of the crime from a pawnshop where the owner knew him. Why would he do so if he planned to use it to kill Ann?

Michael denied any involvement with the killing. He told the jury he had been at his parents' house that night, and they backed him up. Michael's father recited from memory the story of the murder that Jamie had allegedly written, which Michael had read to him over the phone: "The pills didn't kill her, I can't shoot her, she is too woozy. The bitch won't stand still. . . . I've got the butcher knife, and I put it in a plastic bag with Michael's prints on it, because if I go down, I'm taking him with me, and I buried it, but I used rubber gloves so my prints aren't on it."

The jurors were not impressed. Michael's credibility had been irreparably harmed when he admitted that he had testified falsely at Jamie's trial for the motel theft. Meyers told the jury that in conversations with his parents Michael had described details of the crime only the perpetrator could know. When Michael claimed that he had read those details in his wife's journal, the prosecution countered that he was a liar and a perjurer by his own admission.

The jury deliberated for only seven hours before returning with a guilty verdict. On June 29, 2000, a judge sentenced Michael to life in prison.

More than a year after he was sentenced, the Minnesota Supreme Court ordered a new trial. It ruled that even a marriage of convenience must be respected, and Jamie's testimony was therefore inadmissible. The case was sent back to district court, where another conviction was doubtful without the help of the star witness.

Meanwhile, prosecutor Meyers had taken a job with the U.S. Attorney's office in Fargo. "I assume Meyers was the one who pushed to have Michael tried in federal court," says Richard Henderson, Michael's attorney. "Ann Camp had crossed the state line from Fargo over to Minnesota before she was murdered, so they were able to bring charges, and Jamie's testimony would be admissible in federal court."

The reversal of Michael's conviction placed Jamie in the catbird's seat. She had already lived up to her end of her plea bargain and was serving twenty-five years. Now her testimony was required again if there was any hope of a federal conviction. She made a new deal in which her sentence was reduced to sixteen years before she agreed to take the stand.

"We were able to punch holes in her story," says Henderson. "We got some funding to do forensics, and that helped. For example, Jamie stuck with her story that Ann had been shot twice, the first time when Michael snuck up behind her and shot her in the back of the head. We hired a lab to test Ann's clothes, and there was no gunshot residue on the back of her clothing. That pretty well discredited her account of the murder."

The defense again maintained that Michael's only knowledge of the murder came from reading Jamie's account of it. Jamie denied ever writing the story.

"I know it sounds odd that she'd write about a crime she'd committed, but she was a compulsive writer," Henderson says. "She wrote about everything. Her own mother told investigators that the story sounded like Jamie's narrative style."

Nevertheless, the defense was not able to present an alternate theory of the murder. They simply said that Michael was innocent. The jury didn't buy it. He was convicted again and received another life sentence.

Michael's family believes an injustice has been done. They point to the discrepancies in Jamie's story, but even more telling, according to Lowrance, is the contrast between the two individuals.

"Jamie is a sociopath," she says. "Everybody who's come in contact with her says so. She's a stalker, a thief, and a bright, devious person with a long criminal record. Michael was never in trouble until he met Jamie, yet the state claims he planned a cold-blooded murder, then duped her into going along with it. Common sense tells you that isn't so. She's the one without a conscience."

Jamie has been transferred to a prison in another state because of disciplinary problems. If she serves her entire sentence, she will be out when she is forty-six. According to federal rules, Michael is ineligible for parole. He is in Leavenworth prison, where he will spend the rest of his life behind bars.

The Orchid Murder

Early one May morning in 1973 somebody knocked on the back door of the B & B wholesale florist shop, on East Hennepin Avenue in Minneapolis. The owner, Robert Nachtscheim, hadn't opened yet, but he let the caller in anyway, which suggests that it was someone he knew. If he thought it was a friend, he was wrong. The mysterious caller killed him with a shotgun blast to the head. No one has ever been indicted for his murder, but the circumstances surrounding the crime are as convoluted and emotionally charged as any Greek tragedy, and so much cash changed hands because of it that Nachtscheim's killing became a virtual industry—a different kind of Murder Inc.

For ten years before he opened his own business in 1972, Nachtscheim sold flowers for another wholesaler, Midwest Florist Supply Company.

"Bob was a great flower salesman," says his widow, Betty. "He knew the trade inside and out. He didn't just sell flowers to his accounts. He practically ran their businesses for some of them. They relied on him for everything."

Betty worked at Midwest along with her husband. It would later be claimed that she was given a clerical job to keep her super-salesman husband in the fold. That certainly factored into the decision, but there were other good reasons to hire her. She was a competent enough employee and such a stunning-looking woman that men who owned flower shops chose to do business with Midwest just to spend a few minutes in her presence.

Midwest also employed the Nachtscheims' son, Bobby Jr., twenty-one. People dropped around to see Bobby too, but the flowers they were in the market for blossomed from marijuana buds. Norm Wartnick, part-owner and manager of Midwest, suspected that Bobby earned most of his income accommodating them, but he was hesitant to fire him because his dad kept the business afloat.

Robert Nachtscheim Sr. was never paid more than $260 a week, but his employers thought so highly of his abilities that they took out a "key man" insurance policy in the amount of $100,000, payable to the firm, in case he died. In August 1972, Nachtscheim decided to strike out on his own. He and Betty talked about the terms of his departure with Wartnick. They told him to drop the key man policy and threatened to sue if he didn't. Betty later called the agent who had written the insurance, Zola Friedman, and reiterated their demands. Friedman told her he had no power to make Midwest cancel the policy, but he doubted they would keep it now that their employee had left.

Nachtscheim took 90 percent of Midwest's business with him when he departed, leaving the company in desperate straits. It had few assets, but it had a liability that could turn into an asset under the right circumstances. The annual premium on the key man policy, due in April 1973, was $2,650. Interest payable to the policy holder could be applied against that sum, leaving a total of $1,050 due. It was a lot of money for a failing business to pay, and Midwest no longer had an insurable interest in its former employee's life. Nevertheless, on May 13, 1973, at the end of a thirty-one-day grace period, the policy was renewed.

Less than two weeks later, Nachtscheim was murdered.

Detective William Quinn of the Minneapolis police was the first investigator on the scene.

"I always thought it was a planned murder, not a robbery," Quinn says. "Nothing was missing from the shop, and the victim's wallet with about $300 in it was in plain sight where he fell."

So was a box of orchids that Nachtscheim had apparently taken out of the cooler moments before he was shot.

"That was a wholesale quantity of orchids," says Betty, "and I told the investigators what it meant. Another florist had gained entrance on the pretense that he wanted to buy flowers from Bob. Florists often accommodate each other that way."

Betty had a specific florist in mind. She still does. "I have always believed that it was Norm Wartnick who killed Bob," she says. "We were interested in ending the hard feelings that existed between Norm and us because Bob had quit. If Norm had come to the door, Bob would have let him in."

Investigator Quinn was soon joined at the scene by a second detective, Russell Krueger. The two agreed that Krueger would lead the investigation. Krueger had a long and colorful career in local law enforcement, dating back to a time when, in his words, "our size 12 shoe was the only search warrant we needed."

A beefy, pugnacious man, Krueger started out as a vice cop in the 1950s. After several years of trapping prostitutes and gays, he made detective in 1957.

His career languished at that point because the crooks he found himself dealing with didn't provoke the moral outrage he needed to get motivated. The 1960s were the best thing that ever happened to him in that respect. His single-minded efforts to rid Minneapolis of weed-smoking hippies garnered him reams of publicity and a promotion to the homicide division. By the time Nachtscheim was murdered, he had investigated more than three hundred homicides. A videotaped interrogation he conducted was used on a TV cop show as a case study in how to violate a suspect's rights.

Krueger was a throwback to another era in law enforcement, but even his critics—and he had many, both in and out of the department—had to admit that he was an effective investigator. Nevertheless, it was slow going on the Nachtscheim case. There was no hard evidence to be found but plenty of conflicting information.

The evening of the murder Betty called Krueger and told him about the key man life insurance policy. She fingered Wartnick.

The victim's father had other ideas. He banged Krueger's ear with tales of Betty's alleged infidelities and of the animosity that Bob's daughter Angie

Florist Norman Wartnick, alleged killer of Robert Nachtscheim Sr. Photograph by Wing Young Huie.

felt toward her dad. He was as sure that someone in the family was responsible for his son's death as Betty was that Wartnick was the culprit.

Neither party had anything but their certainties to offer, however, and there was nothing at the scene to connect anyone to the crime. There were a few clues—the key man policy, the box of orchids—and the fact that Nachtscheim was killed with a load of bird shot fired at extremely close range. The blast would not have been fatal at more than a few feet because of the nature of the ammunition. That clashed with the theory that it was a planned murder; a hand gun would have been more effective and far easier to conceal. Was it a bungled attempt at robbery? The possibility could not be discounted.

Early in the investigation Krueger and Betty began to socialize at the Blue Ox Lounge in downtown Minneapolis, where Krueger worked as a part-time bouncer. Betty's daughter, Teri Peters, often went along to keep an eye on her mom.

"To tell you the truth, I was worried about her," says Peters, "not only because she was drinking too much for the first time in her life, but because I didn't like the scene there. I especially didn't like Russ Krueger's behavior. I remember him getting into a drunken argument with some people once, and waving a loaded pistol around while he was shouting at them. I was thinking, 'This guy is a cop. He could shoot somebody and get away with it.' Russ was a scary guy. He sure scared me."

Peters was surprised to hear that Krueger was working at the Blue Ox when he and her mother were there. "I always thought he just hung out and drank," she says. "That was how it looked."

In the 1970s off-duty Minneapolis cops were allowed to work at bars. It is forbidden now, for a variety of reasons, including the one that Peters observed. The combination of alcohol and guns was considered too volatile, instances of police officers enforcing bar rules as if they were the laws that they were sworn to uphold had become common, and there were some bars where a cop/bouncer was bound to rub shoulders with criminals.

According to Betty, she and Krueger socialized with gangsters at the Blue Ox, among them the late Ferris Alexander, the Minneapolis-based pornography kingpin. Alexander did a stretch in a federal penitentiary in the 1980s for pornography-related charges. The feds characterized him as an important organized crime figure.

Peters wasn't happy about her mother's involvement with Krueger, but she understood what prompted it. "She wanted to keep him interested in the case. She wanted to make sure he stayed on top of it and checked out any information we came across. And he'd tell her things about the investigation.

I can still hear her saying, 'I've got to go meet Russ because he's going to tell me something about dad.'"

Wartnick has a different view. "Betty Nachtscheim was a beautiful woman, and Russ Krueger was a big clunk," he says. "Did she have some physical attraction to him? I doubt it." He believes Betty's relationship with Krueger allowed her to skew the investigation toward him and away from her family.

Both Betty and Krueger admit to a sexual relationship—a one-night stand that occurred during the investigation. Krueger, a born-again Christian, has since told Wartnick's attorneys that in his opinion the affair was immoral but not unethical.

Inspector Sherman Otto, who was Commander of Criminal Investigations for the Minneapolis police in the early 1990s, when the case got a second look, disagrees. "It was improper, and it was unethical," Otto says.

Betty regrets her affair with Krueger but denies any hidden agendas. "I didn't have ulterior motives of any kind with Russ," says Betty. "I was drinking then, I was unhappy and vulnerable, desperate really, and he was around.

Betty Nachtscheim still frets about who really murdered her husband. Photograph by Wing Young Huie.

That's all." Queried whether Krueger may have had some loyalties to her that compromised his investigation, she laughs. "He had loyalties alright, but not to me or my family."

She believes Krueger was less than thorough because he was protecting Alexander. "Ferris was laundering money through Midwest while Bob worked there," she says. "I think Ferris put Norm up to killing my husband to save the business. Midwest was very important to him."

Its importance, she claims, was based on a quirk of the flower industry. Poets have observed that the beauty of a rose is most exquisite just before it starts to wither. Street people have noticed the same phenomenon, and ragged hustlers peddling almost dead roses have been familiar figures in bars and clubs around the Twin Cities for decades. They go to wholesale florists, buy a few dozen roses destined for the trash bin for next to nothing, sell them for a dollar a bloom, and pocket the difference.

According to Betty, Alexander organized that trade during his heyday as a pornographer, enabling him to wash bundles of money by putting hundreds of peddlers in bars and on street corners every weekend. She claims it was a good deal for Midwest. It allowed them to err on the long side when they ordered, knowing they would never get stuck with large quantities of blooms that had become worthless.

"I guess it's possible that Ferris bankrolled flower peddlers, I don't know," says attorney Randall Tigue, who defended Alexander in court many times. "I dealt exclusively with the free speech issues raised by the pornography charges he faced. He began his business career with a flower shop in downtown Minneapolis."

But Betty was unable to explain why Alexander's connection with Midwest was worth killing to protect. Wholesale florists refer to the street people who pester them for stale roses as "nuts," but they tolerate them, and even extend them credit, because it enables the florists to milk a few last dollars out of their inventory. Midwest was not the only wholesaler that would welcome someone who could organize that business and pay cash up front. Alexander faced many pornography-related charges in his life, but he was never accused of murder, and it was not for lack of investigators probing his affairs. Besides, there were far better suspects, most notably Wartnick.

Soon after the murder Wartnick hired attorney Phil Gainsley to represent him in two matters: the payment of the insurance money, and the investigation itself. Wartnick contacted Gainsley shortly after Krueger stopped by his home for a chat.

Wartnick presented his alibi, which was shaky. He said he had slept in the spare bedroom the night before Nachtscheim was killed, because his wife was having a card party, and he didn't want to be disturbed when she came to bed late. Therefore, no one could verify that he had been home about 6 a.m., when the murder occurred.

Queried why he renewed the key man policy, Wartnick claimed he had intended it as an enticement to persuade Nachtscheim to return to Midwest. He said he planned to offer Nachtscheim the dividends as a yearly bonus and to promise him the full cash value when he reached age sixty-five.

"During the questioning of Mr. Wartnick he was visibly shaken, his body was trembling," wrote Krueger in his report. "He would become noticeably more upset when I would bring up the $100,000 policy."

A few days later Krueger interviewed Zola Friedman, the Prudential agent who wrote the policy. He asked Friedman why Midwest could get insurance on someone who didn't work for them. Because Nachtscheim agreed to be insured when the policy was written, Friedman explained, and since it had never lapsed, no further permission was necessary.

According to Friedman, when he heard Nachtscheim had quit Midwest, he reacted in true insurance agent's fashion—by attempting to sell Nachtscheim a key man policy on himself for his new business. Nachtscheim was cool to the idea, and Friedman admitted that during the conversation Nachtscheim threatened to sue Prudential if the company did not cancel Midwest's policy.

Krueger hammered away at the contradiction inherent in insuring someone's life against their will. "Isn't it a little strange," he said, "that Norm Wartnick paid that premium with just one day left until it would be canceled, and just thirteen days later the insured party is found shot in the head with a shotgun?"

Friedman said he was sorry about that because he considered Nachtscheim a friend, but neither he nor the company had anything to do with his murder.

"All during the questioning the man would mop his brow and wring his hands," Krueger wrote in his report. He said this indicated that Friedman wanted to get something off his chest. Others have observed that wringing of the hands and mopping of the brow, not to mention peeing of the pants, are natural reactions to an interrogation by Krueger. When the detective told Friedman that Wartnick had likewise been nervous when he was questioned, Friedman replied, "Good God, I can believe it. Who wouldn't be under these circumstances."

In December 1973, attorney Gainsley wrote his client Wartnick a letter in which he reiterated his belief that a suit he was about to file at Wartnick's behest was ill-advised. It begins: "As you know, we have refrained from commencing an action against Prudential for the recovery of benefits result-ing from the death of Robert T. Nachtscheim because we have been advised that you are a suspect in the death of Mr. Nachtscheim."

The letter put Wartnick's denial of guilt on the record, as well as some details about Midwest's financial situation, which was grim. It described the possible consequences of filing for recovery—legal hassles, multiple deposi-tions, adverse publicity, plus "embarrassment and humiliation"—but concluded by stating that as soon as the other shareholders in Midwest acknowledged reading and understanding a copy of the letter, Gainsley would commence the recovery action per Wartnick's request.

One year later, after receiving assurances from Hennepin County Attor-ney Gary Flakne that no charges would be filed, Prudential paid up.

Wartnick was an obvious suspect, but he was not the only one. During his in-vestigation Krueger became aware of a party that had taken place at the home of Bobby Nachtscheim Jr. and his girlfriend Debby Feist the night before Nachtscheim Sr. was murdered. Accounts of what occurred there raised ques-tions in the minds of investigators.

Bobby Jr. was interviewed soon after the murder. He told Krueger he had left Midwest at the same time as his father to work with him at B & B. Bobby said he and Nachtscheim Sr. had parted ways that past January after arguing constantly, not only about the business but about his breakup with a young woman from Mound, Minnesota, whom his father liked, and his relationship with Feist, whom his father didn't like. Bobby claimed his father had called him the afternoon before the murder and asked him to return to work, but he had refused.

Then they discussed the party. Bobby initially said he had been drinking until the early morning hours but soon amended that to say he had fallen asleep shortly after midnight. He told Krueger that he had found out about his father's murder when he awoke the next morning.

Feist confirmed his story. She said Bobby had gone to bed around mid-night, about the time the other guests were leaving. She had gone out for pizza and had returned about 1:30 to find Bobby still asleep. They had both been awakened at 7:30 the following morning by a phone call informing them of the murder.

Over the next few days more details about the party were revealed. Among the guests was Dennis Kreuser, twenty, a former B & B employee. He had been paroled from St. Cloud prison, where he was serving time for robbery, six months before the murder. Bobby's sister Angie had arranged for her father to hire him after she became his pen pal and discovered that his release was contingent on employment. They started going together shortly after his release.

According to Betty, her husband had fired Kreuser in March 1973 because of his poor work habits. She said Kreuser had come around B & B a few weeks before the murder and attempted to sell Nachtscheim Sr. some merchandise that he assumed was stolen.

"Bob told him to get out and stay out," says Betty.

Kreuser disputed her account. He claimed he had lost the job because of his relationship with Angie, which infuriated Betty. He said he had overheard Betty demanding that her husband give him five days' notice, so he had tendered his resignation instead.

Angie had accepted an engagement ring from Kreuser at Christmas time, but they were miffed at each other the night of the party. Angie was one of the guests, but she spent much of her time with another young man, Larry Strehlow.

Like several others at the party, drink brought out the worst in Strehlow. That evening he simply went home, he claimed, but that wasn't his usual MO. He was in the curious habit of going to cemeteries and tipping over gravestones when he was loaded. His macabre pastime cost him dearly a short while later.

Roger Nordstrom also attended the bash at Bobby and Debbie's place. He was a high school friend of Bobby's, a gun collector, and a drug dealer who had once lived with Bobby. He had had a run-in with Bobby's parents. Nachtscheim Sr. had loaned his son some money to buy a car. Bobby got so far behind on the payments that his father announced he was coming to take the automobile. According to Betty, when they arrived Nordstrom was standing on the porch with a shotgun.

"He threatened to kill my husband if he took the car," Betty told Krueger.

According to her, they went to the Roseville police, got a police escort, and took the car anyway. Both Nordstrom and Bobby denied it ever happened (Nordstrom flatly denied it; Bobby said he "couldn't recall" it), but the investigators found a record of the incident in the Roseville Police Department's files.

Shortly after Nachtscheim was murdered, Nordstrom left the Twin Cities area permanently.

Kreuser, Strehlow, and Bobby were each questioned several times by different investigators, who discovered that cocaine, pot, and beer were all consumed at the party, and the possibility of robbing Nachtscheim Sr. had come up in conversation. Bobby characterized the talk as "just a bunch of guys shooting the bull." He claims that he told the others it would be easy to get money from his father because Nachtscheim Sr. always hung his pants on a hook in the bathroom before he went to bed and left his wallet, which routinely contained up to $500, in his pocket. Bobby said he suggested opening the bathroom window, which was never locked, and using a long pole to snag the pants.

More than a year later Kreuser told Krueger that it was actually an armed robbery of B & B Florists that was discussed at the party, and Bobby had done most of the talking. Kreuser's information was suspect however, because he was in federal prison when he provided it, and Bobby helped put him there. Bobby sent a friend of his to buy drugs from Kreuser, at Krueger's bidding.

Why Krueger and Bobby conspired to trap Kreuser is a mystery. Was it a genuine effort to solve the crime by putting pressure on a key witness? Was it a way to take a key witness out of circulation before he got someone into trouble? Or was it a clever plot to put a weak link in a position in which any information he offered was nullified? The fact that the latter possibilities cannot be discounted illustrates something fundamental about law enforcement; faulty police work opens the door to all kinds of speculation. Some of it is bound to make the innocent look guilty, and vice versa.

The truth about Kreuser's entrapment may lie in the investigation files, but they are closed because there is no statute of limitations on murder, so technically they concern an active case. In reality the case is cold as death, for several reasons. Decades have passed, so has at least one important figure, and most crucially, key portions of the file are missing. Neither Krueger nor Inspector Otto can explain how they disappeared, but Krueger admits that he kept the files when he left the police department to go to work for the Hennepin County Public Defender's office. He is now retired.

"It was the only homicide case I ever investigated that wasn't brought to court, and it bothered me," Krueger said, "so I took the file." He made the admission in a deposition taken for a civil case stemming from the murder. He claimed he had referred to the file when he made inquiries of his own down through the years.

If that is true, then his zeal after the county attorney decided not to charge the case contrasts sharply with his approach when aggressive police work might have led to an arrest. He claimed his investigation was stymied because he could never interview the man he characterized as "the missing link," Nordstrom. He said he made the rounds of Nordstrom's hangouts and questioned a variety of people about where he had gone but came up with nothing for a long time. When he finally discovered Nordstrom had moved to Austin, Texas, Krueger said he asked for plane fare from Captain Carl Johnson, who headed homicide, but was refused.

"That doesn't sound right on the face of it," says Inspector Otto.

Krueger also claims he called an investigator he knew in the Austin police department and asked him to find Nordstrom, but "the missing link" could not be located. That doesn't sound right either, because a private investigator who was hired in connection with one of the subsequent civil cases found Nordstrom easily.

Nordstrom was deposed in Austin, where he had been living with a listed phone number under his own name and making no efforts to conceal himself. He denied any involvement in Nachtscheim's murder and said there were several Twin Citians who had known his whereabouts but had not been asked.

Any efforts Krueger might have made to get information from Strehlow were frustrated as well. Not long after the murder, Strehlow was found crushed under a gravestone that weighed almost two tons. The Roseville police who investigated his death concluded that he had somehow managed to tip the stone over on himself. The fact that the spot where he died was just a few yards from Nachtscheim's grave, they decided, was mere coincidence.

Wartnick and others have speculated that Strehlow's flattened corpse and its position near Nachtscheim's grave may have been a message to those with knowledge about the killing.

When Kreuser was questioned in 1975, he explained that he had lied to protect Bobby two years earlier because he had considered him a friend at the time. He was willing to offer the truth now, he told Krueger, because his ex-pal had busted him.

He told Krueger that Bobby was not asleep when the party broke up, as he had previously stated. He said Bobby, Feist, and Nordstrom left together about 1 a.m. Kreuser said he asked Bobby what happened after he heard about the shooting, and Bobby simply replied that he was now part-owner of a wholesale flower business.

He also claimed that Bobby had canceled plans to marry the young woman from Mound and had married Feist so she could never testify against him. He told Krueger that when he asked Bobby about his marriage to Feist, Bobby just smiled.

Kreuser's information was intriguing, but it was offered under circumstances that rendered it almost useless to a prosecutor. Those circumstances were cooked up by two people—the lead investigator, who had been thoroughly corrupted, and the suspect that the information concerned. When Kreuser talked, he was serving his second stretch in a penitentiary. He admitted he had lied previously and said he was offering the revised account to even a score.

It was either an unfortunate or serendipitous turn of events, depending on one's viewpoint.

Robert Nachtscheim Sr. was not paid what he was worth when he was alive, but he made lots of money for other people. Maybe he stiffed someone in a former life. If so, his karmic debt must have been unpaid when he died. Once the authorities gave up on solving his murder, he immediately resumed his old role.

The first payment prompted by his death was $100,000—the proceeds of the key man insurance policy that went to his former employers, Midwest Florists. That company had been living off his efforts for years, but his posthumous contribution was not enough to keep it afloat. It soon went out of business.

Prudential's decision to pay on the policy stuck in Betty's craw. In November 1974, she retained attorney Ron Meshbesher. The two of them began to explore the possibility of lawsuits against the insurer and Wartnick.

"It was an intriguing case," says Meshbesher, "but difficult from the evidentiary standpoint. We had motive but nothing else. I thought it was very upsetting that a company could issue a policy on someone's life, then let the policy be taken out of the insured party's control. When Nachtscheim left Wartnick's employ, both Mr. and Mrs. Nachtscheim told the agent they wanted the policy canceled, but there was no way to force Wartnick to cancel it. That's damned strange. It actually creates an incentive."

Meshbesher sat on the lawsuit in the hope that additional evidence would surface. Occasionally he made inquiries of the police, but he discovered that things were worse than he thought. There was some chance that if anything did surface, it would incriminate his client's son, not Wartnick. But Betty remained convinced that Wartnick was the killer. She urged him to act.

Almost two years after she retained him, a reluctant Meshbesher filed an unjust enrichment claim against Prudential, Midwest, and Wartnick. It was a claim he admits smacked of wrongful death allegations because it was based on Nachtscheim's murder. Why wasn't the suit for wrongful death?

"Well, that's an embarrassment to me," says Meshbesher. "Somehow our tickler system went awry, and the statute of limitations on wrongful death ran out."

He admits that the unjust enrichment claim was questionable. "My case would have been based on the proposition that Wartnick acted against the public interest in renewing the insurance and therefore should not have been allowed to benefit. If he couldn't pay, then I'd have said the insurer should. Could we have won? Well, never say never, but I'm glad I didn't have to make that argument."

The reason he did not involves some legal twists that are just as tangled as the criminal aspects of the case. During the pretrial maneuvering, which took years, Gainsley brought Wartnick in for a deposition by Meshbesher. According to Wartnick, his attorney didn't advise him how to handle the questioning until the last moment, and then the advice was cursory at best.

"He just handed me a card and told me to read off it in answer to every question unless he specifically instructed me to do otherwise," says Wartnick. "The card read, 'I respectfully decline to answer that question on grounds that it may violate my rights under the Fifth Amendment of the Constitution.'"

Predictably, Meshbesher asked Wartnick if he had killed Nachtscheim or hired anyone else to do so. In reply, he took the Fifth.

"I was pleasantly surprised to say the least," says Meshbesher. "He had already given a statement to the police, so it wasn't as if he was maintaining silence. It was a big mistake in my opinion. In Minnesota the fact finder in a civil case is allowed to draw an adverse inference when someone takes the Fifth. Without that we'd have never gotten to a jury. The judge said as much in one of his orders. Until then the law was all on Wartnick's side. He owned the policy, he'd paid the premiums, and he had a right to collect."

Years later Gainsley would contend that answering the question would have opened Wartnick to a withering cross-examination by Meshbesher, a premier trial attorney and former prosecutor. According to Gainsley, something Wartnick said could have put him in jeopardy of criminal charges.

In light of the new development Meshbesher began kicking himself all the harder for missing the wrongful death deadline. He asked his clerk to research whether there was any way to remedy his error within the law as written. The answer was no.

Gainsley also gave his clerk a task. He wrote him a memo saying he had instructed his client to take the Fifth and then had been told by Meshbesher that the jury could draw an adverse inference. "How does taking the Fifth affect civil liability?" was his question to the clerk. "Obviously," he added, "I would like your answer to be it does not."

His clerk, an associate who hoped to make partner someday, was glad to accommodate. He wrote a report concluding that liability was not affected by taking the Fifth. Gainsley took him at his word. It would turn out to be a grievous error, because Meshbesher was right, not the clerk.

Gainsley had a long time to remedy his error. The case didn't come to trial for years. But he made no effort to put Wartnick on record denying the crime.

In 1977 Prudential settled with Betty out of court for $75,000 and was severed from the case. Meshbesher began lobbying the state legislature for a change in the wrongful death statute.

"I pointed out a discrepancy," he says. "There is no statute of limitations on criminal cases involving murder, but there was a limitation in civil cases. I portrayed changing that as victim's rights legislation, which it is in my opinion."

The bill that did away with the civil limitation was drafted in Meshbesher's office and written to be retroactive. It became law in 1983. Betty's complaint was immediately amended to include wrongful death.

The case finally went to trial in 1986. In Meshbesher's opinion, Gainsley made another error when he allowed his client to answer queries about the deposition from the stand, rather than having a clerk simply read it verbatim. Thus, Meshbesher was able to repeat his earlier query, then ask Wartnick if he had taken the Fifth in reply.

"Did I ask you whether you killed Robert Nachtscheim or hired someone to do so?" he asked.

"Yes," said Wartnick.

"And did you reply that you declined to answer on grounds that it would violate your Fifth Amendment protection against self-incrimination?"

"Yes," Wartnick said.

According to Meshbesher, that was the turning point of the trial. "You could hear the jurors catch their breath when it happened," he says.

Another moment of high drama came when Krueger took the stand. "It's beyond comprehension," he testified, "that a man can get an insurance policy on another man and two weeks later he's shot in the head and killed." Then he rose from the stand and shouted, "AND THE ONLY MAN THAT BENEFITED FROM IT WAS THAT MAN RIGHT THERE!" and he pointed at Wartnick.

A few days later the jury awarded Betty $2.4 million. It was a Pyrrhic victory. By then Wartnick was supporting himself by refereeing kids' basketball games. The court garnisheed his checks, which barely chipped away at the interest.

In 1988 Wartnick sued his attorney Gainsley for malpractice. He cited the disastrous advice to take the Fifth, the flawed trial strategy that required him to answer in his own voice when asked if he had done so, and Gainsley's failure to conduct an adequate investigation into the crime so he could pose an alternative to the theory that his client killed Nachtscheim for the insurance.

Wartnick's attorneys in the malpractice case hired an investigator, who quickly tracked down Nordstrom in Texas. At trial they presented investigators' reports and depositions about the party at Bobby and Debby's place and what was discussed there. Nordstrom denied any involvement in Nachtscheim's murder, but Wartnick's lawyers' ability to pose a counterexplanation was instrumental in the jury's decision. In October 1994, they found in Wartnick's favor and awarded him $4 million. Two years later, while an appeal was pending, Gainsley's firm settled with Wartnick for $3 million. Wartnick felt at least partially vindicated, but financially it was another Pyrrhic victory. Shortly after the malpractice suit was filed, Betty was granted a judicial lien on the proceeds of any verdict or settlement. After Wartnick won, he moved to have the lien vacated, but in April 1996 he abandoned the effort and settled with Betty for $1.4 million—everything that was left of his judgment after attorney's fees and court costs.

Getting his denial of guilt on the record helped Wartnick overcome a state of depression that he feared was permanent. "I considered suicide many times," he says. "I did not kill Robert Nachtscheim. I want the world to know that."

In the 1980s Betty and her daughter Teri Peters lobbied a bill through the state legislature that gives an employee the right to take over a key man policy.

In 1990–91 the Minneapolis police conducted a second investigation of Nachtscheim's murder. They decided there was not enough evidence to charge anyone with the crime.

Danny's Boat

Danny Seymour was a hard man to choose a gift for on the occasion of his twenty-seventh birthday. He seemed to have everything. He was wealthy, talented, he knew lots of interesting people, two good women loved him, the cream of the underground frequented his New York loft. Nevertheless, he told some friends who had gathered for a party that night that he was practically in a state of despair.

"Nothing can change for me until my money is gone," he declared. "I want to be broke."

That was Danny at his worst, the poor little rich kid whining about his fate. Sometimes he had a way of making people want to slap him in the face, but he usually redeemed himself—with an act of generosity, an insight distilled from his extraordinary life, or his flair for having a good time and seeing to it that everyone else did too.

Before the evening was over, Danny had shown his guests some photos he had taken during the Paris uprising of May '68. He had held the phone out so they could hear Keith Richards sing him "Happy Birthday" from London. He had passed around a signed first edition of *Old Possum's Book of Practical Cats* by T. S. Eliot, and described how it had been presented to him by his mother, the poet Isabella Stewart Gardner, in a fit of drunken largesse. She had attempted to retrieve it many times, offering money or items of value in return, but he enjoyed refusing. She wanted it back because she had decided he lacked the refinement to appreciate it. "No thanks," he'd reply, "we're using it to prop a window open."

A few weeks after the party, Danny plunked down $70,000 cash for a thirty-eight-foot wooden yacht, sailed away—and in April 1973 he disappeared. Rumors soon began to surface among his friends in Minneapolis. He had been hijacked and murdered by pirates. He was living as an anonymous beach bum on the San Blas Islands. The CIA had killed him. The CIA had saved him. Likewise the Mafia, or a cabal made up of both organizations, because their agendas just happened to concur in regard to Danny.

In other words, Danny was doing what he always did. He was living out other people's fantasies.

Danny came from one of America's oldest and wealthiest families, the Gardners of Boston. His mother, the niece and namesake of the art collector Isabella Stewart Gardner, traced her ancestry to Mary, Queen of Scots. Danny's mother studied drama in England and acted on the London stage from 1939 to the outbreak of World War II, when she returned to the United States and began writing poetry seriously. Her decision served as an inspiration to her cousin Robert Lowell. They both went on to become major poets, while their more practical kinsmen got on with the family business—investment banking for the men, marrying well for the women.

Isabella didn't always marry well, but she married often. Her second husband, Maurice Seymour, a Russian Jewish show business photographer, was Danny's father. They lived in Chicago, where Isabella joined the staff of *Poetry Magazine*. One of her duties was to use her name and connections to acquire funding, and that was how she met her third husband, the real estate tycoon Robert H. McCormick Jr.

By age seven Danny was living in a home in which architects Mies Van der Rohe and Walter Gropius, plus every literary light that lived in or passed through Chicago—Karl Shapiro, Dylan Thomas, Reuel Denney, and Galway Kinnell, to name just a few—showed up for drinks. Young Danny, who had been given a camera by his father, began taking their pictures. He had found his vocation.

Later he would gain a reputation in Minneapolis based on his whimsical half-photo, half-drawings, but that phase didn't last long. He soon abandoned original work in favor of what he knew best, photographs documenting the famous people he rubbed shoulders with. A book of Danny's photographs titled *A Loud Song* was published in 1971.

Ted Hartwell, former curator of photography at the Minneapolis Institute of Arts, organized a show of Danny's work in 1967. He put his finger on the nature of Danny's gift. "Some of his photos were excellent," said Hartwell, "but he won't be remembered so much for their quality as for his amazing knack for being in the midst of interesting people and situations, and capturing them on film."

Danny's interesting life did not include much fathering after his mother divorced Seymour, but Isabella's younger brother, George Peabody Gardner Jr., tried to take up the slack for awhile. George, an amateur archaeologist, showed Danny how to search for artifacts during summer hikes on Cape Cod. He taught him how to fish for trout in a stream near the family's Wellfleet estate, and how to sail, first on Wellfleet Bay, then off a nearby point where the seas could be treacherous.

George Gardner had plenty of time to spend with Danny. After graduating from Harvard and rising to the rank of lieutenant commander in the Navy, he took a decade off. Besides tutoring his nephew in what Danny's grandfather, George Sr., dubbed the fine art of fucking around, he went mountain climbing, spent a year in Mexico digging in the Mayan ruins, dabbled in journalism, became a regular at East Coast sailing regattas, and married a Russian ballerina after a stormy courtship.

Gardner made an excellent companion for a young boy, but in the end he proved to be a man of predictable interests, and Danny wasn't one of them. His transformation from surrogate dad to disapproving uncle coincided with the blossoming of his own financial career. In 1955 Gardner became a partner at the investment banking firm of Paine, Webber, Jackson and Curtis, and shortly thereafter his father arranged a seat for him on the board of United Fruit, a company in which the family was a major holder.

Gardner was well qualified for the post not only by background, but because of his Navy contacts. United Fruit had been the dominant power in the Caribbean basin for more than fifty years, but the company was being tested by local insurgencies and had become increasingly reliant on its ties with the armed forces and the intelligence community.

Danny asked his mother if he could drop out of prep school and come home when he was sixteen. You're too young, she replied. A year later he asked again. You're too old, she told him. By then she was living in Minneapolis with her fourth husband, the critic and poet Alan Tate, who taught at the University of Minnesota.

Danny came to Minneapolis anyway. He rented an apartment on Kenwood Parkway not far from his mother's home, set up a tiny darkroom in the basement, and began making a life for himself. His place soon became headquarters for a bunch of young photographers. Two of them, Paco Grande and Steven Arhelger, became his lifelong friends.

Days and nights at Danny's flowed seamlessly into one long party, and the line between work and play became blurry. Danny happened on one of the most startling effects in his repertoire when he lit a joint with a match in the darkroom, and created a flare of exposure across a face floating in a tray of developer. He and Grande used red wine for toner in a series of maroon nudes.

Grande introduced Danny to his first serious girlfriend, Phyllis Cooney. "I inherit half a million dollars when I'm 21," he once complained to Cooney. "Have you ever tried to ignore something like that?"

"Not until I met you," she replied.

Danny's ambivalence about his wealth did not go unnoticed. "He'd be in a room full of people trying to be one of the crowd," says his friend Steve

Kaplan, "but it was always clear to him that the minute he left someone would say, 'Know who that was? Danny Seymour the millionaire.'"

For awhile in the 1960s, Kaplan, Danny, and writer Billy Golfus published a magazine called *In-Beat*, which chronicled the Twin Cities music scene. It featured interviews with big names like Bob Dylan, along with local bands— The Trashmen, The Castaways—and opined on some of the day's burning questions, like "Is Mod out?"

There was a purposeful effort not to let the war in Vietnam spoil the fun at *In-Beat*, but the big issues actually affected Danny deeply, according to Arhelger. "He was as anti-war as anybody," said Arhelger, "but he took the stuff about corporate war criminals personally. It just tore him up. His attitude toward his uncle George was all over the place. He loved him, he felt abandoned by him, he despised United Fruit and everything it stood for; he thought the Gardner money was dirty, but he wanted it anyway. People sometimes dismissed Danny's problems because he was rich, but the guy was really in pain."

Which may explain another aspect of his character. "He was always excessive," Kaplan says, "and he fancied excess, if you know what I mean. That was his self-image, the excessive, burn-out artist. He talked a lot about early death."

He got his wish in that regard, but he never did shrug off the yoke of privilege. The Gardner family's power and influence would provide an intriguing epilogue to Danny's short, strange life.

George Gardner Jr. stood squarely in the tradition of the *filibusteros*, a Spanish term for predatory adventurer, coined to describe the Americans who came to the Caribbean basin to exploit its resources. The classic filibustero was a Yankee named Minor Keith, a ruthless engineer possessed of an odd capitalist genius that didn't kick in until he was facing ruin. In 1872 the president of Costa Rica hired Keith to build a railroad from that country's coffee-producing highlands to the coast.

More than one thousand of Keith's workers died during the first two years of construction, amid jungle conditions so gruesome that he couldn't recruit new laborers. When he was down to a skeleton crew and progress was being measured in inches, he made a deal with the Louisiana prison system to send him seven hundred inmates. Backbreaking work and tropical disease took a heavy toll. All but twenty-five died before construction ended in 1890; thus was a great enterprise born in blood and travail, but it wasn't the Costa Rican railroad.

Keith's project had been plagued by financial crises, resulting in the chronic threat of starvation for his workers. Desperate, he hit on the idea of planting banana trees to feed them, which ultimately led to the formation of a profitable banana export company. Near the turn of the century, when financial problems again forced his hand, he traveled to Boston to make a deal with his main rival, Andrew Preston, the president of the Boston Fruit Company. The two merged interests, forming the United Fruit Company on March 30, 1899.

That same year the first boatload of bananas left Honduras, bound for New Orleans. The bananas belonged to the Cuyamel Fruit Company, owned by Samuel ("Sam the Banana Man") Zemurray.

In 1929, after an unsuccessful price war against Cuyamel, United Fruit decided to merge with its rival, and the Banana Man became the biggest shareholder in United Fruit. When he retired as president of the company in 1951, Zemurray was known as the most powerful man in Central America. He meddled unabashedly in the region's politics, using bribery, intimidation, and mercenary goon squads to get his way. His base of operations, Honduras, remains the region's most reliable U.S. ally. It has served as the staging ground for many U.S. intelligence operations, including the 1954 overthrow of Jacobo Arbenz, president of Guatemala, a democratically elected leftist who made no secret of his desire to throw United Fruit out his country.

Among the idealistic young Latin Americans who flocked to Guatemala to fight "The Octopus" (their term for United Fruit) was an Argentinean named Ernesto "Che" Guevara. He fled just ahead of the coup and took refuge in Mexico City. There he hooked up with Fidel Castro, who was planning a revolution in his home country of Cuba.

Cuba's proximity to the United States had made it ground zero for filibusteros from the nineteenth century on, a tradition that flowered spectacularly in the 1950s, when American mobsters acquired the major hotel and casino operations in Havana. Meyer Lansky operated the Montmartre and the Havana Hilton. Santo Trafficante Jr. grabbed the Capri. Gangsters turned whoring and gambling into industries in Cuba, and took the profits for themselves.

Marquee wiseguys were just the whitecap on a wave of hoods who hung out in Havana. "You walk into one of these Cuban gambling joints," reported *Newsweek* in 1954, "it's like walking on to the set of a Grade-B gangster movie." The similarity was really uncanny at the Capri, where George Raft, who played so many gangsters he began to think he was one, welcomed guests with his patented Scarface snarl.

Another multiple personality, a Chicagoan who usually called himself Richard Cain, was a frequent visitor to Havana. Cain flew there whenever he could get time off from his job as a detective on the Chicago police force. A handsome, glib, tough guy who spoke five languages, Cain was making a career out of playing both ends against the middle. His knowledge of mob activities had already proved invaluable to the police, and by the mid-1950s he had shown the mob that the information he could provide about the police could be just as valuable to them.

Havana in the 1950s was a fantasy world of exotic music, erotic stage shows, and the rush of high-stakes gambling, but when Fidel Castro rode into town on a tank in 1959, the dream was over. The gangsters tried to do business, but Castro refused.

The loss of their Cuban fiefdom enraged the mob. They plotted with the CIA to assassinate Castro. Most historians believe that Trafficante and Chicagoan Johnny Roselli, who were jointly in charge of the contract on Castro's life, quickly saw the folly of the project and simply fed the CIA tall tales of near misses in return for the agency's money. If any credible attempt was made, Cain was the man who made it.

According to the report of a U.S. Senate committee that investigated the CIA in the 1970s, "Cain was connected to La Cosa Nostra, spoke fluent Spanish, and had extensive contacts in Latin America." The committee concluded that Cain had been on Chicago mobster Salvatore "Momo" Giancana's payroll since 1956, and in 1960 tried to arrange Castro's assassination at Giancana's behest. A Cuban hooker of Cain's acquaintance was supposed to seduce Castro and poison his drink. According to the committee, it almost worked.

Mobsters were not the only ones who took Castro's revolution personally. Danny's uncle George had become chairman of the United Fruit board and president of the company shortly after the Arbenz coup in Guatemala. He was considered the kind of bright, well-connected young executive who could clean up the company's tarnished image and boost its profitability. He viewed United Fruit's Cuban sugar mills as the key to increasing revenues. Castro's decision to nationalize them stuck in Gardner's craw.

It is a matter of record that the Cuban refugee force that engaged Castro's army at the Bay of Pigs made liberal use of United Fruit's resources, especially its communications facilities on an island off the coast of Honduras. Rumors about the company's role in the plots to assassinate Castro were rampant but never substantiated.

As his twenty-first birthday approached, Danny began laying plans to leave Minneapolis. By then he and Paco Grande were hanging around the university's studio arts department, where another friend, Jay Hines, taught photography.

The buzz among Hines's students concerned an adventure that was brewing. Danny was going to take Grande, Hines, and whoever else struck his fancy to Europe to make films. About a week before departure, Hines introduced

Danny to one of his students, a freshman named Jessica Lange, who quickly became part of the retinue. Lange and Grande later married.

When Danny and his twelve-person entourage hit Paris, the 1968 uprising was in full swing, but he took only a few shots of the action. He opted instead for pictures of the personalities he encountered in a café on Rue D'Bac, the center of a scene that included British pop stars and political heavies like Danny the Red, who spent their days on the ramparts. Rolling Stones guitarist Keith Richards and his bodyguard Tom Keylock swept through frequently. Richards and Danny began a friendship that they would renew a few years later in the United States.

Lange and Grande stuck with Danny after everyone else left for home. The three of them flew to New York City and took up residence in 1969. Danny moved into a loft on the Bowery with his new girlfriend, a dancer from California named Kate Moore.

Danny and Kate's loft became a rendezvous for photographers. A school of photography evolved there, a kind of documentary surrealism. Photographers Danny Lyons and Larry Clark are associated with that style, along with Danny. All three reflect the influence of Robert Frank, who lived one floor below. Danny fronted the money for Clark's book *Tulsa*, which has become a collector's item.

On the set of Danny's film *Home Is Where the Heart Is, left to right:* Paul Berkowitz, Danny Seymour, Jessica Lange, Paco Grande, and Robert Frank. Photograph by Mark Steenerson.

It was possible to run into anyone from pop stars to buskers at Danny's loft, but the person an occasional guest was most likely to run into was Ernie Holman, a bodyguard-sized black man who was the bouncer and part owner of a jazz lounge. Holman was found dead in his Lower East Side apartment a year after Danny disappeared. He had been shot ten times. Some of Danny's friends were convinced that their deaths were related, but no connection ever surfaced—other than the obvious one. They both used heroin. Drugs had begun to play a central role in Danny's life after he moved to New York, and it became an issue in his relationship with Moore.

In December 1970 Yoko Ono was looking for a place to shoot her film *Fly*. She decided to use Danny's loft, and Danny took the opportunity to make a movie about her and John Lennon.

It opened with Danny's signature shot, an overexposed blur that gradually darkened and focused to reveal an image—Lennon, sitting on the couch playing a tune that he was creating on the spot. An outtake from Ono's film appeared on screen, a fly seen through a magnifying lens, picking its way through a tangled mass of pubic hair.

Danny's film showed Ono auditioning dozens of naked actresses in search of the right backdrop for the fly, a process that involved pointing a light meter at the crucial portion of anatomy, and shouting out readings. Lennon stayed off to the side and cracked jokes in a cockney accent.

It was Danny's best cinematic effort, a portrait of two of the essential figures of an era just as their era was coming to a close. He and Ono discussed a possible collaboration during the filming, but Danny wasn't much interested. He had his eye on a boat, he told Moore. He wanted to sail away for awhile, to clean up. Moore agreed to accompany him if kicking heroin was truly the agenda.

Before they could leave, Danny lucked into one more adventure. His friend Robert Frank had done the cover art for the Rolling Stones album *Exile on Main Street*. The Stones liked his work, and Frank had been invited to chronicle their 1972 tour of the United States on film. He asked Danny to come along as a cameraman.

The Stones were at the height of their fame. They were whisked from city to city in a private jet, grabbing whoever amused them and taking them along for the ride. Frank wanted to film things as they were, and things were pretty earthy. The film, *Cocksucker Blues*, is under permanent injunction by the Stones, limiting it to one private showing per year. Frank has referred to it as a portrait of three people: Mick Jagger, Keith Richards, and Danny Seymour. If so, it makes a fitting epitaph for Danny and his times. They were gaudy, dissipated, and easy targets for criticism but interesting in ways that haven't been duplicated since.

A few months after the tour ended, rumors began making their way to Minneapolis. Danny was lost at sea. Piracy was suspected. His disappearance was part of some larger plot. The CIA was involved, or the Mafia, or both. It sounded like the kind of soap opera Danny might have scripted for his curtain call.

Danny named his boat the *Immamou*, after a Haitian deity, and set sail from Miami in October 1972. Aboard were Moore, her two-year-old son, Jason, and two friends, Susan and Robert Duran. They were bound for Jamaica, Haiti, and South America.

The voyage began idyllically, with frequent stops on beautiful, isolated little islands, but Moore felt duped by the caches of drugs that kept turning up aboard ship, and caring for a two-year-old at sea was a full-time task.

By the time they reached Haiti in March 1973, the Durans had wearied of Kate and Danny's quarrels. They returned to the United States.

Moore decided to stick with Danny for the time being. They set sail from Haiti, bound for Cartagena, Colombia. It was a hellish trip. Foul, dangerous weather plagued them to within a few miles of the coast. There the clouds lifted, and gentle northeast breezes, the fabled "trade winds" of the Caribbean, ushered them into port. But at the height of the gale, a day out of Port-au-Prince, they had to lash Jason into his bunk so they would have one less potential disaster on their hands. Jason's cries were so loud that they rose above the wailing wind, but Moore couldn't go below and comfort him.

When the storm was over, there were still twenty-foot swells and intermittent squalls to contend with. There was no way one person could handle the boat for long. At best one of them could crash for an hour or two, while the other held the rudder with one hand and controlled the main spar with a rope with the other. That was the drill, day and night. The compass spun wildly, the radio went dead, they were blown off course many times, but Danny always managed to get them pointed in the right direction again. By the time they made port, they were sleep deprived and emotionally exhausted.

Shortly after they docked, Moore told Danny she wanted out. I guess I can't blame you, Danny said. He was worn-out too, but Moore's decision put him in a bind. As their recent voyage had demonstrated, sailing the *Immamou* required a minimum of three capable hands, preferably four. Now he was down to one.

There wasn't a seat to be had on a Miami-bound plane for a week, so Moore and Danny had to keep on going through the motions. It was excruciating, Moore recalls, an emotional trial tacked on to the physical ordeal they had just been through. On one of their many strolls around the docks, they met Bob Breckenridge, an American kid who called himself a boat watcher, meaning he stayed aboard rich people's vessels while they took side trips to Bogotá or wherever. Breckenridge was a few years younger than Danny and Moore. He had dropped out of college to see the world and ended up in Cartagena for the same reason most people did, cocaine.

In the early 1970s, when the Colombian cocaine industry was still taking shape, and smuggling routes had yet to be established, Cartagena bulged at the seams with cocaine, much of it in the form of basuco, a raw, cracklike preparation. Warehouses full of coke sat waiting for a buyer—any buyer. For a brief moment in history supply outstripped demand. Throwaway kids who slept in doorways laced their mooched cigarettes with basuco. Macho outlaws, among them a car thief named Pablo Escobar, took advantage of standing offers of one million dollars cash to fly planeloads of refined product into the United States. Anyone with a boat could fill the hold with cheap cocaine and take a stab at getting rich.

For most aspiring smugglers, obtaining the boat was a bigger problem than acquiring the payload, an imperative that drove Caribbean piracy to a new stage. Pirates no longer attacked boats to steal cargo. They hijacked boats to smuggle cargo and rarely left any witnesses to tell the story. The boats were generally sunk after one or two runs.

In 1975 a U.S. House subcommittee chaired by Representative John Murphy of New York heard evidence that more than six hundred U.S.-registered pleasure craft and two thousand crew members had disappeared during the period of 1971–74. A witness testified that bad weather and bad luck might account for twenty missing boats. The rest, the committee concluded, fell prey to narco-piracy.

Danny may have heard of the danger, but he had few options. He could abandon his boat and the way of life it represented, or he could find a crew. He chose the latter. Breckenridge told him he was more than willing to help sail the boat, whatever the destination, and he knew of two experienced sailors who might feel the same. They were French, Moore remembers him saying.

The Frenchmen's names have been blacked out of the files that the Drug Enforcement Agency (DEA), the FBI, and the U.S. Navy compiled on the matter of *Daniel Seymour and Robert Kent Breckenridge—Crime on the High Seas*. Moore vaguely recalls Danny's referring to them as "the two Rs," which sounds like him (he used to tell friends that his five-star prep school education had succeeded in imparting less than two of the three Rs). Raoul and Robert? Ricard and Roland? Moore can't remember. At the time she couldn't have cared less. She was busy preparing for her departure, which finally took place on April 25, 1973.

Before she and Danny parted, they arranged to meet in Miami in June to discuss their relationship. Meanwhile Moore flew to her hometown of San Francisco.

On May 19 someone from a yacht named the *Chesapeake* asked Danny, Bob, and the two Rs to pose for a picture. They were busy preparing to sail but took time to gather on deck for the photo. Later that day Danny signed out of the Port of Cartagena, bound for Colon, Panama, a voyage that should take three days with a following wind, a week if extensive tacking is required.

Danny had promised to call Moore from Panama as soon as the *Immamou* docked there, but weeks passed, then a month, with no word. Moore kept her worries to herself as long as she could and then called Danny's mother, who contacted her brother George.

Gardner began pulling strings. Soon the U.S. Navy, the Coast Guard, the DEA, the FBI, and several branches of U.S. intelligence were in the midst of a highly unusual search for a private citizen's vessel outside the territorial waters of the United States. A letter dated July 24 accompanying the *Immamou*'s description (the author's name was deleted from the FBI file but was most likely Gardner) takes note of "the problems of jurisdiction and other problems as well," and thanks Navy Commander M. K. Phillips for the efforts he has already made.

A photograph taken on the deck of Danny's boat shortly before he left Cartagena. Breckenridge is on the right, Danny on the left, and the two Frenchmen in the middle. Danny and Breckenridge were never seen again. Photograph from author's collection.

How extraordinary were those efforts? According to the U.S. House committee that investigated boat disappearances, they were unprecedented. The committee concluded that the DEA, the Coast Guard, and the FBI, each of which had legitimate grounds for investigating the rash of hijackings, routinely ignored the phenomenon. The Coast Guard had taken note of the exceptional number of disappearances as early as spring 1971 but inexplicably sat on a warning it intended to issue until a committee investigator prodded them on the matter years later. The DEA was concentrating on buy-and-bust tactics, targeting low-level dealers in order to build its statistics, and feared taking on a problem as intractable as narco-piracy. Nonetheless, both agencies joined what amounted to an official government search for Danny's boat. By August 1973 the Caribbean was being systematically combed for the *Immamou*.

Late that month Moore received a letter from a kindred soul she and Danny had met in Jamaica, a hippy named Rico. He and his girlfriend Sarah were still sailing the Caribbean on their ship the *Pogo*.

The letter, postmarked August 23 from Cartagena, began: "I have heard some rather strange stories since arriving here about Danny and crew. I hope everything is as it should be, but if not I should tell you what I know." He explained that a few weeks after Danny sailed from Cartagena he had seen the *Immamou* docked at Port Royal, Jamaica, with only the Frenchmen aboard.

"The big fancy yacht Chesapeake was in Port Royal at the time," he writes. "They knew Danny from Cartagena, and talked to the French fellows about him. They got the story that Danny was too strung out on coke, and had split when they reached the San Blas Islands, planning to fly to New York. But funny thing—when I tried to talk to them about it they claimed to speak no English (one didn't speak very well, but the other spoke perfect English I later learned). All very strange. Another fellow left Cartagena with them, he hasn't been seen either, I understand you haven't heard from Danny, and I'm told people have come here looking for him."

Along with the letter, Rico enclosed the picture taken from the *Chesapeake*, somewhat the worse for wear but clearly showing Danny, Breckenridge, and the two Frenchmen on the deck of the *Immamou* shortly before they sailed.

The news froze Moore. She knew that Danny's uncle should have the information, but her contact with him was through Isabella Gardner. Isabella had divorced Alan Tate. She was living alone in Los Angeles and in fragile shape. More bad news might be the death of her, Moore reasoned, yet George Gardner had to be informed.

Besides worrying about Danny and his mother, Moore had problems of her own. Earning money was something she hadn't thought about for a long time. She had left Cartagena with enough to get by until she and Danny met in Miami. Now she was beginning to wonder whether she would ever see Danny again, but doing anything practical to improve her situation smacked of giving up on him.

One evening, while she was sitting around pondering her predicament, a man named Mr. Brown knocked on her door and solved all her problems.

Brown, a dapper, fiftyish fellow, said he was a detective looking for Danny. "He told me something that I guess sounded a little strange," she recalls, years after the fact. "He didn't say George Gardner had hired him. He said he owed George a favor, and that was why he was trying to find Danny."

But that discordant note was lost in a symphony of upbeat talk. Brown was optimistic about locating Danny and indicated that he might be able to help Moore too. He was a perfect gentleman but with enough flirtatiousness in his manner to charm a young woman. He told Moore that if she used his name, an associate of his who owned a nightclub in the Bay Area would hire her. He inquired if she had any information that might be useful in his search for Danny. She handed over Rico's letter and the picture, but only after he promised they would be returned.

Brown kissed her hand by way of farewell and said something in French. She remembers feeling better after his visit than she had felt in a long time.

Brown was as good as his word. The letter and the picture showed up in her mailbox about a week later. By then she had inquired about the night-club job. It turned out to be a topless joint, and the owner gave her the creeps. She didn't take the job, but just checking it out got her going again. She soon found work more to her liking. She never articulated it, not even to herself, but Brown's visit had prompted her to accept her loss and move on.

Two copies of the picture were sent to Commander M. K. Phillips, U.S. Navy, along with a letter, author's name deleted (one of hundreds of deletions in FBI file 45-11278, most of them accompanied by the explanation that they would "disclose the identity of an individual or an agency conducting a lawful national intelligence operation"). According to the letter, "Dan Seymour is on the left with the hat and the cigarette, and Breckenridge is on the right." Whatever it says about the Frenchmen (almost ten lines' worth) is deleted. Their figures are blacked out in the reproduction of the photograph contained in the file.

On November 27, 1973, about six weeks after Brown visited Moore, the Coast Guard received a tip, which was passed on to several other agencies, including the FBI. The supplier of the tip is identified as "special agent (deleted)." The author of the memo writes that "(deleted) is a pseudonym." The tip came in the form of a brief message written in French and partially translated as "It seems odd to me that 'coast watchers' at St. Bart's would be able to dig up info unobtainable by your guys. I understand the problems though, and am grateful for your help."

The rest of the message is deleted, but it must have specified the *Immamou*'s location. Of the 183 American pleasure craft listed as missing in winter 1972–73, the *Immamou* was the only one ever located. It was spotted in the open sea shortly after the tip was received, and tailed thereafter by a motorized boat.

After they came under surveillance, the Frenchmen altered course and headed straight for the French island of Guadeloupe, a good jurisdiction from their perspective. In early December they docked at Pointe-à-Pitre, where they were immediately arrested by French authorities. The *Immamou* was impounded.

The files only hint at the sequence of events leading to their capture, but it is reasonable to infer that Brown started tracing Danny's boat from Port Royal on the basis of the letter Moore gave him. Either Brown or someone connected with him is the "coast watcher" who spotted the *Immamou*. Brown is the author of the tip.

"A lawyer has been down to Guadeloupe and what he reports is quite terrifying," Isabella Gardner wrote Moore, in December 1973. "He discovered that 2 yachts and several individuals had previously disappeared as a result of the Frenchmen's machinations."

In another letter Danny's mother reports that the Frenchmen are out of jail but must stay in Guadeloupe until a civil action concerning the ownership of the *Immamou* is settled. "The French are notorious for cruelty in getting prisoners to talk," she writes. "*God knows* why the Frenchmen did not tell *something* about Daniel and Keith B—Oh *God* where is he—"

Of course, she knew in her heart where he was and how he got there. The lawyer she refers to in her letter had discovered even more than she conveyed to Moore. Colombian authorities were certain that the Frenchmen had been involved in five murders. The lack of a corpse had precluded prosecution in Colombia. It would ultimately have the same result in Guadeloupe.

Throughout the month that they languished in the Pointe-à-Pitre lockup, the Frenchmen stuck to their story. They continued to stick to it throughout their fourteen-month-long confinement on the island: They had been invited aboard the *Immamou* by its owner, Danny Seymour. He had turned his boat over to them when he and Breckenridge went ashore on one of the San Blas Islands. Both Americans were too strung out on drugs to remain at sea. They had all planned to meet in Miami in March 1974, where Danny would again take possession of his boat.

Their tale reeked of expedience, but it was impossible to disprove. Three bullet holes were discovered in the *Immamou*'s saloon. The Frenchmen pleaded ignorance. Queried whether they wanted to assert ownership of Danny's boat, they answered no. Had they said yes, they would have been charged with piracy, but they knew better.

That was how things stood in January 1974 when Moore was thumbing through *Time* magazine one day and was startled to see Mr. Brown's picture under the headline "Double-Dealer's Death." The story concerned the assassination of well-known gangster Richard Cain, who had been murdered on Chicago's "hairy, scary west side." He had been murdered just a few weeks after he located Danny's boat.

"I was really frightened," Moore says, and her fears were not soothed by the advice she received in a letter from Isabella Gardner.

"For some reason," she wrote, "my brother wants to keep both you and me out of all this. SAY NOTHING TO THE FBI OR ANYONE."

According to the *Time* magazine story, "On the afternoon of December 21st, 1973, two armed men wearing ski masks walked into a sandwich shop where Cain was drinking coffee, and ordered everybody in the place up against the wall. One of the gunmen then shoved a shotgun under the chin of Cain, 49. The hit man fired two blasts, blowing away Cain's handsome face."

Witnesses said the killers were accompanied when they fled by a mysterious woman Cain had been talking to before he was murdered. "Thus ended Cain's remarkable, double-dealing life as a policeman and a mobster," said the article.

The question the story raised but failed to answer was, who killed Cain and why? In death as in life, Cain was an enigma. A Chicago gossip columnist had once described him as "a compulsive adventurer who wasn't happy unless his life was in danger."

A relentless publicity hound, Cain often claimed that his real name was Ricardo Scalzetti, and that he had been born and raised in Chicago's infamous First Ward, just a few blocks from where he was gunned down. Not so, according to the *Chicago Tribune* (in its front-page coverage of the assassination): "An investigator who made an extensive inquiry into his life, said his name really was Cain, and his father came from a family that farmed near Owosso, Mich."

According to the investigator, Cain left high school in Michigan at seventeen, and joined the army during World War II, using a forged birth certificate. Later he would regale gossip columnists with tales of his exploits in the Chinese underground, but he actually served as a company clerk with an army detachment in the Virgin Islands, where he learned to speak and write

Spanish fluently. He worked as a private detective in Dallas and Miami after he was discharged, and developed an extensive network of contacts in both cities' law enforcement communities.

According to a memoir by his brother, Cain worked for a detective agency in Miami that was headed by a Cuban national named Guillermo Buenz, who had many clients in Cuba, among them higher-ups in the Batista regime, which was ousted by Castro. Cain reportedly met Chicago mobster Sam Giancana in 1950 while he was on assignment from Buenz in Havana.

In 1951 Cain went to a polygraph school in Chicago. He joined the police force there in 1952. In February 1959, he made headlines in Chicago twice. The first came when he and his partner raided a prostitute's apartment and claimed they had seized $60,000 in cash, which they turned over as evidence. There was a scandal when the prostitute swore that $90,000 had been seized.

Soon after that raid, Cain was placed on administrative leave when he was caught bugging the office of Mayor Richard Daley's organized crime task force. He immediately went to work for the Cook County state's attorney and made news again when he killed a well-known gangster in a gunfight in downtown Chicago. It was ballyhooed as a brave act by a tough cop, but it would later be revealed as a hit contracted by rival gangsters.

Cain spent the next few years in Mexico, where he worked for the CIA and the State Department. He described his job as "tracing the flow of money into the hands of Central American revolutionaries." He also helped train anti-Castro Cubans for the Bay of Pigs invasion. It was during this period that he masterminded the unsuccessful attempts on Castro's life, according to the House Select Committee on Assassinations.

In his memoir, Cain's brother traces the line of authority for those operations back to Robert Mahue, a former FBI man who specialized in arranging contacts between the CIA and U.S. business interests. Mahue's principal client was Howard Hughes. His main mob connection was Johnny Roselli, who answered to Sam Giancana.

In 1962 Cain returned to Chicago and went to work as chief investigator for the Cook County sheriff's office. He was still working for the sheriff in 1966 when the feds indicted him under the name Rico Scalzetti for his role in a 1963 bank robbery. He ultimately served three years in prison, a concurrent sentence for that crime and another robbery committed while he was working for the sheriff.

When he was released from prison in 1971, Cain publicly assumed a role that he had been playing covertly for years. He became Giancana's chief bodyguard and financial adviser. He had been a prominent figure in Chicago's nightlife, but soon after his release, sightings of Cain in the city's clubs became much less frequent. He and Giancana began spending most of their time in a heavily guarded fortress in Cuernavaca, Mexico. They were dodging subpoenas from government committees that were investigating the plots to kill Castro.

Cain had a chameleon-like gift for learning languages and taking on identities to go with them. He operated under many pseudonyms throughout his career as a double and triple agent. According to his putative boss, Giancana, he was up to his neck in the plot to assassinate John F. Kennedy. According to General Fabian Escalante Font, head of Cuban counterintelligence from 1976 to 1982, Cuban investigators concluded that Cain was a central figure in Kennedy's assassination.

An anonymous police investigator told *Time* magazine that Cain was killed "because he knew too much." He doesn't say what he knew, or why it might have marked him for death.

According to accounts of the murder in the Chicago papers, Cain entered Rose's Sandwich Shop about half an hour before he was killed, sat down at a table, and talked to four unidentified men, one of whom had a very dark suntan. The four men left, and minutes later an attractive woman, midthirties, olive skin, dark hair, dressed in black, joined Cain at his table.

Cain and the woman were talking when two men wearing ski masks came through the door, one toting a shotgun, the other holding a two-way radio in one hand and a pistol in the other. They ordered everybody in the place up against the wall—eight people including the proprietor, the waitress, the woman in black, Cain, and four customers.

The masked man with the radio conferred in hushed tones with someone outside. One of the customers heard a distinct "all clear," and then the masked man with the shotgun put the weapon under Cain's chin and shot him. When the smoke cleared, the other masked man reached into Cain's pants pocket and took something out. A voice over the radio inquired, "How does it look?" "OK," was the reply. "Then come on," the voice commanded. The gunmen left, accompanied by the woman in black.

Two days after the murder, an article appeared in the *Chicago Tribune* under the headline "Cain Was Informer, Federal Aides Reveal." It began by theorizing that Cain may have been killed when underworld leaders learned he was a government informant. "Federal authorities said privately that Cain had provided them with information on and off for years and met with them regularly," said the article. "As recently as a week ago Cain conferred with a federal official here while making the rounds of crime syndicate hangouts as a courier for exiled mob boss Sam (Momo) Giancana, it was learned."

The lowdown on Cain, offered "privately" to the million or so readers of one of the largest metropolitan dailies in the country, may have been what intelligence operatives call disinformation. Neither federal authorities nor their aides ordinarily identify informants, even dead ones. It discourages potential informers. And if Cain had indeed conferred with the feds a week before he was killed, why tell the press about it? Blowing Cain's cover renders any information he might have provided useless.

Nor was there anything new about the allegations. Cain was notorious for working both sides of the street. It was public knowledge that he consorted with mobsters while working for the Chicago police and the Cook County sheriff. Columnists in the Chicago papers routinely referred to him as "two-faced" and a "double agent." He didn't shrink from those appellations. On the contrary, he reveled in the notoriety they gave him. Suddenly, after he was assassinated, the double life he had lived for twenty years was offered up as the mob's motive for killing him.

More tidbits dropped by unidentified federal sources are scattered throughout the many articles concerning Cain that appeared after his death, among them this one: "Cain left Mexico two months ago, and federal agents who keep watch on the movements of hoodlums believe he was on a mission for Sam Giancana."

No one was arrested for the murder of Cain, and to the extent that anyone remembers it now, it is considered a mob killing. Two years later Giancana was assassinated on the day Senate Intelligence Committee staffers arrived in Chicago to arrange for the testimony he had finally agreed to give. His death prompted open speculation that he had been murdered to preclude that testimony.

The intelligence community wanted both Cain and Giancana either dead or out of subpoena range, especially Cain. It was widely understood that Cain could spill the beans on CIA activities dating back to the 1950s. Giancana stayed put in Mexico until shortly before he was killed, but Cain was forever popping in and out of Chicago, a habit that would have resulted in his death years earlier if the mob truly wanted to kill him. A lone gunman with a Mafia contract (the typical mob MO) would have nailed him the first time he showed his face in a place like Rose's Sandwich Shop, a mob hangout he was known to frequent.

But a hit squad of seven people (two killers, the woman in black, and the four men Cain came to the sandwich shop to meet) couldn't strike that fast. They would need ample lead time, which would require keeping track of Cain's travels and prior knowledge that he was heading for Chicago.

The newspapers speculated that Giancana had fingered him, which made sense. According to the feds, Cain had been on a mission for Giancana until shortly before his death, so he would have known Cain's whereabouts and his plans.

Some time during their extended stay on the isle of Guadeloupe it must have occurred to the Frenchmen that they had hijacked the wrong boat. An amazing array of U.S. government agencies were trying to find evidence of piracy and murder to use against them. Cables and courier-delivered letters flew back and forth across the Caribbean, many of them by way of the U.S. State Department.

The FBI alone had four offices working on the matter: the foreign liaison unit, a legal attaché based in Caracas, the Miami office, and the Mexico City office. The Canal Zone offices of naval intelligence and the Office of Strategic Information were both assisting the effort. The American embassy in Paris served as a liaison between the Paris police and investigators on Guadeloupe. It was the embassy's efforts that unearthed a warrant for one of the Frenchmen's arrest on a draft evasion charge.

Many of the memos in the file concern searches and inquiries that had "negative results," but anything that might indicate where those searches took place, or what the inquiries concerned (with one exception), is blacked out.

The U.S. attorney in Miami, Laurence Craig, is copied on everything. Several documents refer to Craig's insistence that he cannot prosecute the Frenchmen without more evidence. A January 1975 memo to the FBI director's office states: "Craig has advised that based on the facts known to date there is no evidence of a crime on the high seas. While Seymour and Breckenridge appear to be missing there is no corpus delicti or other evidence of death."

A related inquiry into the fate of the U.S.-registered yacht *Royal Star III* and the French yacht *St. Georges* was opened. The documents concerning those boats are heavily censored, but apparently they are the other two vessels the Frenchmen hijacked. A March 15, 1974, memo from the FBI's legal attaché in Caracas raises the possibility that Breckenridge was involved in one of those hijackings: "Inquiries are underway to determine if Breckenridge was a crew member aboard the *Royal Star III* at the time of the crime, or whether he went aboard as caretaker after the yacht was brought from Santa Marta to Cartagena," says the memo.

It all came to nothing though. About a year after the Frenchmen were seized, a cablegram from Paris advised the U.S. attorney in Miami that one of them could be held indefinitely on a draft evasion charge if that was his pleasure. U.S. Attorney Craig didn't acknowledge the suggestion. He merely advised the FBI's legal attaché in Caracas on May 6, 1975, that he was declining prosecution. He cites the lack of hard evidence, which made it extremely unlikely that either man could be convicted. There remained only one impediment to the Frenchmen's release. A few days later they appeared in court in Pointe-à-Pitre. The magistrate asked them again, for the record, if they claimed ownership of the *Immamou*. They answered no, and he told them they were free to go.

By the time Danny had disappeared, rumors about him were nothing new in Minneapolis. Hearsay about his adventures had been filtering back for years — from New York, where he was at the center of a circle of photographers and filmmakers; from Spain, where he was living in a cave, making a film about flamenco music; from London, where he was dating an Australian movie star; from Switzerland, where he and Keith Richards had checked into a clinic to have their blood purified.

Sometimes he would appear in town to offer up some token of his amazing knack. A bunch of Danny's Minneapolis friends were his guests at a backstage party when the Rolling Stones played Met Stadium in 1972. That same summer he showed his film about Lennon and Ono in the backyard of a house on Irving Avenue in Minneapolis. People remembered those occasions when the veracity of gossip about him seemed questionable. Anything can happen when it comes to Danny, was their attitude.

Rumors flew even thicker after he disappeared, each one more melodramatic and unlikely than the last, but in broad outline they proved to be pretty accurate. Somehow a few snippets of fact made it through the barrier that George Gardner erected, and friends who had been hearing about Danny's escapades for years used them to intuit the rest. It couldn't have been a simple misadventure or even a bloody example of modern piracy. It had to be connected to some of the central dramas of the times: cold war politics, the CIA/Mafia axis, the assassination of John F. Kennedy.

Eventually wishful thinking superseded intuition, and Danny was resurrected. He had been seen walking the beach in San Blas. Somebody spotted him splashing around in a lagoon in the Dutch Antilles. He had kicked heroin, chucked his inheritance, and grown a beard. He was making a new life for himself in the islands.

Only one rumor met the barest standards of plausibility. It had a few brush strokes of detail that rang true, and a secondhand source, a Minneapolitan named Chris Hamley, who had done a stretch in a Mexican prison in the late 1970s. Hamley's cell mate was another gringo, and the two of them passed time swapping stories. Hamley told about Danny's disappearance.

His cell mate knew of the case. He had spent some time on Guadeloupe during the Frenchmen's stay there. According to him, the Frenchmen must have reasoned that their fate depended on how well they could pass as innocent sailors. Instead of hiring a competent attorney, they told the magistrate they were broke, and settled for the colonial equivalent of a public defender, a law clerk who made a monthlong project out of getting them released from the island's dungeonlike jail.

According to Hamley's cell mate, it took nerve and resolve to go through with that plan. A good solicitor could have sprung them with a few phone calls, and they could have hired one. It was common knowledge in some circles that they had plenty of money stashed in Martinique.

Once they got out of jail, they had to watch themselves carefully. They were in the public eye. The story they had told the press of the legal nightmare that befell them when they tried to help two strung-out Americans, plus the aura of danger that hung about them like smoke, combined to make them celebrities on Guadeloupe. Especially the Corsican-looking one. He cut a wide swath through the ladies of Pointe-à-Pitre's yachting set during his months of confinement to the island. Nothing could help his pug-nosed pal in that department though, so both of them lived off the Corsican's conquests while they feigned poverty.

By early 1975 it was apparent that they would soon be released, but they had to play their parts out to the end. That meant they would need to hitchhike a boat ride to Martinique when the court freed them. According to Hamley's cell mate, many a wry joke was made about the brave soul who would dare take them aboard, and in the end it was a woman. She and the Corsican had gotten cozy as their departure from Guadeloupe grew imminent.

She was dark-haired and sexy, according to Hamley's cell mate, about thirty-five, olive-skinned, living on a yacht with two men he took to be gay because of their disinterest in the affair she was having. One of them rarely showed his face on shore. The other was more outgoing, a drinker, one of those strange people who have given themselves up to the sun. He was middle-aged, but his face looked like a road map etched in old rawhide.

The day of the Frenchmen's departure finally came, after an evening of drinks in a tavern and fond farewells all around. Hamley's cell mate was on the dock with the others. They watched the boat glide slowly out of port, the Corsican on deck with an arm around his new lover, his putty-nosed partner standing nearby, smiling a pinched little smile, and the leather man at the helm.

A few months later Hamley's cell mate saw the sun worshiper again, in a bar in Trinidad. Being a little drunk and feeling garrulous, he greeted him thusly: "Well, I see you survived your cruise with the pirates."

The man cocked his head, quizzically. "What do you mean?" he said. "You know, the Frenchmen—the ones who sailed with you, from Pointe-à-Pitre."

"I have no idea what you're talking about," he replied. "You have me confused with someone else."

His tone was polite enough, but something in his stare made Hamley's cell mate agree that he was indeed confused, even though he knew he wasn't. The man locked eyes with him for a few more moments. Then he picked up his drink and walked to the other end of the bar.

Not long before Danny was reported missing, his half sister, Rosa Van Kirk, Isabella Gardner's daughter from a previous marriage, was beaten almost to death in New York. She suffered brain damage and spent the rest of her life in an institution.

Isabella Gardner's health declined rapidly after her children's misfortunes, but she continued to write. In 1979 she published a collection of new and selected poems, *That Was Then*, which was nominated for the National Book Award. The new work in the book concerns people she had loved, or who had been important in her life. One is dedicated to George Gardner, the kid brother with whom she had always felt a special bond.

These lines are from the title poem, in which she reminisces about summer days on the beach with her children:

My daughter then five, now in
Bedlam, chased butterflies and thirty years
ago my infant son, now for some years
lost, was happy too. I washed his diapers

George Gardner was loathe to have his nephew declared officially dead while his sister was alive, but soon after her death in 1981 he did so, and Danny's estate was divided. It consisted of films, photographs, and possessions, but very little cash. Gardner hired a crew to bring Danny's boat to Boston, where it was sold.

When George Gardner was queried about his relationship with Richard Cain for this story, he replied, "I have nothing to tell you about that."

The Difference

A famous St. Paulite once observed that the rich "are different from you and me." His equally famous pal's glib response, "Yes, they have more money," is what makes the exchange between Fitzgerald and Hemingway memorable, but Fitzgerald was right. Jay Gatsby had a ton of money. Tom Buchanan was rich.

So was Russell Lund Jr., the only son of the founder of Lunds Inc., the Minneapolis food, oil, and real estate empire. Lunds is a family-run enterprise, and Russ's father hoped that Russ Jr. would run it someday. Instead, he failed to participate in the business in any meaningful way. His own son's 1991 appointment as president and CEO was accompanied by Russ Jr.'s removal from the board, a position he had held all his adult life until then. It was final acknowledgment that the leadership of Lunds had skipped a generation. Russ, who was fifty-eight, told friends that it didn't bother him a bit.

Guns, ham radios, and electronic snooping devices were Russ's passions. He dressed in faded jeans, sweatshirts, and sneakers, and enjoyed tinkering with machines. He drove two vehicles, an old brown Chevy van festooned with aerials, and a motor home, in which he often disappeared for months at a time. He flew fighter jets during the Korean War, and survived two plane crashes as a civilian aviator.

Russ had numerous friends, many of them fellow gun collectors and ham radio enthusiasts. He was intellectually curious and a good conversationalist if the topic engaged him, silent and standoffish if it didn't. He had an explosive temper, signaled by an alarming reddening of his face. Traditional religion wasn't his cup of tea, but he belonged to several New Age sects at various times. A reputed skinflint, he secretly gave thousands of dollars to food shelves. His family made a fortune appealing to the epicurean fancies of newly affluent, post–World War II Twin Citians, but Russ, whose net worth was estimated at $12 million, had a palate that could charitably be described as pedestrian. Nora's budget restaurant on West Lake Street was his favorite eatery.

Russ was always moody, but the drowning death of his five-year-old daughter in 1974 seemed to darken his temperament in some fundamental way. His second arrest for shoplifting, in 1981, resulted in a court-mandated psychological evaluation. He was diagnosed as a kleptomaniac.

He never stood trial for the 1992 murders of his estranged wife and her lover, but he surely killed them. The only question is how his entitlement enabled him to spend the remainder of his life in relative comfort and freedom. If you or I commit the ultimate crime, we have handcuffs and the clank of the jailhouse door to look forward to. The cops had to make an appointment to see Russ, and they were not allowed to ask any questions.

According to Coleen Rowley, FBI gadfly and *Time* magazine's 2002 Woman of the Year, the way Russ's lawyers represented their client exemplifies the low ethical standards of the legal profession. In a January 2003 speech at Hamline University Law School, she claimed that they used the shield of attorney-client privilege to hide his crime from the police for twenty-four hours.

That's debatable, but they did arrange to have Russ committed to a mental institution before the police were officially informed of the murders, and doctor-patient confidentiality protected him from investigators after that. Rowley said their actions illustrate the inferiority of the legal profession's ethics to those of law enforcement. "Law enforcement ethics overlap basic human decency," she said. "Legal ethics did too, originally, but over time that changed."

Whatever the merits of the two ethical codes, the evidence suggests that Rowley has her facts wrong. Russ's lawyers defended his interests zealously, but if there was any impropriety, it was committed by a law enforcement officer before they got involved.

The way his case was handled certainly serves to confirm Fitzgerald's observation that the rich are different from you and me. Official misconduct, if it touches our lives at all, is usually a problem for us. It's more likely to solve one for them.

Marry in Haste, Repent at Leisure

At the beginning of the go-go eighties a tiny flight school based at Flying Cloud Airport outside the Twin Cities morphed into Flight Transportation Corp., a charter airline specializing in package tours to the Cayman Islands. The founder was Russell Lund Jr., whose skill as a pilot and access to capital should have made him the CEO, but didn't. That title belonged to a flamboyant loudmouth and incorrigible chiseler named William Rubin. Russ settled for the title of vice president, one rung beneath Rubin's lover, Janet Karki, a whiz with numbers and the executive vice president.

Russ's failure to thrive at Flight Transportation mirrored his inability to find a niche in his family's business, but for different reasons. Lunds Inc. bored him. The charter airline intrigued him, but the company's business plan obviated any need for his capital, and his pilot's license wasn't very useful either. The airline never flew anywhere. It was a paper facade that fabricated phantom revenues to lure real investment.

For awhile it was a spectacular success. Shrewd bankers gave the company loans that were never paid, to buy airplanes that were never purchased. Reputable law firms papered transactions that didn't happen and got stiffed for their fees. Three stock offerings backed by phony revenues yielded more than $30 million.

Rubin assembled an exotic car collection that included a Lamborghini, a Ferrari, and four custom-designed Cadillacs. Karki had drawers full of jewels, including $100,000 worth of diamonds given to her by Rubin. As the fraud became more elaborate, more Flight Transportation employees became party to it.

Eventually, bilked investors got the attention of the U.S. attorney's office. In 1983 the feds closed Flight Transportation Corp. and seized its comparatively meager assets. Five hundred thousand in cash disappeared shortly before Rubin and Karki were arrested. Karki's jewels went missing before the plaintiffs' attorneys could find them, but they did locate Rubin's car collection. He lost it in a civil suit.

In 1985 the two were indicted on multiple counts of felony fraud. They made bail and continued living together in the upscale suburb of Plymouth. Meanwhile, one Flight Transportation employee after another faced charges.

In 1986 Rubin and Karki were convicted in what was portrayed as Minnesota's largest fraud trial ever. They were jailed to await sentencing, and as they languished in separate cells, Assistant U.S. Attorney Tom Heffelfinger told Karki about the secret life her lover had been leading right up to the moment they entered the courtroom together.

Rubin had wooed and wed another woman while he was out on bail and living with Karki, a manicurist from Maple Grove named Crystal Pladson. According to Pladson's neighbors, Rubin showed up to pursue the courtship in a variety of flashy cars, the same ones he had forfeited earlier in a civil settlement (no one ever figured out how he got his hands on them again). He gave Pladson thousands of dollars' worth of jewelry, including pieces that once belonged to Karki. Shortly before the trial began, Pladson and Rubin eloped to South Dakota for a surreptitious wedding.

Karki was enraged by her rap partner's duplicity. Before she was sentenced, she provided prosecutors with hitherto unknown details of Flight Transportation's affairs. She had been acquitted of sixteen of twenty-eight counts of fraud, but now she confessed to committing many of those crimes and implicated Rubin in acts from which he had escaped conviction as well. Karki was first to be sentenced. She received twenty-five years. It was the longest term ever meted out to a white-collar criminal in Minnesota, but records are made to be broken, and a month later hers was. Rubin got thirty-five years. The judge took into account the information Karki gave investigators after learning of her lover's marriage.

Flight Transportation Corp. was a veritable tar baby of corruption. Just about everyone who touched it came to grief. The company's attorney and five former employees besides Rubin and Karki either pleaded guilty or were convicted of charges relating to the scam. The court-appointed receiver admitted stealing some of the assets he was in charge of distributing.

Russell Lund Jr. was one of the few who emerged unscathed. Prosecutors and law enforcement officers agreed that Russ was a pawn and a dupe and such a dunce when it came to business that he couldn't possibly have been culpable.

Nevertheless, for years after the trial Russ figured strongly in rumors that Flight Transportation Corp. flew cash to offshore banks for rich Twin Citians so they could evade taxes. His wealth, the fact that he speculated in foreign currencies, plus his interest in ham radio and guns, added up to a recipe for suspicion, but it was the resentment that the rich inspire, the other side of the coin from the deference they take for granted, that gave those rumors legs.

Russ left a packet of information about the Flight Transportation affair with a KSTP-TV reporter shortly before he murdered his wife and her lover. The killings short-circuited any plans the station might have had to follow up. The contents of the packet have never been made public.

She's Divorcing My Father

On the surface Russ's marital problems looked mundane compared to his former boss's. He was married to Beverly Martin for nine years. The couple had three children, including his eldest son, Russell T. ("Tres") Lund III, president and CEO of Lunds Inc. Martin described her 1967 divorce from Russ as amicable but declined to answer when an investigator asked whether her former husband had ever threatened her. She described him as obsessed with three things: ham radio, surveillance, and detective magazines.

Martin and Russ stayed on reasonably good terms after they split up, and Martin became friendly with Russ's second wife, Barbara.

Russ married Barbara Berglund in 1968. They had two children, a daughter who drowned at age five, and a son, Robert, an officer at Lunds. They split p in 1989. The separation was Russ's idea, but the decision to make it permanent was mutual.

According to Russ's friend Rod Larson, Russ's persona was an impediment to his wife's social aspirations, and his appearance served as a daily reminder of their incompatible goals. At six feet three, 185 pounds, Russ was a handsome, potentially elegant-looking man. Barbara wanted to dress him in tailored suits and designer jeans, but Russ preferred sweatshirts, khakis, and sneakers. His shabby attire was emblematic of a deeper rift in their marriage. "Russ was just happy to talk with the common guy," Larson told investigators. "He was happy talking to the maintenance guy who was over fixing something on the house, and to Barb that was just not acceptable."

Larson explained that Barbara considered him tolerable because he was well educated and drove a Mercedes, but the people who really interested her were the rich. "Barb liked to hang around with the status people, the Daytons and the Pillsburys," he explained. "Russ did not want to do that, and that's where they grew in different directions."

But there was no bitterness between them, he added.

That seemed to be the case, at first. Russ agreed to pay Barbara's legal fees, plus maintenance, while their divorce was finalized. He voluntarily gave her both the couple's homes, one in Orono, another in Aspen, Colorado, and bought a house for himself at 2301 Sherwood Hills, Minnetonka. He chose it for its hilltop location, which made it ideal for pulling in radio signals.

Soon Russ was happily ensconced in his new digs, which neighbors described as "a pit." The yard reverted to a tangle of native flora, and his three-car garage was so stuffed full of electronic equipment that he had to park his battered van in the driveway. The house was cluttered with unpacked boxes of belongings, clothing that lay where it fell when he changed, and mail, much of it unopened. Only his gun collection was properly stored.

Larson introduced Russ to Pam Fox, a legal secretary, and she became a regular guest at his house. His estranged wife continued her career as a high-end real estate agent in the Lake Minnetonka area. She split her time almost equally between Orono and Aspen, and in 1990 began seeing Kevin Kelly, a lawyer/lobbyist from Des Moines.

Kelly, forty-seven, a former Iowa legislator and a championship swimmer, was six years younger than Barbara. Russ seemed to like Kelly, despite his profession. He wasn't fond of lawyers.

He came to especially dislike attorneys Robert Due and Larry Katz, the second legal team his wife hired to represent her in the divorce. Unlike her first attorneys, Due and Katz were aggressively seeking more than Russ was offering. Their efforts were spurred by the death in February 1992 of Russell

Lund Sr. They wanted a careful accounting of how Lund Sr.'s assets were distributed.

Russ bitterly resented their demands for information. In July 1992, a subpoena was issued to Lunds Inc. seeking numerous personal and corporate records, and according to Von Martin, an officer at Lunds, the company was preparing to comply.

Lund Sr. left everything to his grandchildren when he died. Russ was said to be comfortable with that decision, but he may not have wanted the fact that he had been cut out of his father's will memorialized in a divorce record.

"She isn't divorcing me," he told Martin. "She's divorcing my father."

The Crime of the Century

By summer 1992 the relationship between Russ and his estranged wife had soured so thoroughly that she had given up her real estate career and was avoiding the Twin Cities. She came to town occasionally to visit family and friends and to discuss strategy with her lawyers. She was unable to strategize with the lawyers over her phone because Russ had tapped it, she told attorney Due. She also told him that Russ had entered her Orono home in her absence and looked over some papers pertaining to the divorce.

Those papers concerned a contempt of court hearing scheduled for August 18. Due had brought the action against Russ because he was $35,000 behind on Barbara's legal fees, and $10,000 behind on her maintenance payments. Apparently Russ was withholding the money to pressure his wife to abandon her quest for information.

Russ had begun to dwell on that pending court date. He told Martin that he might well end up in jail. He agonized about dying behind bars for lack of proper nutrition and wondered aloud if prisoners in the Hennepin County lockup could order meals from Nora's.

On Friday, July 31, Barbara and Kelly arrived in Orono for a rare visit. Their agenda consisted of a few social engagements and one last effort to come to an agreement with Russ about the divorce. They planned to leave the following Wednesday.

According to Larson, Russ had high hopes that a settlement would be reached while they were in town. He canceled plans that he and Larson had made to go to an air show in order to concentrate on talks with Barbara. He had come to think of Kelly as a voice of reason in those discussions and was glad for the opportunity to sit down with the two of them.

Over the next few days Russ told several people that progress was being made, but there must have been some big sticking points. Barbara told Martin that she and Russ had had a long, rancorous phone discussion on Saturday. It became so tiresome to her, Barbara said, that she purposely made a remark that angered her husband, knowing he would hang up. She told Martin she couldn't think of any other way to end the conversation.

On Monday, Russ and his son Robert visited Barbara and Kelly at the Orono home. According to Robert, everyone got along. Barbara and Kelly took a boat ride, while Russ and Robert fiddled with a generator in the garage. That evening Russ called Fox. Although he didn't say so directly, he left her with the impression that a settlement was imminent. Fox agreed to meet Russ at his home on Wednesday evening.

On Tuesday, Russ had a conversation with Larson. He grumbled about attorneys and remarked that they like to generate paper and controversy, and the more of each they created, the more they billed. He indicated his displeasure with Barbara's attorneys and said that the money they were being paid was wasted in view of the fact that he had offered a generous settlement before they got involved.

Later that day he called Barbara and left a message, which would soon be seized as evidence by investigators. It was Russ's final settlement offer, a flat $4 million. "I would be very glad to renounce all of my father's wealth," he said. "It doesn't mean anything to me because I didn't earn it, as we've discussed. And then we could have, I guess, what I'd call an ordinary divorce, where your lawyers didn't have to go after my family."

Subsequent events suggest that $4 million was not enough, and Barbara was prepared to instruct her attorneys to proceed with the subpoena of Lunds Inc.'s records. But it may have been in response to that message that Barbara and Kelly agreed to meet with Russ once more before they departed on Wednesday.

A few minutes after 3:00 p.m. Wednesday, Russ walked into the First Bank Ridgedale. According to teller Rosalind Nice, who knew him from past discussions they had had about foreign currency rates, he seemed edgy.

"He stuttered a little bit," Nice told investigators. "He'd start talking and not finish, and it seemed like he was very concerned that he was going to hold up the line. He kept looking back over his shoulder." He seemed unsure of what kind of transaction he intended to make, and Nice remembers him saying, "I'll have you so confused by the time I leave they'll know Russell Lund was here."

The bank's records show a deposit of $8,284 made into one of Russ's accounts at 3:15.

About an hour later Fox got a call from Russ that disturbed her. "He said, 'Don't come out to the house tonight, things are falling apart with Barbara.'" She told investigators that his voice was shaky, but he was firm about her not coming. "I couldn't imagine what happened between then and Monday night, when there seemed to have been a civil discussion between Barbara and Kevin and Russell," said Fox, "but he wouldn't elaborate."

Barbara and Kelly were due back in Aspen Wednesday evening. When they didn't show up, Kelly's children from a former marriage began calling members of the Lund family in a fruitless effort to find them. They were unable to reach Russ.

At 4:30 p.m. the next day, Minneapolis attorney David Rosten called Richard Setter, chief of the Minnetonka police. According to Setter's report, Rosten said he wanted to meet at the Radisson Ridgedale Hotel at 6:45 that evening to tell Setter about "the crime of the century that was occurring in my community."

Despite the urgency that Rosten's use of the present tense seemed to indicate, the attorney refused to meet earlier or to divulge any details. They had to meet at 6:45 on the dot, he insisted.

Chief Setter alerted Lieutenant Mike Olson and Sergeant David Peterson that he was going to a meeting to receive information that might pertain to a crime. He asked them to be available throughout the evening, but he went to the hotel alone, so his is the only account of what occurred there.

Setter never mentions that he and Rosten are personal friends, although that can be inferred from his narrative. He writes, "As I entered the hotel I noted a person whom I knew as David Rosten. He was seated with a man later identified as Michael Grostyan, a private investigator."

According to Setter, he and Rosten "made small talk" while they waited for well-known Minneapolis criminal attorney Joe Friedberg, who arrived at 7:00 p.m. The attorneys then informed Setter that there were two dead bodies at 2301 Sherwood Hills, Minnetonka.

"They further related that both had been dead since yesterday around noon, 8-5-92," Setter writes. "I asked what the cause of death was, and they stated multiple gunshot wounds. . . . They identified one of the victims as Mrs. Russell Lund and the other as Kevin, last name unknown, from someplace in Iowa. When I asked, they confirmed that the Lund victim was associated with the Lund grocery chain. None of the three indicated that they had seen the bodies to confirm the deaths, yet I was informed by Mr. Friedberg and Mr. Rosten that the family was being notified of the deaths as we spoke. This was being done even though they indicated that they had not personally been at the crime scene. I asked if any other people had been at the crime scene, and they said they didn't know."

Setter reports that the attorneys "seemed concerned about ethical issues." He asked if they knew the whereabouts of Russell Lund. They said they couldn't tell him. He asked if they represented Lund, or anyone else. They declined to answer, nor would they reveal how they had become aware of the crimes. They conferred privately at one point and then said that they had some physical evidence to turn over.

"I told them that I did not want to take receipt of any evidence, and based on the severity of the criminal offense, that I wanted to call my staff, especially Lt. Olson and Sgt. Peterson to the scene. . . . At 7:40 p.m., Mr. Grostyan, the private investigator, went out to the parking lot, and in the presence of myself, Mr. Friedberg, Mr. Rosten, Lt. Olson and Sgt. Peterson, opened up the trunk of a vehicle and removed a stainless steel revolver in a plastic bag and turned it over to Sgt. Peterson. The revolver had what appeared to be blood on the barrel and cylinder."

The curtain of secrecy that would become the hallmark of the investigation into the murders of Barbara Lund and Kevin Kelly had already come down. Key questions that were never answered would dog the investigation from day one. Exactly when did the victims die? Why were the police informed more than twenty-four hours after the murders occurred? And most important, where was Russell Lund Jr., and why wasn't he under arrest?

Russ Lund with his attorney Joe Friedberg. Copyright 2003 Star Tribune/Minneapolis-St. Paul.

"I hate to investigate crimes that involve the rich," says Lieutenant Arlen Holland, a Minnetonka detective who was part of the investigation team. "It really slows things down."

What the Maintenance Man Saw

The police compiled a six-hundred-page file on the investigation into the murders of Lund and Kelly. It reveals that five people and perhaps a sixth knew about the murders long before the police were informed. It contains an analysis of the crime scene that shows graphically how the murders were committed.

"It was spooky," says Holland, "truly awful. It began in the basement, which was crammed full of junk, even more so than the rest of the house. We can only guess why they were down there. Maybe Mr. Lund marched them down at gunpoint. Mrs. Lund was the first to be killed. She was shot three times, once in the head, which would have killed her instantly. Kelly was apparently nicked by the first bullet fired at him, and fled up the stairs with Mr. Lund in pursuit. He was hit once more on the run, but neither of those wounds was fatal. You could follow the trail of blood and see that he was picking his way through the junk, looking for an escape. At one point he was trying to get out the side door, but he gave up. He probably thought it was locked. We discovered that it was jammed because it was hung crooked, and of course in his panicked state he didn't figure that out. If he'd have pushed hard, it would have opened. Then he'd have been in the yard, and everything might have come out differently. As it was, Mr. Lund just cornered him and shot him down. He was able to reload, so it must have taken awhile."

Kelly had four wounds from three shots. The last bullet passed through his upraised hand and his tightly closed eye into his brain, "a defensive reaction to an anticipated shot," according to the postmortem. The blood on the pistol that was turned over to the police on Thursday evening was analyzed and found to be Kelly's, indicating he had been shot at close range.

Little is known about Russ's activities from Wednesday when the murders took place until the following Saturday morning. A teenage neighbor said that she heard gunshots and saw Russ speeding away in his van shortly before noon Wednesday, but investigators discounted her story because it didn't jibe with the time line they constructed.

"We think the murders were committed between 1:00 and 4:00 p.m.," says Holland. According to him, it is quite possible that the victims were dead when Russ went to the bank, which would explain his nervous behavior there. The money that he deposited might have been slated to play some role in the settlement.

From the time he left the bank until the next morning, Russ's whereabouts are a mystery. Members of his family later told friends that they believed he stayed in the house with the bodies for some time, dictating letters and winding up his affairs. He was certainly there at 7:40 Thursday morning, when an alarm was tripped at his house. Security personnel called in response, and Russ answered to assure them everything was OK.

He turned up at the Lunds corporate offices about 8:00 a.m. to drop off some tools for Robert, who was late for work that day. He waited around, and at about 10:30 asked an executive secretary to take two letters that he wanted to dictate. One was to a television station concerning the Flight Transportation affair. The other was to a credit card company, contesting a charge.

Robert still hadn't arrived when he finished dictating, so he left. He called Robert around noon to see if he had gotten the tools. He called Robert again at 4:00 and asked him to make sure that both he and Tres Lund were at the offices at 6:00, because he was coming by to speak to them about something important.

His request indicates that he was unaware of a message that had been left for Tres an hour earlier. According to the Lunds employee who took that message, Russ's divorce attorney, Peter Watson, and a psychologist, Donald Pastor, said they were coming to the offices at 6:45 to hold an urgent meeting with the Lund family.

At about 6:00, just as Tres was leaving to pick up his sister for that meeting, an employee handed him a note requesting him to call his father at Fairview Hospital. He called immediately, and Russ asked him if he had talked to Watson and Pastor yet. He said he hadn't, and asked what was wrong. Russ said it was better if the news came from them.

The sequence of messages suggests that Russ was originally determined to break the news to his family himself. Those plans were changed by someone else, and Russ was informed after the fact. By 3:00 p.m. two meetings had been organized, one to officially inform the police of the murders, and one to tell the family. They were orchestrated to happen simultaneously. Everyone involved was instructed that punctuality was important. They all came on time except Friedberg.

Russ was admitted to Fairview Hospital after 11:15 a.m., when he left the corporate offices, and before 6:00 p.m., when his son reached him there. He signed himself in, and he was free to come and go.

Watson began the meeting at the Lunds offices by telling Russ's children that Barbara Lund and Kevin Kelly had been killed at their father's house. He said that Russ was in a mental health facility, and a criminal attorney had been hired to represent him. Pastor said that Russ had come to his office that afternoon with a gun, intending to kill himself. According to Pastor, they spent five hours together before Russ was persuaded to hand the gun over.

Russ's daughter Kim later told investigators that Watson and Pastor stuck strictly to facts. When pressed, they resisted drawing any conclusions about the killer's identity. "They told us they were protecting us so we wouldn't get too involved," she said.

By the time the meeting at the Lunds offices ended, the Minnetonka police had begun drawing up a search warrant for Russ's home. They would soon enter the premises, find the bodies, and inform the media of the killings. In his announcement, Chief Setter claimed that the crimes had been discovered on the basis of an "anonymous phone tip" received at 7:00 p.m., the first of many falsehoods that found their way into the record. Psychologist Pastor's claim that Russ spent five hours with him on Thursday afternoon is another. Russ was at the Lunds offices until shortly before noon. Three hours later, meetings were being planned without his knowledge, which suggests that he was already hospitalized.

The murders and Russ's suspected involvement were page-one news on Friday morning, August 7. Newspaper accounts said Russ's whereabouts were unknown, but by 6:00 that evening a TV station was reporting that he had been admitted to the Fairview Hospital under an assumed name. A hospital spokesman would neither confirm nor deny the report. Setter said that his department was checking all area hospitals in response to several such reports but had turned up nothing.

Meanwhile yet another meeting was held. The maintenance man at the downtown Minneapolis building where Friedberg has his offices saw Friedberg, Rosten, and Russ enter the elevator from the garage about 4:30 p.m. Friday. "They acted like they didn't want to be seen," he told investigators. Less than half an hour later he spotted Russ leaving the building alone, via a stairway that leads directly to the street.

Investigators later received an anonymous tip that a meeting had been held at Friedberg's office on Friday, beginning at 11:30 a.m. The female caller, who refused to identify herself, said a lawyer who specializes in ethical issues was in attendance, along with Friedberg, Rosten, and Russ.

On Friday evening Friedberg struck a deal with Hennepin County Attorney Dan Mabley. The lawyer said he would allow his client to come to the Minnetonka Police Department to be fingerprinted and photographed on the condition that he would not be arrested or questioned.

Russ came to the police station on Saturday morning as arranged, accompanied by attorney Rosten. Along with his mug shot and fingerprints, he voluntarily gave a sample of his blood.

"I asked Rosten if he knew where any bloody clothing his client had been wearing was located, or where we might find Mr. Lund's Chevy Suburban," says Holland. "He said, 'That's a good question.' I asked if that meant he didn't know where those items were. He said, 'No, that means it's a good question.' But he didn't tell me where anything was."

He didn't have to tell him where to find Russ's blood-splattered shoes. They were still on his feet. They were seized as evidence. Later that day, police, acting on a tip from the maintenance man, discovered Russ's van parked in the garage of Friedberg's office building.

Special Treatment

The Minnetonka police file is peppered with references to vain attempts to interview the victims' families. A press release issued six days after the murders states: "There appears to be a systematic effort on the part of the family members of Russell T. Lund Jr., Barbara Lund and E. Kevin Kelly not to speak with the police department, either in person or through their attorneys. This has caused a need for additional resources on the part of the Minnetonka Police and Hennepin County Sheriff's crime lab to obtain and verify crucial information which would have been otherwise available."

The Lunds' reticence and Russ's commitment to a mental health facility led to suspicions that there was a conspiracy to get Russ off the hook on an insanity plea, and his family was behind it. Russ's attorneys were certainly laying the groundwork for an insanity defense, but the family had nothing to do with it. They were trying to minimize damage to the business, and they had been advised that the less said the better. Tres later told the *Star Tribune* that the public was supportive throughout their ordeal, but according to investigator Holland, managers at the Lunds grocery stores fielded dozens of calls from people who were incensed by the perception that a cold-blooded killer was receiving special treatment because of his family's prominence.

The investigation quickly bogged down over issues of physician-patient and attorney-client confidentiality. Press releases put out by the Minnetonka police show their mounting frustration with a case in which there was no question about the identity of the perpetrator but significant doubt about their ability to gather evidence. They especially needed information about Russ's frame of mind before the murders. Only the people who knew him well could provide it, and they weren't talking. Worse yet, the police were being accused of cutting Russ too much slack. The media kept the delayed report of the murders and the mystery of Russ's whereabouts after they were committed on the front burner.

"I wish to state that there is no special treatment being given to any person or persons and this case is being investigated as would any other homicide case," says a press release by Chief Setter. "We have no explanation as to why there was a coordinated reporting of the deaths to police and the family members."

According to another release, "The question of why there was a significant delay in reporting the deaths to police, who was responsible, and what took place during this time period continues to be investigated."

On August 13 the police served a search warrant on Fairview Hospital, seeking records that would confirm Russ's presence there. It was immediately contested on the basis of physician-client privilege. The next day they presented the hospital with notice that they were seeking Russ Lund and had probable cause to arrest him. Although it takes a tough tone, it is essentially a toothless plea for cooperation, and it was ignored.

The investigators' frustration was compounded by the fact that Russ's presence at Fairview was an open secret reported daily in the media. But far from being appreciative of the fragility of his situation, Russ chafed under unfamiliar hardships. On Saturday, August 15, he showed up at his friend Rod Larson's Mound home, along with attorney Rosten.

"He said he needed some good food, so he was going to the Dairy Queen after he left my house," Larson told an investigator who interviewed him two days later. "He said Fairview wasn't a very good place because he was forced to watch soap operas, and they kept wanting to put pills and needles in him. His attorney told the hospital that if they put one needle or pill in him he'd sue their ass, so he's the only one up there who's not a vegetable."

When Russ arrived unannounced at Larson's home, Larson had already been informed that an investigator wanted to interview him. He had retained an attorney.

"Russ felt real bad that I had been drawn into this," Larson said, "and when he found out that I had an attorney, he said 'you shouldn't have to go through that expense because of me.' I said the attorney was a friend and wasn't charging me, and he laughed and said, 'My faith in mankind has been rejuvenated—an attorney that will do something for a friend without charging.'"

Larson gave Russ a hug before he departed and assured him that he didn't believe Russ had done what he stood accused of.

Alarmed by Russ's ability to show up in the far suburbs in search of a more agreeable cuisine, Hennepin County prosecutors demanded that Friedberg bring his client in on August 19. Russ was arrested and briefly jailed before bail of $400,000 was set. It was an unusual step to take before a suspect is formally charged. Prosecutors characterized it as a safeguard, although the bond was chump change for Russ. It did have one effect, however. To return to the Fairview psych ward, he had to acknowledge that he was a patient there. His passport was confiscated (the prosecutor cited his "foreign contacts"), but no restrictions were placed on his domestic travel.

A week later he checked himself out of Fairview and flew to Hartford, Connecticut. He wrote a $22,000 check to a mental health facility called the Institute for Living and then stopped payment because he didn't like the food. He flew back to Minneapolis and checked into Fairview again, three days after he had left, and one day after his fugue made headlines.

On August 29 he was charged with two counts of first-degree murder and placed under arrest. Bail was reset at $12 million, the highest bond ever required in Minnesota, so high it took Russ more than a week to post it. He spent that time in jail.

He was back in the hospital on September 10, but he had had a preview of what the rest of his life would be like. Although he was on suicide watch, he managed to get his hands on a plastic bag. On the night of October 30, 1992, he pulled it over his head, cinched it at the throat, and suffocated himself.

Twelve days of jailhouse food and the certainty that takeout was not an option may have played a role in his decision, but Russ was a tortured soul. He was particularly distressed by the fact that his eldest son wouldn't take his calls. When he asked Beverly Martin about the family's standoffish attitude, her reply, "What did you expect?" couldn't have been very comforting.

He told Martin that when he pulled the trigger on his wife, he actually believed he was killing her lawyer. That would have been good evidence for the defense, but insanity pleas are notoriously difficult to sustain. Russ told one of his fellow clients at Fairview that he had done something wrong and contrary to his values, which indicates that he knew right from wrong. A trial would likely have ended in his conviction, and his whereabouts after the murders might have been revealed as well. Inquiries about where he had been, who had helped him, and whether any crimes were committed in the process were dropped after his suicide.

More than a decade has passed, but those questions remain unanswered. The people who could answer them still aren't talking. "I'd love to discuss the case with you," says Rosten, "but the three of us attorneys, Joe Friedberg, Peter Watson, and myself, vowed that we would not talk about it, and I'm bound by that."

Friedberg declined as well, and Watson did not return calls, but three documents in the voluminous file shed some light on Russ's whereabouts after the crimes.

The first is Chief Setter's report, which is curious in some respects. Although he alerted two of his officers that he was going to a meeting to receive information about a crime, he went to the meeting alone. It was a well-orchestrated rendezvous, timed to coincide precisely with the meeting at the Lunds offices, but the most important attorney, Friedberg, showed up fifteen minutes late.

According to the report, Setter and Rosten "made small talk" until Friedberg arrived, while Grostyan sat silent. Only the three men who were present know what they talked about, but Friedberg's absence suggests that it might not have been small. Smart attorneys absent themselves from conversations when they don't want to hear what is being discussed.

Once Setter was informed of the murders, he called officers Olson and Peterson because he "didn't want to receive any evidence." He helped draw up the affidavit for a search warrant but made a point of reporting that he did not participate in the search. "I remained outside of the home as the officers entered and began to search the crime scene," he writes.

According to Holland, Chief Setter, who is now a private investigator, is an affable, outgoing man, a gun collector, a good politician, and not the type to fade into the background. "He was good at talking to groups and getting to know key people in the community," Holland says. "We got a lot of calls here from people who said they knew the chief and wanted to talk to him." He had been the chief of the St. Louis Park police and took the job in Minnetonka only after he secured his pension, an astute move by a sharp self-promoter.

Nevertheless, Setter made a point of remaining slightly removed from the active investigation of what was certainly the biggest case of his career. Why he might have done so is suggested by two other documents in the file, neither of which concern the murders directly. Instead, they concern a related obstruction of justice investigation.

On August 20, 1992, a former client at Fairview contacted the Minneapolis FBI office. The agent who interviewed him begins her report by reiterating the man's claim that he was under treatment for drug addiction at Fairview, and there was nothing wrong with his sanity. The informant says that while he and Russ Lund were in the mental health ward together, Russ told him that he had gone to the chief of the Minnetonka police after the murders, confessed, and showed him the weapon he had used. The chief had advised him to contact an attorney and sent him on his way, still armed.

"Mr. —— thought it odd that the Minnetonka Police did not arrest Lund or take the murder weapon at that time if this was true," says the report.

The FBI informed the Hennepin County prosecutors about the claim, and on August 9, 1992, a detective from the sheriff's department, Charles Kelly, interviewed the informant again. Kelly asked him why he had contacted the FBI.

"He stated that in conversation with Mr. Lund he was led to believe that Mr. Lund was a long-time personal friend of the Minnetonka Police Chief," Kelly reported. "He felt it was necessary to contact an agency that did not have any known ties to Russell Lund."

When Kelly was contacted for this story, he said, "If I didn't think that what the man told me was worth considering, I wouldn't have put it in the file." Queried whether he could believe that an officer of the law would tell an armed man who had just admitted to a double murder that he could keep his pistol and he was free to go, Kelly chuckled and replied, "Facts is facts."

Setter proved just as affable and politic as Holland had described him. "I'd be glad to discuss the Lund case with you," he said. "Of course, I'll have to weigh my responses in regards to the family, and I'd want to contact them before we speak. Call back in a few minutes."

All attempts to reach him after that were in vain.

Had attorney Rosten been willing to talk, the first question would have been how he got involved in the case. Friedberg is one of the best criminal lawyers in Minnesota. Watson was Russ's divorce attorney, so they already had a relationship. What Rosten brought to the table is unclear.

Queried about the possible misconduct of his friend Chief Setter, Rosten seemed shocked that documents relating to that matter had found their way into the file. He inquired about the source. When he was told that it was someone who had been in the psych ward with his client, he had some advice: "I'd be very skeptical about what somebody like that says."

But even a skeptic has to concede that the report of Setter's involvement has the ring of truth. It is a tale of two things we all know to be real: the conflicts that can arise between duty and friendship, and the deference habitually shown to the rich. It begins when Russ, red-faced with rage, corners Kelly and fires the shot that kills him, which is overheard by a neighbor. He flees the scene in his van, horrified by what he has done, the murder weapon still in his possession. He contacts a friend of his, a fellow gun collector and the chief of the Minnetonka police, and blurts out a confession.

The disclosure puts Setter on the horns of a dilemma. His responsibilities as a police officer are clear. He has to disarm Russ and take him into custody. Morally it's a tougher call. A friend has placed his life in Setter's hands. He doesn't want to arrest him, because he knows that Russ has waived crucial legal rights. He can't take the gun, then let him go. That would be tantamount to an admission that he had a perpetrator in his clutches and turned him loose.

Duty tugs one way, friendship another. Deference tips the balance. The chief comforts himself with the assumption that Russ is no random killer, so lives are not in danger, even if the chief has failed to live up to his professional obligations. He sends Russ on his way, after instructing him to contact an attorney—not just any attorney, but one who will make a priority out of concealing the chief's involvement without sacrificing Russ's interests.

Both those objectives were quickly addressed. The Lunds and the police had to be informed simultaneously. If the family was told first, they would become material witnesses, subject to intense questioning. If the police found out first, the Lunds might tell investigators something that would undermine an insanity defense. A strategy of silence minimized the family's involvement and precluded the inadvertent opening of any avenues of inquiry that might lead to the chief.

Setter and Rosten didn't make small talk when they met. Rosten told Setter how the situation had been handled, while Friedberg made himself scarce.

There is plenty in the file to contradict that version of events. The investigators pegged the time of death at 1:00 p.m. at the earliest, probably later. If Russ committed the murders in midafternoon, stayed with the bodies overnight, spent the morning in the Lunds offices, then spent five hours with Pastor, he didn't have time to see the chief. The same informant that told the FBI about the chief's involvement said Russ had told him he contacted Watson first, and it was Watson who put him in touch with Rosten.

Moreover, when unrelated parties come forth with inside information about a high-profile crime, it is rarely of any value, according to investigators. A letter in the Lund file addressed to Hennepin County Attorney Michael Freeman from "A Citizen" is a good example. It tries to tie the murders to the Flight Transportation affair and repeats the rumors that the airline was a money laundry for the rich. Although it is written in a knowing tone, there is not a hint of how that knowledge might have been obtained, or how it might be verified.

According to Holland, whatever went on at Flight Transportation was unrelated to the murders. "There was nothing to that alleged connection," he says.

Holland was unaware of the aborted obstruction of justice investigation, or the claims that led to it. "That makes it interesting," he says. "Yes, the chief might have known Mr. Lund. It kind of explains . . ." He trailed off without explaining what it explains, and declined to elaborate.

One thing it explains is the vow of silence Russ's attorneys took. They were roundly criticized by columnists in the *Star Tribune* and the *St. Paul Pioneer Press* for ignoring ethical and humane considerations, but they never said a word in their own defense. Rowley even raised the possibility that one of the victims might have been saved had the police been informed in a timely way (according to the postmortem, they both sustained wounds that would have caused instant death).

The chief's alleged involvement also explains the attorneys' preoccupation with ethical issues, even though their representation of Russ raised no ethical flags.

"Professional ethics forbid an attorney to disclose a crime that a client tells them he's committed unless the client gives his express permission," says Professor Douglas Heidenreich of the William Mitchell College of Law.

According to Heidenreich, attorneys can and should counsel such a client to turn himself into the police, but that would have been unnecessary in Russ's case. He had already turned himself in. The attorneys' silence protected Chief Setter, not their client or themselves. Their only ethical problem was whether to snitch on Setter. Ten years after the fact they are still not willing to do so.

The passions that were loosed when Russ and Barbara Lund's marriage fell apart—love, rage, avarice, jealousy, cupidity, unresolved conflicts between father and son—were potent but not unusual. What distinguishes Russ's crime from an ordinary middle-class murder is the proximate cause. People who don't have a fortune to argue about may find it hard to understand why Barbara couldn't take the $4 million she was offered and live happily ever after. Russ's attitude is even more incomprehensible. He could entertain the prospect of giving up everything he had—in the abstract. In the event, he drew the line at $4 million and then committed an atrocious double murder when his wife rejected his offer. Why didn't he offer her a few more millions to abandon her quest for information, and try to get by on the $5 million or so he'd have left?

Those are the real mysteries that surround the murders of Barbara Lund and Kevin Kelly, and only the rich know the answer.

A Prayer for Uncle Charlie

In 1923, two inmates at the Leavenworth Federal Penitentiary made a deal. One of them, Charles Allen Ward, was a powerfully built man of thirty-seven. The other was a wealthy snob named Herbert Bigelow, the fifty-three-year-old president of Brown & Bigelow, a calendar manufacturing company in St. Paul.

Ward had lived out a kind of cowboy-movie dream in the gold camps and gambling halls of the last frontier before he was imprisoned. He had mined and prospected in Nevada, punched cows in Arizona, bounced disorderly patrons from saloons in the Southwest and Alaska, served as quartermaster in Pancho Villa's army, and made a fortune, only to squander it on a monumental spree that ended in his imprisonment.

Bigelow was in Leavenworth for tax evasion—and terrified of the other convicts. "He's a miserable piece of humanity, but I'm going to help him," Ward told a fellow convict.

Ward was handy with his fists. His past inclined most of the inmates to respect him, and those who didn't thought twice before they crossed him. Early in his sentence, Ward made short work of a bully from Hawaii nicknamed "Pineapple," who had threatened him. The fight won Ward a reputation as a good man to have for a friend but a bad one to have for an enemy.

Ward promised to safeguard Bigelow in prison in exchange for a chance to make good in his employ when he was released. Ward held up his end of the deal, but Bigelow tried to renege on his several times. Ward never let him.

Ten years later Ward became president of Bigelow's company. He achieved fame as a man who had risen from humble origins and a shady background to found an industry and to make a second fortune in the process. But his past haunted him. The suspicion that he had never severed his underworld contacts and may have been responsible for two murders stuck with him until the day he died.

At the time of Ward's death, in 1959, a Hollywood screenwriter was at work on the script for a film based on his life. Clark Gable was eager to play the leading role, but Ward's widow put a halt to the project, fearing that her children might be kidnapped if their wealth and circumstances were publicized.

The script was destroyed, but it probably wouldn't have been very accurate anyway. Ward spent the latter half of his life evading questions about the first half. The evidence suggests that he was an intriguing mix of iron will and sentimental hokum—shrewd, ruthless, fearless, ambitious, admirable in many ways, and sinister in others.

He was one of the wealthiest men in America when he consented to an interview with the *Saturday Evening Post* in 1938. He had decided to set the record straight about certain matters, he said. He promised the straight facts and seems to have kept his promise. When the reporter probed some aspects of his life, he simply refused to comment, but the answers he did provide check out.

"I was born in 1886, christened Charles Manning, and raised on the Seattle waterfront," Ward told the *Post*. "My mother was Rosemary Manning. She married a seaman named Ward when I was 14. The man gave me his name, but not much else. We quarreled all the time. By then I was running errands in saloons for a living. I guess you could say some of my chores were of a pretty dubious nature."

Charles Ward shortly after his release from Leavenworth. Photograph from author's collection.

The reporter asked Ward to elaborate about those chores, but he declined. An advertising industry trade paper said he had been a plucky shoe-shine boy who had the nerve to ask bar patrons for a quarter rather than the usual dime, a tale that has the ring of one of Ward's latter-day inventions. He told his prison friends that when he was young, he had earned a living beating up penny-ante gamblers who wouldn't pay their debts, and arranging liaisons with prostitutes for sea captains. He also recalled that as a youngster he had eaten so many half-rotten jack mackerel scavenged from the docks that the thought of swallowing another morsel of fish made him gag.

He left home in 1903, at the age of seventeen, and never looked back. When he heard his mother had died many years later, he didn't send flowers.

He headed for the huge, sparsely populated American Southwest, where, in the words of one historian, "there wasn't a wire fence from the Gulf of Mexico as far west as a man could ride." Gold mining, silver mining, and cattle raising were the principal industries; gambling was the principal pastime.

Ward's first destination was Nevada, where his experience on the Seattle waterfront provided him with one marketable skill—the ability to throw rowdy drunks out of saloons with a minimum of fuss. He plied the bouncer's trade in Carson City and Virginia City and then headed south to the area that ultimately became his stamping grounds, the four-hundred-mile stretch of desert that straddles the Mexican border from El Paso to Yuma. Though his travels would take him as far as Saigon, Yokohama, and Nome, Ward was always drawn back to the border country. More than half a century later, he would spend the last day of his life at his southern Arizona ranch.

In 1904, the borderlands were wide-open territory. Arizona and New Mexico had yet to join the union. To the south lay the vast, ungovernable Mexican states of Chihuahua and Sonora—thousands of square miles of mountain and desert, where the only law that mattered was administered at the whim of a bandit who called himself Pancho Villa. The Mexican singers who entertained in the joints where eighteen-year-old Ward worked often sang of Villa's exploits.

Men went by their nicknames in the border country; only a greenhorn inquired about anyone's real name. Saddle tramps carried lariats called "lass-ropes." A man's tack was his pride and joy, and a true cowpoke never parted with his saddle. An Arizona schoolteacher who was trying to define the word "traitor" in 1904 wrote a lesson in which she characterized Benedict Arnold as "the kind of man who'd sell his saddle."

An anonymous eyewitness's tale of an Arizona shoot-out was included in a book that was compiled during the New Deal by the Federal History

Project. The writer was a traveler stranded in Benton—a town where Ward later claimed he had worked as a bouncer.

"The shootout happened on Thanksgiving day, 1906," the traveler wrote, "at Jess Fisher's Gambling Hall, where a fellow who called himself Jack the Ripper tended bar. Fisher and the Ripper had quarreled earlier in the day, then they patched it up and went off for a holiday dinner. They returned in good spirits, but soon were hurling curses at each other again, shouting to be heard over the din at the tables. There were about fifty patrons in the place, including three unarmed hostesses. Everyone else carried either a Colt or a Luger automatic, the latter being a pistol which was gaining in favor at the time.

"The bouncer called on a Mexican singer to take the stage and calm things down, but in the midst of the first song Fisher drew his Luger and shot out the coal lamp chandelier, plunging the place into total darkness. Bullets flew. Gun smoke filled the air. I crawled across the floor and tried to hide behind a cast iron stove, but the bouncer, a husky young fellow, got there first. He let me crouch between his legs while the first volley was exchanged, then picked me up and flung me toward the door. 'There ain't room for two here,' he said. I tumbled into the street and took cover behind a watering trough. From there I could see nothing, but what I heard told the story."

The bark of the Colt and the zing of the Luger were distinctly different sounds. Soon each zing was followed by an ominous-sounding thunk. Four thunks and the Colt barked no more.

They carried the Ripper out and laid him on the wooden sidewalk. A doctor examined him by the light of a full moon and declared him officially dead. A court of the citizenry was hastily convened outside Fisher's Gambling Hall, and the proprietor was declared innocent of any crime.

The bouncer rode past on horseback while court was in session. "Where're you headed?" the traveler asked, hoping to show that he held no grudge for the rough way he had been tossed from the hall. "Damn well out of here," the bouncer replied.

Ward left Arizona in 1906 with a resolve to see the world. He made his way to the coast, hunting, camping, and punching cows along the way. He signed on as a seaman in San Francisco and then shipped out aboard a series of tramp steamers bound for the Far East and Alaska. Young Ward was, by his own description, a "red-blooded sport" who spent his pay like any sailor in port. He wound up in Alaska in 1908 with little money and few prospects. He resumed the trade that had become his mainstay—working saloons in Valdez, Fairbanks, and Nome, and rubbing shoulders with men who talked incessantly of gold.

The men had come north to prospect. They panned the Alaskan mountain streams, chipped away at the hillsides, and in most cases spent everything they earned driving away the oppressive isolation that was the central fact of their lives. When they were sober, they talked about the big strike back in Nevada, in an area they called "the southern Klondike."

Ward left Alaska in a first-class compartment on a steamer bound for San Francisco. He later claimed that he had made the acquaintance of a newspaper man named Jack London aboard the steamer, and had stretched out and done nothing for the first time in seven years.

When Ward arrived in Nevada in spring 1910, the gold boom was reaching its peak. Some of the richest ore ever mined had been found twenty-five miles south of Tonopah. Gold worth millions was being extracted from claims the size of baseball diamonds.

At the heart of the lode was a tent city named National. "In 1910," says a history of the state, "National attracted a rougher class of laboring men than any other camp in Nevada." National was fast becoming the archetypal "high-grade camp"—a place where the ore was rich and life was dangerous. Used as a noun, "high grade" meant very rich ore; as a verb, it meant "to steal."

High-grading was a way of life in the mines that surrounded National. The drifters and hardscrabblers who worked there knew that a ton of rock chipped out of Radiator Hill would bring a minimum of $100 (as opposed to $45 from the California mines). The gold from a single ton had brought sums as incredible as $12,000. A chunk of rock the size of a fist could be worth a fortune. The fifteen silver dollars that miners received as their daily wage (and which they joked about "pissing away" nightly in Tex Rickard's saloon) were little more than an incentive to see how much they could high-grade.

It has been estimated that half of the gold extracted from Radiator Hill left in the miners' possession. Everyone except the mine owners approved of the practice, and the owners' hired guards were far less fearsome than rival gangs of high-graders. Ward never divulged the details of his work in National. He simply said he worked there and did some gambling like everybody else.

"In the Spring of 1910 work in the National Mine consisted of a 12 hour shift six days a week," according to a state history. "The first shift began before sunrise. A hundred men worked in the mine, and every one of them highgraded. A young miner might go to work with the best intentions, but he would see the other miners stealing, and he'd see his shift boss stealing, and soon he'd be highgrading too."

Ward lived in a tent and cooked over an open fire, paying as much as fifty cents for a dozen eggs, and forty-four cents for a pound of bacon—five times the price twenty miles away in Winnemucca. He shared expenses with a friend named Jim, a mechanic from the East Coast whose last name Ward either never knew or never revealed.

"We were fellow soldiers of fortune," Ward told the *Post*.

By the time Ward arrived, the days of easy high-grading were over. It was no longer possible to walk through a cursory search wearing a body harness that held up to seven pounds of rock. A clothes-changing room with a steel door separating it from the main tunnel had been installed. It was monitored by guards, and miners had to leave ore behind the door or have it confiscated. They were strip-searched before they left.

The men took to hanging pocket-sized tobacco sacks full of ore under the seat of the portable privy in the mine and then retrieving the bags when the privy was hauled out and dumped. The company caught on and simply stopped providing a privy. Instead, a shallow drainage ditch was dug along the wall. It flowed out in a channel under the tunnel door.

"As we came off shift we'd drop all manner of packages into the foul muck," wrote one miner, "tins, rag bundles, Bull Durham sacks. After the guards left we came back carrying iron rods with hooks on the end, and went fishing for our prizes."

In November 1910, Ward and his friend Jim left National. He never said how much money he took with him, but subsequent events indicated that he had plenty. According to the state history, if he and his friend were average miners, they departed with $5,000 apiece—a small fortune.

They headed for Tonopah, where Nevada's marriage and divorce industry was in its nascent stage. The town was full of beautiful women who had come west to prospect for rich husbands. Winter was a four-month-long shindig in Tonopah, but Ward and Jim left the party early, drawn to the Mexican border by word of a bonanza awaiting shrewd investors.

"I doubled my roll at the roulette wheel," Ward bragged to the *Post* reporter. "Then we headed for El Paso. The Mexican Revolution was in full swing, and there was money to be made."

There was no more colorful man among the Mexican insurgents than Pancho Villa. The eldest son in a family of Mexican peasants, his given name was Doroteo Arango. He was a few years older than Ward and had been born into even lowlier circumstances.

Arango had lived rough in the sierra since 1903, when he had killed a wealthy landowner in his native Durango, allegedly to avenge his sister's honor, possibly to steal some cattle and cash as well. From that day forward, he had been a hunted man—in theory. In fact, the hired guns who pursued him quickly learned that chasing Villa meant some dust in the face and a few days' pay, but the reward for catching him was eternal.

The ballads and legends of Arango's native hills embellished the adventures of famous bandits who robbed from the rich, gave to the poor, and spent their off-hours in the company of beautiful women. It sounded pretty good to Arango, who did his best to live up to tradition. As he drifted west into Chihuahua, he heard tales of the outlaw Pancho Villa, twenty years dead but still living in the hearts of the peasants. According to legend, Villa was reincarnated as a riderless stallion in times of trouble. The image so enthralled Arango that he reinvented himself as Pancho Villa. He even sent a message back to Durango, urging his family to change the family name to Villa.

Villa was a bandit if there ever was one, but the bitter lot of the Mexican peasantry genuinely enraged him. He and his band were quick to side with the insurgents when revolution began to stir. He soon rose to the rank of general. Villa and his handpicked squad of one hundred bodyguards—"los dorados" (the golden ones)—became the most feared soldiers on either side of the civil war.

As a general, Villa assumed the schmaltzy persona that he is still remembered for—distributing loot to the needy, caring for the orphans of war, and tearfully granting amnesty to enemy prisoners in reward for the brave but losing battle they had waged.

His second in command, Rodolfo Fierro, was Villa's enforcer, and no sentimentalist. Many photos of the Mexican revolution show Villa in the foreground, gesturing magnanimously toward an off-camera crowd. The tall hombre who has his back is Fierro, whose nom de guerre was "el carnicero" (the butcher).

Villa put Fierro in charge of administering the amnesties he granted, a dual management process that functioned to preserve Villa's image while maximizing the practical value of taking prisoners in the first place. Fierro and his commander were well aware that among the rank and file the line between insurgent and defender of the status quo was a thin one, often hinging less on ideology than on which army promised better rations and more booty. They also knew that sheer numbers counted more than anything else when armies clashed.

Fierro asked each liberated prisoner his preference: Would he like to soldier for Villa, or return to the bosom of his family? Those who volunteered for the insurgency were issued a horse, a gun, and three bullets. Fierro assumed that those who opted for home and hearth would be heading for their old regiment. They were executed.

When Ward and his friend Jim arrived in El Paso, the rebels and the Federales had gathered their forces in anticipation of a decisive battle. The rebel army under Villa camped across the Rio Grande from the El Paso smelter, on the outskirts of Juárez. The Federales were garrisoned at the Juárez bull ring.

Both armies relied on guns and supplies purchased in the United States, chiefly in El Paso. Anyone who cared to buy cheap on one side of the river and sell dear on the other could call himself a supplier. Commerce was brisk. El Paso youngsters earned good money selling tinned sardines to Mexican soldiers. Middlemen made solid profits dealing in dry goods. The Schneider & Sons ammunition factory in Clint, Texas, put on extra shifts to keep up with orders coming in from Mexico.

Burros laden with goods forded the Rio Grande and headed for Villa's command post all day. Gringos of every stripe, from curiosity seekers to guns-for-hire, strolled through the rebel camp, gawking. They maneuvered around fly-bitten steer carcasses hung up on racks in the sun, and stepped carefully over piles of burro flop that competed for the flies' attention. Hard-eyed rebel soldiers squinted at them from beneath their sombreros.

Ward and Jim were drawn to a crowd watching a team of burros pull two Ford station wagons across the river toward Villa's end of the camp. When the cars arrived at Villa's tent, he had his purser pay the car dealer in gold. Then he directed his translator to ask who among the assembled Americans might be interested in the job of converting the station wagons to armored cars. Ward and Jim volunteered. Under Jim's direction they did an impressive-looking job, using cotton wadding and sheet metal.

When they were finished, Villa told them to name their fee. It was a double-edged proposition, offered by a man famous for both his generous nature and his quick, murderous temper.

Jim asked for a sum of money. Villa gestured for his purser to pay him. Then he looked at Ward.

Ward hesitated for a moment and then told Villa that he wanted to join his army and be given the hides of all the cattle that were slaughtered to feed the men, as long as he served. Villa asked his translator to repeat Ward's request, just to make sure he had heard it correctly. According to Ward, he roared with laughter and answered, "si."

"He thought it was damn funny," Ward told the *Post* reporter, "but the opportunity I'd spotted was no joke."

Ward rode with Villa off and on for three years, soldiering for fortune all the way. He salted down the hides and sold roughly eight hundred of them every month to leather dealers in El Paso—at four to six dollars per hide.

When some of Villa's officers realized what a good thing Ward had going, he cut them in on the deal to buy their silence.

Villa made Ward and Jim his quartermasters, with the additional duty of transporting the armored station wagons between encampments. Villa often went along for the ride, and he used the vehicles as mobile command posts during battles. Villa felt invulnerable inside his "iron cars."

Ward and Jim spent an average of ten days each month acting as Villa's procurement agents in the United States. They often rode trains hundreds of miles through contested territory to reach the border. They had to be ready to defend themselves against armed men from all factions, who agreed on little but their hatred for gringos. A guard of two soldiers traveled with them whenever they carried gold; otherwise they were on their own. Ward was mute on the subject, but according to histories of the Mexican revolution, anyone who functioned in the capacity he did had to kill to survive.

Technically noncombatants when they were in the field, Ward and Jim wore arms and shared in the everyday life of the rebel soldiers. They cooked beans and beef over open campfires and slept in bedrolls around the coals. An evening's entertainment consisted of drinking mescal and singing songs to the accompaniment of a guitar. Every night, the encampment rang with the anthems of Villa's army, "La Cucaracha" and "Adelita." Another favorite was the nameless battle cry that rallied campesinos to follow the banner of their charismatic leader, Francisco Madero: "Mucho trabajo, poco dinero, no hay frijoles, Viva Madero!"

A contingent of long-haired Yaqui Indians known as Las Cucarachas (The Cockroaches) smoked marijuana, a habit that soon became the hallmark of Villa's army. Gringo recruits like Ward, Tom Mix (later a movie star), Tracy Richardson, and Sam "The Fighting Jew" Dreben turned up their noses at locoweed and mescal. They drank American whiskey purchased in Texas, often with the proceeds from sales of marijuana they brought across the river with them.

Villa and his soldiers lionized Madero as a man born to privilege who had devoted himself to the liberation of the Mexican masses. Word of Madero's assassination in January 1913 brought Villa out of a brief exile in El Paso to reassemble his army. He got word to the troops by dispatching trained carrier pigeons to the ranches and mountain towns where they lived.

Ward and Jim received word less dramatically, on the American side of the river. Ward may have hesitated before riding off to risk his life again. He had $70,000 stashed in Texas banks by then, but something—loyalty, adventure, or money—lured him back.

"Pancho was a hard man," he later told a fellow inmate at Leavenworth, "but I'd still ride to hell for him."

The rebels took Juárez for the second time and then turned and advanced on Torreón. Victorious there, they headed for Chihuahua City. Villa rode the railway with a forward contingent. Ward and Jim traveled with the main force, driving Villa's armored station wagons. As they headed south across the high plateau of Durango, Ward saw his friend's vehicle come to an abrupt halt. He went back to see what had happened and discovered Jim dead at the wheel. A sniper's bullet had passed through a slit in the sheet metal and struck him between the eyes.

Ward knew there and then that he'd had enough of the Mexican revolution. Abandoning the station wagon in favor of a fast horse, he rode for the border, spurred on by the thought of Villa's reaction when he discovered just how safe he had been in his iron cars.

In 1916, at the age of thirty, Ward could look back on a life of spare circumstances and close calls. He felt like going on a spree, and that was what he did. By his own account he raised hell all over the Southwest for the next several years, and inevitably ran afoul of reformers.

The kind of people Ward hung around with were described as "desperados, highwaymen and border riff-raff" by a Denver newspaper, which decried the scarcity of law and order in Arizona. The newspaper named no names and specified no crimes, but implied that the young men in question stood squarely in the path of commercial progress in the great Southwest.

As the clamor to curb the hell-raisers grew, Ward gradually depleted his bankroll, but he was far from idle. He owned a racetrack in Colorado, and a stage line headquartered in the gold mining town of Oatman, Arizona. He later hinted to a fellow convict that he had done a little hijacking as well.

Ward told the *Post* that agents of the U.S. government dogged his every step. "They tailed me everywhere," he said. "I was kind of flattered. But if a load of opium or cocaine was smuggled across the border, Charlie Ward came under suspicion. And all this time I was simply being a red-blooded sport, trying to get a kick out of life."

In 1918, Ward was arrested at a party in a Denver hotel room. He always maintained that federal agents planted the cocaine they seized there, and that his conviction was the result of perjured testimony. The case against him must have been weak—it took the feds two years to bring him to trial and then not for trafficking, but for possession. The judge nonetheless sentenced Ward to ten years in prison, reviling him as a man "beneath contempt." The judgment was hyperbole, but the words stung.

In 1955, Ward reflected on his courtroom plight in an interview with Jack Mackay of the Associated Press: "After the high, wide, and handsome life I led, I was bound to have enemies. Nobody believed me. I guess my vagabond life was too flavored with fringe adventure to defend my innocence."

Ward entered prison stone-broke and chastised. He had spent the last of his money in a vain attempt to remain free. Near the end he had been cadging drinks on Denver's Curtis Street skid row.

In his 1938 interview, Ward told about a turning point in his life that came less than a week into his sentence. He was sprawled on an upper bunk at Leavenworth, staring at the ceiling. It was a bleak January evening. Outside, the jazz age was dawning. Flappers were flapping, revelers were swilling bootleg hooch, and men with half his guts and ambition were getting rich. Inside, his cell mates were playing dominoes on the floor below him with all the spirit they could muster. It was quite a come down for a red-blooded sport.

He was angry, he said, but not despairing. He had prospered in difficult circumstances before, and he was pretty sure he could do so again. He weighed his options as calmly as he could. Escape was a slim possibility. But he would most likely be shot as he fled, and if he weren't, there would always be a price on his head. The only prudent course, Ward concluded, was to become a model prisoner, make parole in the minimum four years, and then succeed on the outside and reclaim his good name. All he needed was one more chance, he was sure of that, and while he waited for it to materialize, he set out to perfect the personal qualities that would aid him in his quest.

Morris "Red" Rudensky, an ex-convict who knew Ward at Leavenworth and later wrote about him in his book *The Gonif* (coauthored by St. Paul newspaperman Don Riley), remembered Ward as a man of great inner strength who reinvented himself at Leavenworth.

The image Rudensky paints of the imprisoned Ward would be recognizable to Ward's business colleagues and chamber of commerce buddies years later. It was at Leavenworth that he adopted the personality that is still the template for success in the corporate world. Whether he had encountered the type in his peregrinations or made it up himself is unknowable, but as usual he knew where the main chance lay. Ward seemed to be everywhere at once in Leavenworth, Rudensky wrote, talking, listening, manipulating, organizing, and most of all, exhorting the men to think positive and stop selling themselves short. He must have been his own best audience for those performances. It was his way of remaking himself. By the time he left prison, the judge would have hardly recognized him.

He also studied electrical engineering and learned enough to be placed in charge of Leavenworth's electrical system. It was a position of trust, because he had to be allowed outside the gates, and because a blackout in a prison can spark a riot. The job virtually assured Ward of parole.

In 1923, two years into his sentence, Ward confided a bit of prison gossip to Rudensky. "There's a scared guy named Bigelow in here, and he's a miserable piece of humanity, but I'm trying to get in a cell with him," Ward said. "The cons have him scared to death. He's got a calendar company or some damn thing, up in St. Paul."

"What do you care about him?" Rudensky asked.

"He might offer me a job when I get out," Ward replied, "and if he does, I'll take it."

Wealthy by birth, arrogant and patrician in manner, Bigelow was the type of man that the other convicts took special pleasure in tormenting. Ward told the *Post* that he monitored Bigelow's plight carefully and waited until he was desperate before offering the bargain that would reshape both their lives. The opportunity that he spotted in the person of Herb Bigelow must have sparked off a memory of his high-grading days. "The moment I saw him," Ward told the *Post*, "something inside me said 'grab this guy Charlie. He can pull you out of the muck.'"

Ward, a prison wheeler-dealer, had no trouble arranging for Bigelow to become his cell mate. Bigelow's fears faded under Ward's protection, and his true personality emerged. He was bone lazy. Ward offered to take over his business correspondence for him, and Bigelow eagerly agreed. Ward soon

Herbert Bigelow in 1930.
Courtesy of the Minnesota
Historical Society.

learned a wealth of key information about the company's employees, their backgrounds, their strengths and weaknesses.

Bigelow had little interest in discussing the business, but Ward pressed him, claiming he needed facts to correspond effectively. Over the two-year period that they shared a cell, Bigelow and Ward had many long conversations about every facet of Brown & Bigelow. It isn't a stretch to say that Ward had a hand in running the company before he ever laid eyes on its St. Paul headquarters.

In April 1924 Ward stood at the gates of Leavenworth and waved goodbye to Bigelow, confident of the relationship they had developed. He expected a good job and a secure future when he was released a month later.

Bigelow met Ward at St. Paul's Union Depot on a Sunday in May. It was a fragrant spring morning, but Ward smelled a rat. Bigelow's manner was cold. As they drove to his White Bear Lake estate he said little, but just before they arrived he offered Ward $25,000 cash to forget about their deal. Bigelow had discussed Ward with his senior executives, and they had advised him that such a man could never fit into the culture of Brown & Bigelow.

Ward refused the $25,000 offer. Bigelow just nodded, but his disappointment was obvious. After a wordless lunch they drove back to town and stopped at a boarding house near the company's plant. Bigelow arranged for a cheap room.

"I wanted a day or two's rest," Ward said, "but he wouldn't hear of it. He told me to show up for work at 7:30 the next morning, and left."

Ward was assigned the job of feeding raw rubber into a processing machine, for $25 a week. His fingers bled from the rubber's friction; the pain in his hands was so intense that he couldn't sleep. "That's when I realized Mr. Bigelow was trying hard to get rid of me," Ward said.

Less than a week after his release from Leavenworth, he lay awake one night, thinking about jumping a freight and returning to the Southwest. Instead, he decided to play the hand that fate had dealt him. "Charlie," he vowed, "you will push weaker men aside. Someday you will sit at Bigelow's desk running the whole show."

From that moment on, Ward approached his career the same way Villa approached a battle—no quarter asked, none given. He was foreman of the rubber line within a month. A few weeks later, the superintendent of the novelty division was stricken with appendicitis, and Ward was assigned to substitute for him. When the man returned to work, he was the ex-superintendent.

"I saw that if I didn't get rid of the men above me one at a time, they would get rid of me eventually," Ward told the *Post*, "so I used facts, figures and argument to convince Mr. Bigelow that I was the better man for the job."

As Ward's inexorable rise continued over the next nine years, he perfected a management style that was part Villa and part Fierro. His shrewdest move was to create his own squadron of loyalists within the company—dozens of ex-cons who held jobs at every level.

As soon as he gained a position of authority, Ward put out word to his prison contacts that any inmate who wasn't afraid to work could get a job at Brown & Bigelow when he was released. Many of them didn't make the cut, but Ward, who fired employees that displeased him without a moment's notice, remained loyal to the ones who did. Those men owed everything they had to him, and anyone in the business hierarchy who tried to hold him back had to contend with them. Thus, an executive who found himself in the uncomfortable position of being Ward's putative superior was caught in a pincer movement. Ward was after his job on one flank, and key people he depended on were busy providing Ward the facts and figures he needed to take it on the other.

They also had to deal with Bigelow. Within a year of Ward's release Bigelow and Ward were friends once more. It was one of the ups in a strange, up-and-down relationship. Several executives went to Bigelow and asked him to fire Ward at various times, but he always refused. Ward moved in with Bigelow in 1928 and seemed to exercise a huge influence over him from then on.

An article in the *Minneapolis Journal* quoted Ward as saying, "I worked with Mr. Bigelow, ate with him, lived with him on his farm out near Hudson. Of course I kept rooms at the Athletic Club, but most of the time we spent on the farm."

Ward told the *Post* that over time he managed to put his allies in every key position in the company. "The treasurer was the hardest man to dislodge, because he was Mr. Bigelow's brother-in-law, but I finally succeeded in doing it in 1929," he said.

Ward displayed great respect for Bigelow in public. Privately he seems to have disdained him. Bigelow was just lazy in prison. Outside he was a lazy playboy who openly promoted employees based on their wives' looks and availability. The business was little more than a way to get sex for him.

Ward, by contrast, was a no-nonsense manager whose sporting days were far behind him. There was only one way to prosper under his command, and that was by working just as hard as he did. He would later be lauded as a champion of the wronged and downtrodden, but he had no pity for the women who were victimized by his boss, and nothing but contempt for their husbands. Many an executive who thought his spouse had earned him a sinecure in Bigelow's bed found himself in a breadline after Ward took over.

As time passed, Bigelow became more and more content to let Ward make all the major decisions. He named Ward executive vice president and general manager in 1932, a year when the Depression hit Brown & Bigelow hard. The firm began losing money—a quarter of a million dollars per year. The sales force fell to fewer than four hundred men.

Publicly, Ward remained loyal, but in private he criticized Bigelow for his poor business sense. "I keep getting promotions," Ward wrote to Rudensky, who was still in Leavenworth, "but Bigelow is such a stubborn little man I don't know if it's worth it. He won't spend a penny. If he would the calendar business would boom!"

In June 1933, Bigelow and Ward had their last falling out. Ward reminded Bigelow of the year his novelty division had turned in a profit of $342,000, and of how he had been rewarded—with a bonus of $250. "You're not very good at paying your debts," Ward said.

When Bigelow replied by threatening to cut Ward's $12,000-per-year salary, Ward turned on his heel and walked out. He later insisted that this seemingly rash act was a calculated move. If so, it worked. The board of directors called a special meeting, and instructed Bigelow to rehire Ward. When he objected, they told him he had no choice.

Bigelow and Ward (wearing cap) were friendly when this photo was taken at Bigelow's White Bear estate. Courtesy of the Minnesota Historical Society.

From then on Bigelow was a figurehead, meddlesome but irrelevant. A few months later, he went on a hunting trip to northern Minnesota, where he drowned, along with a guide and the wife of one of his executives, when their canoe capsized on Basswood Lake. The terms of his will made front-page news in the *Minneapolis Journal* ten days later, under the headline "Prison Friendship with Bigelow Brings Ward Third of Estate." Bigelow had altered his will to leave Ward more than $1 million and a controlling interest in Brown & Bigelow.

That was the beginning of the most unsavory aspect of the saga of twice-born Charlie Ward. His past fueled speculation that he had done away with Bigelow. The will, which had been changed shortly before Bigelow's death when they were on the outs, lent credence to the story. Rumor had it that Ward and Bigelow had gone fishing in the wilderness, but only Ward returned. That clearly is not true—both the *St. Paul Dispatch* and the *Minneapolis Journal* place him hundreds of miles away in St. Paul at the time of the accident. But Ward had plenty of underworld connections and a cadre of ex-cons inside the company who would do anything he asked. No criminal investigation was ever undertaken, but from then on the theory that someone had murdered Bigelow at Ward's behest would be part of his legend.

The board of Brown & Bigelow immediately named Ward to succeed Bigelow as president. Ward made two quick moves. He divested the company of Bigelow's far-flung and unrelated subsidiaries and raised salaries across the board.

Ward's first appointment to a vice presidency went to Richard Rupp, a skilled pressman. Rupp didn't have a criminal record, but people often assumed that he did. "As soon as they found out you worked for Brown & Bigelow," Rupp recalled in 1985, "they'd ask why you'd been in the slammer."

He remembered Ward as "a rough, tough, generous guy, a tremendous bull of a man. He could be brutal if he had to. He made men, but he got rid of them, too, if he became disenchanted."

Ward's old friend Rudensky was released from Leavenworth, after thirty-three years in prison. Ward hired him as a copywriter. A banker named A. J. Peters, whom he had met at Leavenworth, was hired to run the accounting department. Another ex-con, Arthur "Wickey" Hansen, formerly a machine gunner for the Capone gang, found employment at Brown & Bigelow. Three years later Hansen would figure in speculation about a second murder in which Ward was rumored to be involved.

Under Ward the company soon went from $5 million in annual sales to more than $60 million. One reason for the growth was that Ward virtually invented a new industry, remembrance advertising. He saw the advantages of a new product called plastic and expanded the business to include such items as pens, cups, figurines, watches, and lighters, all embossed with a business name or an advertising slogan. The idea of leaving eye-catching little doohickeys around a potential customer's desk was brand-new when Ward realized its potential.

Ward gave generously to charities. Every mention of his giving seems to be accompanied by a disclaimer stating that his largesse was anonymous and behind the scenes, and that he loathed publicizing it. Nevertheless, word leaked to the press and became part of his public image. The Little Sisters of the Poor, animal shelters, and orphans were his favorite causes, but according to some who knew him, he gave large sums spontaneously to people who were down on their luck. Ray Brand, who managed Brown & Bigelow's calendar division, told a trade magazine about one of those occasions.

"Once I was riding in a car with Mr. Ward when we heard on the radio about a farm family whose home had burned," said Brand. "When we got to the office he got that family into a house and taken care of. He picked up all the bills, but it was never publicized."

Each Christmas, Ward threw a holiday dinner for the orphans of St. Paul. More than five hundred children were his guests at these affairs. Ward personally supervised the menu, arranged for entertainment, and even carved the turkeys. The meals were rounded off with dozens of pies and gallons of ice cream, and just as the last spoonfuls were devoured, Santa Claus arrived with gifts for every child.

Ward had run Brown & Bigelow for more than four years when he consented to the interview with the *Saturday Evening Post*. His Cinderella story and his charitable giving had been well publicized. Now he thought the time was ripe to dispel an image of which he had grown weary—that of the eternally grateful protégé of Herbert Bigelow.

"I've suffered from this convict-befriending legend for years," Ward said. "It's about time someone set the record straight. First, Herbert Bigelow tried to welsh on the promise he swore to me in prison, and then he handed me a crippled business."

Ward said that he had done more for Bigelow than Bigelow had done for him: "I saved his business, and before that I saved his life. I was protecting him from a pack of wolves in Leavenworth, and he knew it."

That's all true, but in return Bigelow had given Ward the opportunity to become the man he was when the interview took place: an eccentric, famous, larger-than-life figure who had settled into a life of opulence.

The contrast between his business success and his hard-guy past worked to his advantage, and he purposely leveraged it by cultivating the speech patterns of a B-movie gangster. "He used words like 'dese,' 'dem,' and 'dose,'" wrote John Thornton, a sales manager at Brown & Bigelow, in a memoir of his days under Ward. "He told us how to handle the competition: 'Cut dere troats, and bleed 'em white,' he'd say."

Ward put in twelve-hour days, but he took frequent vacations as well. He sunbathed in the nude and often headed for seashore nudist beaches to relax. He had all his teeth capped with gold, a cosmetic flourish that accentuated his imposing physical presence. As he approached his midfifties he was a barrel-chested man, six feet tall, two-hundred-plus pounds, with bushy black eyebrows, a shiny bald head, and a year-round deep suntan. On social occasions he wore tailor-made Western outfits and a ten-gallon hat. His costume included a diamond stickpin, a big diamond ring, a diamond-encrusted wristwatch, and a holster monogrammed in diamonds with his initials, in which he carried an ivory-handled six-shooter.

In 1940 he married Yvette Saunders, the former wife of Minneapolis restaurateur Charlie Saunders, the owner of Charlie's Café Exceptionale. The couple would have three children, the first of them born when Ward was fifty-four. He and his family lived on a two-thousand-acre farm near Hudson, Wisconsin. *Life* magazine called it "the showplace of the Midwest." The parties he threw there for up to three hundred people always included a multi-course meal featuring fresh-killed game and prime rib. He had a huge garage on the property that housed his collection of expensive cars, along with a bright red fire engine. A corps of armed guards patrolled the grounds. Ward himself carried a loaded pistol at all times.

The occasions were usually business related, but the guest list always included a few celebrities to make them more memorable. "I've been to a lot of parties in my day," Gene Autry told the editor of the *Hudson Star-Observer* on one such occasion, "but this one takes the prize. These Wards are real people."

Charlie Ward, who had been a rough, tough guy in his day, certainly had developed a warm and gracious exterior, but his management style evolved along a different tangent. He became almost capriciously ruthless toward his employees.

"It was against his nature to be a true friend," wrote Thornton. "At the slightest provocation he could scornfully fire any employee regardless of position and length of service, dismiss him permanently from his mind without the slightest regret, and never give him another thought. Amazingly though, replacements served him with the same dedicated loyalty as those he fired. Each felt his position was secure and his chain to Charlie Ward's heart was unbreakable. He often said to me, 'get rid of your enemies or dey will get rid of you,' yet he never recognized his own worst enemy, himself.'"

According to Thornton, many of the highly trained people Ward dismissed started competing businesses. That, and Ward's spendy ways, would eventually bring Brown & Bigelow down, but not until after Ward's death.

Like many millionaires, Ward dabbled in king making. He was drawn to Floyd B. Olson, a former county attorney in Minneapolis, who was elected governor of Minnesota under the banner of the far-left Farmer-Labor Party in 1930. Olson was a popular and charismatic public official who had a real shot at the presidency of the United States, partially due to Ward's patronage.

Olson's background appealed to Ward. He came from a tough, immigrant neighborhood in north Minneapolis, a mainly Jewish community where he got to know the Jewish gangsters who ran the city's organized crime in the 1920s and 1930s. His tenure as Hennepin County attorney came during Prohibition, and like many law enforcement officials of that era, he had little interest in prosecuting the owners and patrons of speakeasies, or the bootleggers who supplied them with booze. That never hurt his standing with the voters, but he did come in for a fair amount of criticism from the muckraking press, which enjoyed its heyday during Olson's career.

Those same newspapers often praised him for his forward-looking ideas about the roots of crime. Olson was convinced that poverty and bad luck put more lawbreakers in the dock than evil intentions. He often joined defense counsel in their pleas for mercy, a practice that brought him to the attention of Ward.

The men became good friends. Although Olson's radical politics didn't appeal to Ward, the more he learned about him, the more he liked him personally. He contributed to Olson's gubernatorial campaign and leaned on his executives to do the same.

Walter Liggett was the editor of a weekly called the *Midwest American* that was critical of Olson. In the book *Stopping the Presses*, Liggett's daughter, Marda Woodbury, writes that her father believed justice was bought and sold in Minneapolis when Olson was the county attorney. Liggett, a staunch supporter of the Farmer-Labor Party, thought that Olson had compromised the party's principles for political gain once he was elected governor. In September 1934 he wrote a front-page editorial titled "Why I No Longer Support Gov. Floyd B. Olson."

The editorial and subsequent articles criticizing Olson came at an inopportune time for the governor and his patron. By 1934 Olson had become the odds-on favorite to lead the Depression-spawned Progressive Party into the 1936 election. President Franklin D. Roosevelt feared a challenge from the left and thought that a ticket headed by Olson, with Louisiana governor Huey Long running for vice president, would be particularly potent. All the Progressives needed was a backer with deep pockets, and Ward was ready to take that role. The opportunity to be the power behind President Olson was too good to pass up from Ward's perspective, and the idea that a small newspaper published out of a south Minneapolis storefront might throw a monkey wrench into their plans must have enraged both men.

Howard Guilford, a radio commentator who had attacked Olson's alleged ties with the underworld, was murdered in September 1934. No one was ever indicted for the crime. The following spring Liggett published an account of being tailed around town by a spooky-looking individual, who Liggett claimed was a member of the Detroit-based Purple Gang.

"Are some of the Governor's friends contemplating silencing me as Howard Guilford was silenced?" he wrote.

According to Woodbury, a friend of Ward's offered Liggett a bribe to stop attacking Olson. The man, whose name she does not disclose, allegedly handed Liggett $300. Liggett published an account of the incident under the headline "Mr. Ward Helps Us Spread the Truth." Liggett wrote that he would use the money to give gift subscriptions to influential people.

In December 1935, Liggett was shot to death in the alley behind his apartment. The drive-by shooting took place in front of his family as they were getting out of their car. In her book, Liggett's daughter concludes that the murder was committed by Minneapolis gangster Isadore "Kid Cann" Blumenfeld. She speculates that "someone bankrolled an expensive murder involving at least two cars and five hoodlums." She as much as fingers Ward.

"The general belief was that Ward was completely reformed," she writes. "Still, Brooklyn prosecutor William O'Dwyer accused Ward of having ties with Murder Incorporated, and after Los Angeles police arrested Bugsy Siegel in 1940 they found papers showing that Ward had lent Siegel at least $150,000. Bugsy was certainly part of Murder Incorporated, as well as a frequent visitor to St. Paul."

Woodbury also describes an attempt to extort money from Ward by accusing him of Liggett's murder. The would-be extortionists were arrested, and among the details of their plot that emerged was the allegation that Ward's employee Wickey Hansen was the hit man for the Liggett murder. When they entered their guilty plea, the extortionists claimed they got all their ideas from well-publicized accusations made by Liggett's wife, and had no independent information.

Cann was tried for Liggett's murder and found not guilty. Nevertheless, Woodbury makes a convincing case for his involvement. What she fails to explain is why Ward or anyone else would have had to "bankroll" the hit. Cann was capable of gathering two cars and five hoods all by himself.

She also fails to take into account the social dynamics of the Twin Cities' Jewish community of that era. It included some gangsters like Isadore Blumenfeld but also far more left-leaning intellectuals and activists of every stripe—Socialists, Stalinists, Trotskyites, Max Schactmanites, Anarcho-Syndicalists, Farmer-Laborers. Many of them had grown up with Olson. They liked him personally, and they liked his politics. A whispered suggestion or even a careless remark by one of them could have been enough to motivate Cann, who craved acceptance by the respectable members of his community.

Olson outlived Liggett by about a year. His political career came to an abrupt end when he was diagnosed with cancer in 1935. Ward footed the bills for the most advanced treatments, but Liggett's condition was hopeless. He died in 1936, and his lieutenant governor, Elmer Benson, succeeded him.

Many politically astute Twin Citians thought that Ward should run for governor in the next election. The Depression was at its height, and the crowds who lined University Avenue for Olson's funeral procession jostled for a chance to touch Ward as he rode by, perhaps hoping that some of his magic

Left to right: Mrs. Floyd B. Olson, her daughter, and Charles Ward in 1937. Photograph by the *Minneapolis Journal.* Courtesy of the Minnesota Historical Society.

would rub off on them. "We love you, Charlie," they shouted as they reached for his cashmere coat.

Any thoughts of running for office passed quickly, but Ward remained politically influential. In 1938, *Time* magazine called him "the Progressive Party's Dark Angel." From 1936 to 1939 a parade of men with big names and big ambitions courted him, including a pair of potent political rivals, Governor Elmer Benson of Minnesota and Representative Bob La Follette of Wisconsin, each of whom wanted Ward's support for a third-party ticket.

At the same time, Twin Cities power brokers, who had spurned Ward's efforts to join their inner circle, began to display a keen interest in him. In their opinion, Benson was a nightmare, far worse than the personable Olson. The *Saturday Evening Post* quoted a Minneapolis banker who was a member of the elite Minnesota Club: "Charlie has shown that he is honest and able, and the powerful kind of man we need to throw out the Benson crowd," he said. "I think we are all ready to eat crow and admit that we were snobs."

There is no record of how Ward responded to their overtures, but he didn't have much enthusiasm for Benson.

In May 1938, President Roosevelt invited Ward to the White House. They chatted in the Oval Office, then dined together on the presidential yacht. Ward never talked about what was discussed, but a few weeks later he gave a barbecue at his estate in Hudson, with both Benson and La Follette in attendance. Ward made sure that Benson, a man known for his volatile temper, had plenty to drink. At one point, Benson and La Follette almost came to blows—an incident Ward cited when he explained why neither man had won his support.

Roosevelt was reelected in a landslide, Harold Stassen became governor of Minnesota, and Ward settled into a comfortable life as family man, millionaire, Minnesota Club member, and country squire.

Ward had mellowed considerably by then. Somehow, despite his reticence on the topic, he had become famous for his generosity to charities. He was fond of showing visitors the numerous commendations and signed photographs that adorned his office walls, including a personal greeting from Pope Pius XII.

"That shows what a few important people think of Charlie Ward," he would say.

He wasn't shy about giving advice. The walls of Brown & Bigelow were adorned with signs that featured his personal slogans: "When you stop being better, you stop being good," and "Let live and live." Worse yet, he constantly exhorted his employees to get plenty of exercise and to follow his example when moving from floor to floor at the company's plant. He never walked up the stairs, he ran. The first clue that his health was failing came in 1955, when he had an elevator installed for his own use.

In May 1959 he took a trip west with his wife. They spent a few days at a vast spread they owned in Arizona. Their ranch encompassed land he had roamed with his cow-punching buddies half a century before. On May 26 they took a train to Los Angeles to check on one of Ward's interests there. He died in his sleep in a Beverly Hills hotel room that night, three days shy of his seventy-third birthday.

In a codicil to his will, Ward described his life in syrupy terms: "Each day was filled with beneficence and the busy life of building a business, and each night spent in the quiet peace of a clear conscience."

But surely it wasn't that simple. Until he was thirty-seven, each day was filled with the busy life of a soldier of fortune. It included barroom brawls, prison fistfights, high-grading gold, punching cattle, sailing the seven seas, and fending off bandits while he transported goods for Pancho Villa. As for the quiet peace of a clear conscience, he told friends that he never forgot the words of the judge who called him "a man beneath contempt." In effect, Ward spent the rest of his life trying to prove him wrong. Whether he ever accomplished that to his own satisfaction is debatable.

Of all the charities he supported, the one that engaged him personally was the annual Christmas dinner for St. Paul's orphans. He threw himself into those occasions, beginning weeks before, when he helped scour orphanages and foster homes to make sure no child was left out. By all accounts the dinners were lavish, hang-the-expense events, and probably the high point of many a dreary young life. The smiles on the orphans' faces after Santa distributed his gifts were almost thanks enough for Ward—but not quite. He always gave a brief inspirational speech to end those affairs, and when he had finished and the applause had stilled, he would remain silent for a few moments, lost in his own thoughts.

He had plenty to reflect upon—the feel of the breeze through the window of a railway car as it highballed across the Mexican desert, the magical way chunks of rock fished from the muck could turn into pure gold, the look on an executive's face when he found out that his wife had sold her honor for nothing. After a few pregnant moments of silence, Ward would request a favor of the assembled children.

"Please stand up," he would say. "Now put your hands on your hearts, and say a little prayer for Uncle Charlie."

Portrait of an Heiress at the End of Her Career

There are ghost towns all over Arizona, and the municipality of Ajo, 120 miles west of Tucson, almost became one of them. Ajo was on the cusp of extinction three times.

In the early twentieth century Ajo consisted of some clapboard houses and a few commercial enterprises that served local ranches, but cattle grazing in the region is chancy. Several rainless years had driven most of the cattlemen out of business by 1911. The town's population fell below fifty, and the future looked bleak for Ajo. Then, a technology was discovered that turned it into a boomtown.

The foothills around Ajo are striped with orange rock (the town's name is a Spanish rendering of an Indian word meaning "colored clay"), and as far back as the eighteenth century, explorers had recognized that the coloration indicated rich copper deposits. A few miners made money over the years by chipping away at the exposed ore and packing it out on mule trains, but the easy pickings were long gone by 1911, when a leaching process was discovered that made it possible to work the rock efficiently. The New Cornelia Copper Company was organized a few years later, and a mining operation was established outside Ajo. One of the partners was Chester Congdon, who had made a fortune in the iron mining business in northern Minnesota.

The New Cornelia Mine bore Congdon's trademark. It was a huge open hole. Mercifully, the ore that was gouged out of the Minnesota countryside was shipped east for processing. No such luck for Ajo, where a smelter was a key component of the operation. Soon five thousand miners lived in company shacks near the lip of the pit, a mile from Ajo, their view of the nearby mountains obscured by the fog of green vapor that emanated from the smelter's hundred-foot stack.

The town that sprang up next to the mine was called Cornelia. Ajo proper was situated on top of a copper deposit that the company had designs on. When a fire of mysterious origin destroyed the old town, the new one took its name.

Two world wars and the industrial expansion that followed them boosted the price of copper dramatically. The New Cornelia partnership netted hundreds of millions in profit before prices began to fall in the 1970s. When the mine shut down in 1985, there was still plenty of copper left, but it was no longer worth the cost of extraction. Ajo quickly became nothing but a collection of shacks, most of them abandoned.

Ajo flirted with ghost town status once more, but it had a few things going for it than no one could have imagined during the heyday of copper mining. It was scenic, if you didn't mind the open pit and the old smelter that loomed alongside it. When that smelter ceased operations, the mountains reappeared. So did the majestic organ pipe cactuses that dot the nearby desert and give the national monument a few miles south of town its name.

And Ajo is almost a crossroads. The freeway to San Diego from Phoenix and points east is not far from town, and the highway to the Mexican border and beyond to the Sea of Cortez and the coastal village of Puerto Penasco is Ajo's main north-south street. By the mid-1980s Puerto Penasco was being developed into Arizona's Riviera, so travelers passed through Ajo regularly.

Demographics played into Ajo's hands as well. America's aging population was looking for someplace warm and cheap to retire. Mining shacks in Ajo went for $10,000 to $15,000. Medical costs were rising, so the proximity to Mexican doctors became another attraction.

Soon the elderly were flocking to Ajo, among them Marge and Wally Hagen, a couple from Minnesota who moved there in 1986. Marge was in her midfifties. Her husband was twenty years older and in poor health. They fit nicely into reborn Ajo, a community of four thousand people, the majority of whom were retired.

Marge quickly became a familiar figure around town. She joined church groups, started a quilting circle, and began sharing her expertise in crocheting and knitting with some of the local women. When Mary Duran told Marge that her neighbor, Felipa Romero, had cancer, Marge brought Romero gifts of food and chocolate. When Marge found out that there were elderly Catholics in town who were too infirm to go to church, she persuaded a priest to come from Phoenix for a special mass. It was held in the Hagens' home, which laity and cleric alike gazed on with undisguised admiration. Marge had decorated it with an artist's flair.

Marge helped George Skinner patch up a quarrel between two acquaintances of his who hadn't spoken for years. When Marge invited friends over for dinner, they left talking about the delicious food she had prepared. Her social dexterity, the way she organized charitable activities, and the things in which she excelled—quilting, the needle arts, interior design, gourmet cooking—made folks wonder if Marge, who was tight-lipped about her past, might be a genteel lady, perhaps a finishing school graduate.

The members of Ajo's tight little law enforcement community wondered if she was a scam artist. The Hagens came to their attention a few months after they arrived, when sheriff's deputies had to confiscate some of Marge and Wally's possessions to satisfy a judgment. The action came about as a result of a lawsuit filed against them because they had written more than $50,000 in bum checks.

Marge's husband certainly wasn't culpable. Wally didn't look strong enough to sign a check. He became almost completely housebound within a year of their arrival, and when he did get out, people noticed that he had an ashen pallor. Marge popped across the Mexican border regularly to purchase the alternative medicines that she used to treat him. She had devised his regimen personally and confided to her new friends that it was the only thing keeping him alive. He suffered from multiple illnesses including cancer, she explained.

Like many of Ajo's residents, the Hagens had arrived in a motor home. People lived in those vehicles while they picked and chose among the mining shacks and then parked them in the desert outside their new homes. The Hagens paid to store theirs in a commercial yard secured by a fence, an expense that was out of reach for most of their neighbors.

Four years after the Hagens arrived, Ajo almost became a ghost town again. A plague of arson fires, more than forty in a twelve-month period, created a climate of near hysteria. Most of the fires were in abandoned houses, but people were frightened that their own homes might go up in smoke. They feared for their lives. Real estate prices actually fell, and the possibility that the town might empty out was real.

"Ajo was on edge, that's for sure," says David Alan of the Pima County Sheriff's Department, who investigated the arsons.

Ajo's ordeal by fire began about 2:00 a.m., on July 9, 1990, when a Pima County deputy noticed flames inside the commercial yard at Del Sur Enterprises. At least two vehicles were on fire, she reported.

In fact, four vehicles were consumed by flames that night: a dump truck, an automobile, and two motor homes, one of which belonged to the Hagens. Investigators discovered that a hole had been cut in the yard's chain-link fence. Fires had been deliberately set inside both motor homes and had spread to the other vehicles. All four were totally destroyed.

"The perpetrator used an accelerant, probably kerosene," says Alan. "Marge filed a claim for their motor home, but the insurer was aware that there was an open arson investigation, so they dragged their feet on paying."

Meanwhile, the arson continued. "Sometimes we'd get two fires a night," says Alan, "but generally speaking they were more spread out—one every couple days, maybe a week would go by with none, then all of a sudden there'd be two more."

Shortly after the fires began, Alan and another deputy were on patrol when they spotted a wisp of smoke coming from an abandoned house. They alerted the fire department and then entered the house in time to discover the arsonist's method. It was relatively sophisticated. Charcoal briquettes had been piled in a closet, doused with accelerant, and ignited, giving the arsonist plenty of time to flee the scene before the house went up in flames.

Pima County is five thousand square miles of desert with one city, Tucson, and not much else. Alan is one of only twelve investigators stationed in and around Ajo. A few border patrol officers live in town, and the highway patrol is on call in an emergency, but the outbreak of arson stretched law enforcement's capabilities to the breaking point. Alan and his colleagues wondered if they were fated to stand by helplessly while a pyromaniac brought Ajo down.

"We're spread so thin here that our investigations aren't the kind you see on TV," Alan says. "There's no such thing as putting surveillance on somebody, for example. We just don't have the manpower, and it wouldn't work in a small town anyway. At a point we began to suspect Marge strongly, but there wasn't a whole lot we could do. She was seen in the neighborhood of several fires. I saw her a couple times, and we had some verbal exchanges. I got the distinct impression that she was taunting me. It was as if she knew that I knew she was the perpetrator, and there wasn't a dang thing I could do about it. She was laughing at me, that's how it felt. Her eyes were dancing as we talked."

An obvious question presented itself, however. If Marge's motor home was destroyed for insurance, why were the rest of the fires set? "She never debriefed me on her rationale," says Alan. "But I'll tell you one thing. Marge was one strange lady."

Alan didn't know the half of it then, but he did have some knowledge beyond his personal observations. "We were getting clippings in the mail, anonymously, about arson fires that had happened in other places where she'd been living," he explains. "There was a bank in Colorado that burned while she lived there, and some homes she'd lived in, in Colorado and Minnesota. A man who owned a restaurant in Queen Creek, Arizona, called and told us that Marge wanted to buy a house he had there, and when he refused to sell, it burned down."

The Hagens lived next door to Mark Indivik, a border patrol officer. "I can't remember if Mark had words with Marge or not," says Alan, "but all the law enforcement personnel in the area knew she was our suspect."

That may have been why Indivik was a light sleeper. He was dozing fitfully the night of March 24, 1991, when he heard a noise outside. He looked out and spotted Marge leaving his yard, with her dog on a leash. He dressed and went out to check his house. A rag soaked in kerosene had been jammed into the frame of his crank-out window. Indivik called Alan.

"We immediately put people in the alley and the house," says Alan, "including a deputy with a flash camera, inside." They closed the window, pulled the curtain, and sat down to wait. Less than an hour later Marge walked up to the window, struck a match, and lit the rag.

"The rag flared up, everyone yelled, and they pulled the curtains back and took a picture just as she turned around and ran," says Alan. "I guess we hadn't thought the picture thing out very well—all we got was a photo of a flash off the closed window—but everything else went down just the way we planned. Marge was tackled in the alley, and placed under arrest."

It was a process Marge was familiar with, although it took her by surprise on that occasion. Her previous arrests had been anticipated, which gave her

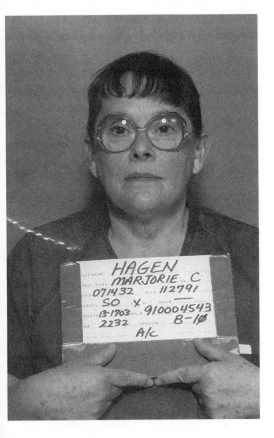

Marjorie Hagen after her arrest in Arizona. Photograph courtesy of the Pima County Sheriff's Department.

some time to prepare. She had devised an ensemble to wear when the law came to get her. A squat woman with plain features and dark hair, Marge always donned sunglasses that had oversized frames, and a cowl-like scarf tied in a floppy knot under her chin. She affected the same look when she showed up for her trials. Her supporters thought it was stylish.

"I thought she looked like a murderer from central casting," says Dan Mabley, a judge in Minneapolis. Mabley prosecuted her for arson in 1983 when he was a district attorney, but his recollection of her menacing persona dates back even further.

"I was a young prosecutor in the Dakota County attorney's office when the famous murder case against her was moved there in 1979," Mabley says. "It was tried in a courtroom next to my office, so I saw her regularly. I thought her appearance would hurt her. Obviously I was wrong. I was surprised how quickly the jury acquitted her."

Marge burst into the headlines when her mother, Elisabeth Congdon, was murdered at Glensheen, the family's Duluth estate. Marge and the man she was married to at the time, Roger Caldwell, were both tried for the crime. Caldwell was convicted. Marge wasn't. Their cases received national attention and established Marge's lawyer, Ron Meshbesher, as one of the leading criminal attorneys in the country.

When Glensheen was built in 1909, Chester Congdon and his heirs had yet to acquire the millions that the New Cornelia Copper Company would earn for them, but they were already immensely wealthy. Elisabeth was one of six children of Chester and Clara Congdon. She dropped out of Vassar to be with her mother when her father died. Glensheen, a forty-room mansion overlooking Lake Superior on the outskirts of Duluth, would be her main residence for the rest of her life. Glensheen's gothic exterior always looked like a set for a murder mystery, but the Congdon family's life there was idyllic until Marjorie came along.

Elisabeth was a spinster. She went east to adopt two infant children during the Depression, "foundlings" in the parlance of the time. Records indicate that the first foundling, the one she named Marjorie, was born in North Carolina in 1931. How and where Elisabeth found her is unknown. She found another daughter, Jennifer, a short time later. The two girls grew up together at Glensheen, but they weren't close. Jennifer was tall, fair, and lovely. Marjorie was short, dark, and malicious.

Marge showed sufficient signs of incipient pathology as a child to worry her mother, among them incidents of petty theft and vandalism, the attempted poisoning of a horse, and a possible arson fire. Elisabeth took her out of a boarding school in Massachusetts when she was eighteen and put her in the care of psychiatrists at the Menninger Clinic in Kansas. She left there after a few months for an outpatient counseling program at Washington University in St. Louis.

Marge met her first husband, Richard LeRoy, in St. Louis. She told him she was studying nursing at Washington University, a white enough lie, but an early augury of her keen, some would say unhealthy, interest in disease. She would later tell acquaintances that she was a trained nurse. Marge and LeRoy married in 1951.

The marriage, which lasted twenty years, must have been happy in some ways. The couple had seven children and raised them in a comfortable home on Fremont Avenue S., in Minneapolis's lake district. LeRoy earned good money as an insurance executive. Marge had an income of $500 a month from trusts. Nevertheless, they were in constant financial trouble. Elisabeth bailed them out time after time.

One major expense was the speed skating and equestrian lessons that Marge insisted on giving her kids. They all became competitive skaters, and during the 1950s and 1960s Marge was a fixture at local arenas and rinks. It was at those events that she became acquainted with another couple whose children skated, Wally and Helen Hagen.

LeRoy thought his wife's obsession with turning their children into championship skaters was a little nuts, but it paled in comparison to her other habits. According to a deposition he gave for their divorce, her purchases of everything from oriental rugs to thoroughbred horses cost over $1 million, most of which was paid by her mother. He also stated that her habit of proclaiming her wealth and ranting about her prejudices alienated their friends. She particularly despised 1960s-style protesters, but she wasn't fond of people of color either. He didn't mention the fact that their garage burned down mysteriously in 1966.

Marge may have offended the people they socialized with as a couple, but she could be charming when it suited her. She made friends in the speed-skating set who would stick with her through her upcoming tribulations. The Hagens and others attended her trials dutifully and supported her in every way they could.

Shortly after her divorce from LeRoy, Marge bought a house in Marine-on-St. Croix, Minnesota, and hired a contractor to do extensive remodeling. He and Marge had an affair, but it ended badly. The man filed liens against the property for the $100,000 that Marge owed him. She bought another home in Englewood, Colorado, and moved there.

In May 1975, Marge's house in Marine burned down. She claimed she had been in Colorado at the time, but a lengthy investigation uncovered conclusive evidence that she had flown to the Twin Cities and set the blaze. She was never charged because of an oddity in Minnesota law. At the time it was not illegal to burn your own house down if you didn't profit by it, and Marge had let her insurance lapse. The fire did destroy the only asset her ex-lover could have claimed to recover his $100,000, however.

Eight years later, a determined prosecutor named Dan Mabley managed to shoehorn evidence of Marge's long history of wrongdoing into her trial for arson, in Hennepin County, Minnesota. "Most of the information about her involvement in other fires came from the two Bureau of Criminal Apprehension investigators who worked the case I prosecuted," Mabley says. "When they first presented the case to me, they already knew about the fire in Marine. I asked them to do some follow-up, and they found out about other fires she'd been connected with."

One of those fires occurred soon after the arson in Marine. A woman of Marge's description was seen in the vicinity of a bank in Englewood, Colorado, that was deliberately set ablaze. She was investigated but never charged.

It was during this period that some third-generation heirs, including Colorado attorney Thomas Congdon, filed a lawsuit attempting to exclude adopted children from inheriting after Elisabeth's death. If they had succeeded, it would have disinherited both Marge and Jennifer, plus all their offspring, but the Minnesota Supreme Court ruled against them.

The suit is indicative of a conflict Marge had to deal with. As a child, she had led a life of immense wealth and privilege, but her aunts, uncles, and cousins didn't think she deserved it. Her behavior suggests that she might have agreed.

She told an Arizona probation officer who had to write a pre-sentence report about her that Elisabeth had plucked her out of an orphanage in which she had been placed after her biological parents died in a car accident. She described them as lower-class drunks. She was less than a year old when she came to Minnesota, so someone must have discussed her origins with her, probably while she was being chastised for one of her frequent misdeeds.

As soon as she was old enough to spend, she became a spendthrift, and punishment did not deter her. It had the opposite effect. Marge learned early that wild spending was a shortcut to punishment. She is surely a pathological arsonist, another repulsive trait that manifested itself before she reached adulthood. When she thought the occasion demanded it, she cut herself.

Everywhere Marge went she developed a circle of friends who found her charming and generous, but people as diverse as her biographer, prosecutors, investigators, journalists, and their audience seem to delight in believing the worst about her. Maybe they dislike her because she is rich. She appears to loathe herself for the same reason, although she rarely misses an opportunity to announce that she is an heiress.

In 1976 Marge met Roger Caldwell at a single-parents meeting in Golden, Colorado. Caldwell was a baggy-eyed lush from Latrobe, Pennsylvania, who had moved west with his first wife and stayed after their divorce. He had worked sporadically as a salesman until he met Marge. She told him she was rich. They were married, and he assumed his working days were over.

The couple moved to a ranch in the mountains, where Marge knitted and read histories of English royalty all day, while Caldwell drank himself into insensibility, usually by midafternoon. When he felt the need to get outdoors, he drove to the nearest bar, a few miles away, and drank there for awhile. Sometimes that turned into a three-day bender. He thought he had died and gone to heaven.

But, alas, it was soon paradise lost. Marge had inherited the capital from one of her trusts, hundreds of thousands of dollars, and blown it. Elisabeth was still a sucker for her eldest daughter, but by then she knew it, and she had taken steps to insulate herself from Marge's eternal pleas for cash. Trustees had been placed in charge of those decisions, and the answer was always no.

The news that they were broke gradually seeped into Caldwell's booze-saturated brain and so enraged him that he became physically abusive. Marge filed assault charges against him several times, then dropped them before he could be arrested. She showed up in a Denver hospital on one occasion with injuries she initially claimed had been caused when a horse kicked her. She later told the doctor that her husband had beaten her.

When they weren't fighting, they spent a lot of time trying to make real estate deals, all of which fell through because Marge couldn't pry any money loose. The bank foreclosed on their ranch, and they moved into a motel in Golden, Colorado. That was where the plot that would result in Elisabeth's murder was allegedly hatched.

First they tried gentler means. Marge sent Caldwell to Duluth in May 1977 to meet with a trustee for the Congdon fortune and an attorney who specialized in estate work. Caldwell's mission was to convince them that he was a hard-headed business man who needed $750,000 so he and his new wife could start a horse-breeding ranch in Colorado.

According to documents connected to his trial, Marge tarted him up for the occasion in high-end Western garb—fringy buckskin, turquoise jewelry, a string tie with a silver clasp. Caldwell, who later told a reporter that he hated horses and couldn't run a ranch if his life depended on it, must have felt as foolish as he looked. After he was turned down flat, he took a cab to Glensheen, where Elisabeth's personal secretary grudgingly allowed him a brief visit with his mother-in-law. There is no record of what they discussed, but he was not invited for dinner.

A month later, Elisabeth, who was partially paralyzed and had a nurse in attendance twenty-four hours a day, returned to Glensheen from the family's summer home in Wisconsin. The date was Sunday, June 26, 1977. Her regular nurse had the night off. Vilma Pietala, a nurse who had worked for Elisabeth until she had retired a few months before, was called in for the shift.

At 7:00 a.m. the following morning the regular nurse came to work and discovered Pietala's bloody, beaten body at the foot of the stairs that led to Elisabeth's bedroom. Elisabeth was in bed, smothered to death with a pillow that was still lying on her face. A wicker case and a gold coin were missing from the bedroom, and a cameo ring had been taken off the victim's finger. There were indications that one or both women had put up a struggle. Pietala's car was missing.

By that afternoon the news had gone out that one of Minnesota's most prominent citizens and her nurse had been brutally murdered. A media frenzy the likes of which Duluth had never seen ensued. Marge and Caldwell came to town and set up headquarters at the Duluth Radisson Hotel, where Marge quickly found herself at the center of the furor.

Several of Elisabeth's relatives had called the Duluth police as soon as they heard what had happened, and said they suspected Marge. They told about her past misdeeds and said she was in bad financial trouble. Her sister, Jennifer, explained that Marge's relentless demands for money had been stonewalled recently, but that she stood to inherit more than $4 million when her mother died.

A Duluth detective who met with Marge and Caldwell on June 29 noticed that Caldwell's lip was cut, and his hand was swollen. The next day—the day Elisabeth was buried—the newspapers reported that the two were suspects.

Marge confronted the accusations publicly. She bitched to reporters about the way the police were treating her and Caldwell, and about their dire economic circumstances. She said it was a scandal that an heiress such as herself was virtually penniless. Queried why she didn't get a job, she replied, with some justification, that she was unemployable.

Reporters didn't have a chance to question Caldwell. In sharp contrast to his wife, he laid low—as well he might have. Marge had visited several realtors in Colorado over the weekend the murders took place. She had a solid alibi. Caldwell had none. Marge told investigators and the press that her husband had been with her, but she had visited the realtors alone, and she had only vague and contradictory explanations of where Caldwell was at the time. Caldwell simply clammed up.

He should have cleaned up. The police searched their room at the Radisson and found a receipt from a gift shop at the Twin Cities airport dated the day of the murders. A clerk at the shop identified Caldwell from a photo. She told investigators that he had purchased a leather garment bag, and she had watched him place in it a wicker case like the one that was missing from Elisabeth's bedroom.

Pietala's stolen car was quickly located in a parking lot at the airport, and then a Duluth cabby identified Caldwell as the fare he had dropped in the vicinity of Glensheen the night of the murders. Investigators searched Marge and Caldwell's motel room in Golden and found a Duluth Radisson envelope addressed to Caldwell in his handwriting, containing the gold coin that was missing from Elisabeth's bedroom. It would later be determined that his thumbprint was on it. The motel clerk said it had come in the mail a few days after the murders, and he had delivered it to the couple's room in their absence.

By then Marge and Caldwell had moved to the Holiday Inn in Bloomington, Minnesota, near the Twin Cities airport. On July 5 police entered their room with a search warrant. They found the missing wicker case, the cameo ring, and the garment bag that the clerk remembered Caldwell buying. On July 7, Caldwell was arrested for the murders of Vilma Pietala and Elisabeth Congdon.

After they took Caldwell away, Marge moved in with one of her sons in a Twin Cities suburb. An incident occurred there that provides a glimpse into Marge's psyche. She phoned an old friend from her days as a speed-skating mom and said she had just been attacked. Her assailant, she claimed, was a man with a badge and gun, who had slashed her repeatedly with a razor.

A few days later she told the Duluth newspaper that the man with the badge had warned her not to assist in her husband's defense, or he would return and finish the job. Police who investigated the incident concluded that her wounds were self-inflicted. She continued to insist the attack was real.

Whatever happened, it did not deter Marge from helping Caldwell. She told a friend that he had been at a public library the day he would have had to fly to Minnesota in order to commit the crimes. She told Duluth reporters that although she could not account for his whereabouts on the night the murders occurred, he had awakened her in their Colorado motel room at 7:00 a.m. the following morning, hours before he allegedly purchased a garment bag in the Twin Cities airport. She said her mother never owned any gold coins, and suggested that the whole coin story was a setup. She explained that Caldwell had stayed at the Duluth Radisson a month before the crimes, when he sought money to start their horse ranch. The trustee had asked for some self-addressed envelopes at that time, and the ones Caldwell had provided were from the hotel.

The bogus attack by the imaginary cop raised questions about Marge's sanity, but a decision she made shortly thereafter showed her to be canny and well informed. She hired Twin Cities lawyer Doug Thompson to defend her husband and retained Ron Meshbesher as her counsel.

Thompson was a competent, hard-working attorney with a reputation for strong closing arguments. Meshbesher was a step up from there. He was capable of charming juries with his ironic sense of humor and succinct arguments, but he took a scholar's approach to making his case. He had a reputation for researching forensic assumptions, finding their flaws, then tearing into seemingly unimpeachable evidence and destroying it. He also had a knack for finding expert witnesses who could undercut the prosecution's arguments in fundamental ways.

Meshbesher knew very well that if Caldwell was convicted, Marge would be indicted for the same crimes. He and his staff devoured every detail of Caldwell's trial.

Prosecutor John DeSanto built his case carefully, first documenting Marge and Caldwell's financial woes and then revealing that Marge had executed a handwritten, notarized will shortly before the crimes that gave her husband

Roger Caldwell leaves the Crow Wing County courthouse. Photograph courtesy of Steven Kohls, *Brainerd Daily Dispatch*.

control of more than $2 million of her anticipated inheritance. DeSanto portrayed the will as an incentive to murder Elisabeth. The jury cringed when he brandished the brass candlestick that was used to beat Pietala to death.

DeSanto made much of the missing gold coin that had been mailed to the defendant in Colorado, the only scrap of physical evidence that linked Caldwell to the scene. He called Colorado Bureau of Investigation agent Steven Sedlacek to testify and walked him through his extensive training and experience before asking him whose thumbprint was on the envelope in which the coin was mailed. Sedlacek replied that the print matched Caldwell's exactly.

Thompson countered that his client had been framed, possibly by his wife. He observed that Caldwell's fingerprints were not found at the scene, only on an envelope with a dubious link to the scene. DNA analysis was the stuff of science fiction at the time, and Thompson was able to point out that blood found on the stairway, which DeSanto claimed was Caldwell's, was simply the same type as his client's and about thirty million other people. He made a five-hour-long closing argument, but it was unsuccessful. It took the jury less than twenty-four hours to find Caldwell guilty of both murders. He was sentenced to consecutive terms of life in prison.

Marge and her attorney Ron Meshbesher arrive for her murder trial in Hastings, Minnesota. Copyright 2003 Star Tribune/Minneapolis-St. Paul.

A few days later Marge was arrested and charged with conspiracy to murder her mother. Her trial commenced on May 1, 1979. It had been moved to Hastings, more than two hundred miles south of Duluth, in Dakota County, because of the sensational publicity surrounding the murders. A coterie of supporters showed up for Marge on day one, and many of them, including her fellow speed-skating parents Wally and Helen Hagen, were there every day of the sixteen-week trial.

DeSanto began by building a base of testimony about Marge's financial problems and her continual battles with her mother over money. He relied on the same evidence and strategy he had used against Caldwell, but he also had a bombshell in his arsenal. A doctor who had served as Elisabeth's personal physician testified that Marge had attempted to poison her mother in 1974.

According to the physician, Marge knew her mother was diabetic but insisted on giving her marmalade on some bread she had made for her. When a nurse arrived the next morning, Elisabeth was comatose, and there was real concern that she might die. A blood test indicated the presence of a tranquilizer in her system, enough to account for her dangerously low blood pressure and weak heartbeat.

There was not much for a defense attorney to say about that, but Meshbesher ripped into the prosecution's theory of how the murders were committed, in essence turning Marge's trial into a second trial for Caldwell. He showed that the trustees and other heirs had far more to gain from Elisabeth's death than Marge did. One of those heirs, Thomas Congdon, had hired a private detective named Tom Furman, ostensibly as a bodyguard. Meshbesher cross-examined Furman and revealed him as a crook and a liar. In the process he managed to suggest that Thomas Congdon and Furman had framed Marge and Caldwell. Furman refused to answer several questions on the grounds that it might incriminate him.

The worst blow the prosecution sustained was the revelation that the thumbprint on the envelope containing the gold coin was not Caldwell's. The print had not been preserved carefully enough to use in evidence against Marge. All by itself that could have hurt DeSanto's case, but Meshbesher allowed a photograph that was taken when it was fresh to be used and put a forensics expert on the stand who testified that there were "gross discrepancies" between Caldwell's print and the one on the envelope. DeSanto's attempt to discredit the testimony on cross-examination was a dismal failure. When Meshbesher's expert stepped down, the major evidence in both cases had been revealed as false.

Marge, who had sat impassively during the weeks leading up to the impeachment of the fingerprint evidence and had often buried her nose in a detective novel during testimony, allowed herself a brief smile. Her supporters couldn't hide their elation. Newspaper accounts refer to them as a group of women, but there was at least one man among them. Wallace Hagen was a handsome fellow, in a benign, harmless-looking way. He had been cheating on his wife for years. Hiding his infidelities had never been much of a problem, and it was even less of one now. Helen was rapidly sinking into Alzheimer's disease. Shortly after the trial ended, she went to a nursing home. If Hagen and Marge spent any time together during the trial, it went unnoticed, but they must have been laying some plans.

In his closing argument Meshbesher reminded the jury that several witnesses had described Marge as intelligent, a characterization that the prosecution did not dispute. Then he told them that two certifiable morons could not have devised a murder plot less intelligent than the one the prosecutor had described.

He pointed out that every important piece of evidence used against both parties to the alleged conspiracy had been seized from motel rooms days after the murders. According to the prosecution's theory, Caldwell had taken the garment bag, the cameo ring, and the cumbersome wicker case stolen from the victim's bedroom to Colorado. Then, he had brought them back to Minnesota, where the police found them, along with the gift shop receipt that placed him at the airport (no evidence was ever presented that he had been on an airplane the day of the murders, although DeSanto said he was). The receipt, Meshbesher reminded the jurors, turned up on a dresser in a Duluth hotel room in plain view of anyone who walked in with a search warrant. Would an intelligent murderer place it there? he asked. Would two diabolical plotters haul the only evidence that existed against them halfway across the country twice in order to present it to the police?

He used Marge's contradictory stories of where her husband had been when the murders were committed to his advantage, by telling the jury that an intelligent plot would have included a well-rehearsed alibi for both parties. He said Caldwell was probably gone on one of his binges, and Marge had been lying out of embarrassment. He mused upon the leaps of imagination required to execute a will in order to motivate a murderer just a few weeks before the murder, and then to have it notarized so that there is a witness who can testify that it exists.

In DeSanto's closing argument he had again alluded to the mailing of the gold coin, which he had characterized as a "signal" of some kind. A signal to whom, about what? was Meshbesher's question. He reminded the jury that there was no evidence Caldwell ever possessed the coin, but assuming he did, why would he mail it to himself? The prosecution said he was on the way to the Twin Cities when it was posted, to catch a plane to Colorado. Obviously he would arrive before the coin did. Then, if the prosecution was correct, he had rushed back to Duluth with his co-conspirator, forgetting all about the fact that a piece of incriminating evidence was heading for their Colorado residence in the mail. And where did Caldwell get the envelope? Did he stop at the Radisson in midflight from the murders and grab it from the lobby? Did he bring it with him to the scene in his pocket? If so, why wasn't it bloody and crumpled? And most important, why didn't the thumbprint on the envelope belong to him?

Throughout his closing argument, Meshbesher made frequent references to the state's discredited star witness, agent Sedlacek. In doing so he sowed doubt about every other witness they put on the stand. He reminded the jury of a point he had made during the trial: Marge had an income of about $40,000 per year from trusts before her mother died, and it would increase to about $50,000 due to her mother's death. He asked the jurors if they thought she had murdered a woman for whom she had always demonstrated great affection for a paltry $10,000 per year? The large lump sum she supposedly would inherit was tied up in civil litigation, and several other heirs stood to gain more than she did no matter how those suits turned out.

The jury deliberated for thirty-six hours before finding Marge not guilty on all counts. It was a devastating blow for DeSanto. He had lost two cases in one.

Marge's children had filed a lawsuit trying to gain her inheritance while the cloud of guilt hung over her. Once she was cleared, it was settled, but most of what she received went for legal fees.

Three years later the Minnesota Supreme Court ordered a new trial for Caldwell. He had been in prison almost five years by then and was eager to make any deal that guaranteed him he wouldn't go back. DeSanto needed a conviction badly, even the kind of cosmetic conviction that would result from the plea bargain he offered Caldwell.

In July 1983, Caldwell pleaded guilty to two second-degree murders and was sentenced to time served. As part of the bargain he had to confess fully and completely to the crimes, which he did. He claimed he had gone to Glensheen to steal some jewelry, an idea that had occurred to him after his first visit, and had committed the murders in a panic, when Pietala saw him and started screaming. He said he had grabbed the closest thing he could find, a brass candlestick, and beaten her to death. That fit the prosecution's scenario, but his recollections about the rest contradicted the verifiable facts in several ways. He explained that away by claiming he was stone drunk when he broke a window and entered the mansion and couldn't remember the details.

He did not implicate Marge, although he had many derogatory things to say about her.

The minute Caldwell walked out of the judge's chambers, he told waiting newspaper reporters that he was innocent. He continued to do so until the day he died, May 17, 1988, when he slit his wrists and bled to death on the floor of a lady friend's apartment in LaTrobe, Pennsylvania.

Whether he killed Congdon and Pietala remains unknown. "All I know is what Roger told me," says his older brother Howard. "He left me a note when he committed suicide. It said 'I want you to know I did not kill those women,' and that's the way I'm looking at it. He'd told me earlier, 'I might be stupid, but I'm not that stupid. Why would I murder the old woman? She was almost dead as it was. And if I'd have wanted that coin, I'd have put it in my pocket. Mailing it just incriminates me.'"

If Caldwell was guilty, the murders should say something basic about his character. They bore all the earmarks of a one-off committed by a violent drunk—poor planning, sloppy execution, little if any thought to an alibi—and not the work of a congenital criminal. On the other hand, a macabre murder committed in Colorado years later hints that there may have been more to Caldwell than meets the casual eye.

Howard Caldwell never got to know his brother's offspring, but he heard quite a bit about one of them. "Roger got married, and he and his wife moved out west when he was a young man," he says. "I stayed in LaTrobe, so I didn't see much of them. They had three kids. His ex-wife is dead now. She was murdered by their daughter, in Littleton, Colorado. Oh yes, it was in all the papers. People sent me clippings. The daughter's name was Chrissy. She suffocated her mother, put her in a box, then she filled the box up with rock salt, and nailed a lid on it."

Apparently Chrissie made a shrine out of the box containing her mother's preserved body. She decorated it with dozens of lit candles and then went out on a date. The police found the body a few days later, after they discovered Chrissy, dead, in a car parked by the side of the road. She had shot herself.

Wally Hagen revealed his relationship with Marge to his three children shortly after his wife was placed in a nursing home. He was seventy-two, and Marge was forty-nine. It was the beginning of a decade of discord between the Hagen children and Marge. They were shocked that Wally was abandoning their mother and blamed Marge for alienating them from their father.

According to a doctor who examined Helen Hagen when she was admitted to the nursing home, she was in good shape except for her dementia and would probably survive for years. In fact, she lived only a few months. In

March 1980 she unaccountably went into a coma and died. The duty nurse said old friend Marge had visited the night before and had been seen feeding her baby food out of a jar. An autopsy determined that she had died of pneumonia, but it didn't include a toxicology exam.

"I don't believe for a moment that Margie killed Helen Hagen," says Meshbesher. "She died of natural causes." Meshbesher acknowledged that his former client was a tad eccentric, but he didn't have a bad word to say about her.

"I've always found her to be gracious and charming," he said. "I've been to her house for dinner a few times, and she was just an excellent cook. Would you like to see a sweater she knitted for me?"

He explained that he keeps the sweater in his office for two reasons: as a memento of one of the biggest victories of a long and successful career, and because it graphically illustrates a side of Marge that few people know. It's a thick, handsome, tightly knit garment, light gray with a subtle cream-colored pattern, the work of someone who has raised a craft to the level of an art. "She enjoys doing this kind of thing for her friends," Meshbesher said. "She has a generous nature."

Meshbesher chuckled when he heard Mabley's description of his client as a murderer from central casting. "It's in the eye of the beholder," he said. "She looked like a soccer mom to me."

Mabley's jaundiced view of Marge is not confined to her appearance. "I once commented to a colleague that Marjorie Hagen probably committed more crimes and got away with them than any other person I've known in my career in criminal law," he said, "theft, fraud, arson, murder, blackmail, bigamy, perjury, false reporting of crimes. It seemed that almost every day she did something illegal."

Mabley and Meshbesher clashed in court over Marge's next misadventure, a trial for fraud and arson. Newspaper reports of her 1983 arrest on those charges took note of the fact that she gave the name Marjorie Hagen when she was taken into custody. That set some inquiries in motion. Investigators discovered that she and Wally Hagen had wed in North Dakota in 1981, while she was still married to the imprisoned Caldwell. Authorities there decided not to pursue extradition, but she cannot set foot in North Dakota for fear of arrest. "A fate worse than death," Meshbesher observed, after settling the matter for her.

After their marriage, the Hagens decided to live in the Twin Cities suburb of Mound. According to court records, they agreed to buy a home there in January 1982. Marge called it "Cranberry House" because of its crimson exterior. The price was $59,000. There is some evidence that the proceeds from an insurance scam were used for the $8,000 down payment. They obtained a bank loan for $14,000 and took out a contract for deed with the sellers for the remaining $37,000. It was due one year later, in January 1983.

By late summer 1982, they had decided to sell Cranberry House. Marge told friends that Hagen's failing health made it difficult for him to walk upstairs to their bedroom. She made arrangements to purchase another home nearby and entered into an arrangement with Clayton and Geraldine Kulseth to buy Cranberry House for $88,700, which meant a tidy profit for the Hagens. The deal called for the buyers to take over the bank loan, which still had $13,700 owing; enter into a contract for deed with the Hagens for $60,000, payable over ten years; and give the Hagens $15,000 cash.

The closing took place on September 1, 1982. The buyers agreed that they would not move in until September 15, so the Hagens could clean the place. Meanwhile the Hagens insured their new house for $70,000.

The cleanup consisted of an aborted attempt to varnish the wooden floors. The varnish was slopped on over deep scratches, dust, and even piles of dirt, and the job was abandoned with half of one room untouched. It didn't do much for the appearance of the place, but it did coat a few hundred feet of floor with incendiary material. The purchasers took one look and asked for all the keys. As of September 14 they supposedly had them.

At 6:45 a.m. the next morning, firefighters were called about a blaze in progress. Cranberry House was burning. It took hours to put out the flames, and when they were finally extinguished, the roof and the interior had been damaged beyond repair.

Fire marshals investigated the charred structure. The doors were relatively intact and locked from the inside. "Flammable liquid patterns" were discovered, indicating the use of an accelerant such as gasoline. The marshals wrote a report that stated there was "no possible accidental cause that could account for the fire."

During their investigation, they interviewed Marlys Annis, who lived down the street from Cranberry House. She told them that she had walked her daughter to the school bus stop while the blaze was in progress. When she reached the corner, she saw Marge parked there in a pickup truck (the Hagens had purchased the new truck with the $15,000 the buyers had given them). According to Annis, Marge asked, "What's going on down there?" Annis told her that her house was on fire. Marge had no visible reaction, so she repeated herself. "Your house is burning down," she said.

Marge replied that it wasn't her house anymore, she had sold it two weeks ago. Then she drove away.

The State Bureau of Criminal Apprehension began an arson investigation. Agents learned that Marge had begun hounding the home's insurer days after the fire. She was particularly interested in who would be getting the insurance money—her or the new owners. Although there is no indication of it in the record, the agents must have prodded the insurer to settle up and make sure the Hagens received some of the proceeds.

The transcripts of the agents' interviews, first with Hagen, then with Hagen and Marge together, reveal a noose slowly tightening. Hagen tried to provide an alibi for Marge for the morning the fire was set, but the agents got him to admit she had awakened earlier than he, and had gone out. They asked Hagen what the couple's financial circumstances were. He said they were "comfortable." Marge echoed that characterization when she returned home a short time later, but the agents seized bank records showing that they had written numerous NSF checks over the past few months and had a negative balance in their account.

The agents had a physical confrontation with Marge when she attempted to slip something down her pants so it couldn't be confiscated. It was a key to Cranberry House. Both Hagen and Marge had claimed they had turned all the keys over to the new owners.

One of the agents inquired if Marge had purchased any gasoline recently. She said she had, for her pickup truck. He asked if she had put any in a gas can. We don't have any gas cans, she replied, but Hagen corrected her. We do too have one, he said, remember? Marge just sighed and explained that she had forgotten all about it.

In January 1983, the American Family Insurance Company paid off on the purchasers' $70,000 policy. The proceeds were divided between all parties who had suffered a financial loss: the couple the Hagens had purchased the home from, the new owners, and the Hagens. The Hagens' contract for deed was paid off, and they received $16,000 cash. Another search warrant was quickly issued, and a check in that amount was recovered from Wally Hagen's wallet. It was the last element the investigators needed to make their case. The couple had profited from an arson.

Marge was arrested for arson and insurance fraud. Apparently there was no thought of holding Hagen responsible. "He always struck me as a man who was totally lost," says Mabley. "He came across as a very kind person who'd fallen under the manipulative and charming spell of his wife."

Meshbesher defended Marge again. It was an uphill battle. Her failure to get rid of the key was such a monumental blunder that it calls the conceptual basis for Meshbesher's closing statement four years earlier into question. Yes, one could now argue, it is possible for two conspirators to retain incriminating items and then practically make a gift of them to the police—if one of them is subconsciously determined to punish herself, and the other is too drunk to know the difference. Intelligence doesn't count for much under those circumstances.

Meshbesher had won Marge's murder case by studying Caldwell's trial. Mabley began his preparations by studying Meshbesher's approach to Marge's trial. He could almost smell his opponent's strategy wafting in from the future. Meshbesher would portray Marge as a high-profile patsy for a greedy insurance company and a law enforcement establishment that felt cheated by her acquittal in the Congdon case. Mabley's task would be to illustrate a pattern of behavior that eliminated any reasonable doubt about her culpability. His argument would conclude with two important pieces of evidence: the key she had kept and denied having, and the indications of arson the fire marshals had detected. But it would begin with as much information as possible about Marge's past.

There was plenty to be discovered. Marge didn't come to trial until November 1983, almost a year after she was arrested. "It seemed that the longer I worked on the case, the more anecdotes and stories I heard about her illegal activities," Mabley says. "Some came from the police. Some came from Marjorie's children, and the Hagen children—and much of it came from the other Congdon heirs. They told me about many criminal and just plain bizarre acts she'd committed over the years."

Some anecdotes, though intriguing, were clearly inadmissible. Mabley couldn't mention a caretaker's recollection of Marge as a child trying to poison a horse she had grown tired of. There was no way to allude to the fire at a Duluth department store that was set shortly after the store was told not to allow fifteen-year-old Marge to charge on her mother's account. Her alleged attempt to poison her mother was out, as was any suggestion that she had murdered Helen Hagen. Meshbesher tried to exclude all testimony about Marge's past, but the judge allowed five instances of alleged arson and/or insurance fraud into evidence.

The first was the 1975 fire at Marine. Mabley told the jurors that Marge's alibi, that she had been in Colorado, had not survived the most rudimentary investigation. She had purchased a round-trip ticket in her own name from Denver, for a flight that put her in the Twin Cities area when the fire was set. She had rented a car under her own name at the airport and logged seventy-four miles, the distance to Marine and back. A friend of Marge's from Colorado, Judy McCoy, told investigators that a year after the fire Marge had told her she had deliberately burned her Minnesota home.

Mabley disclosed that in 1977 Marge had received an $80,000 insurance settlement, based on the claim that her home in Bailey, Colorado, had been burglarized. He presented evidence that many items purportedly stolen had been reported destroyed in the fire at Marine. Others, he showed, had been

lost or destroyed before the alleged burglary, and still others were simply fictitious. Marge's pal McCoy said she had seen several items that were reported
stolen in Marge's home after the burglary. According to McCoy, Marge said
her insurance claim was "in the sack" because the adjuster was a friend of her
family's from Duluth.

McCoy told investigators that she had been in Marge's home one day in
1976 while an extensive remodeling job was under way, and workmen were
on the premises. As the two women sat in the living room chatting, a newly
installed pane of glass fell to the floor and shattered. Marge told McCoy
she should cut herself with a shard of glass and then run outside screaming
that she had been injured. The construction company's insurer would settle,
Marge assured her, and cutting one's self was easier than it seemed.

Two 1979 arson fires that damaged property Marge had contracted to
purchase were placed in evidence. Both fires occurred less than forty-eight
hours before the scheduled closings. Investigations revealed that Marge could
not have paid the earnest money required to close one of the deals and had
postponed closing on the second several times due to lack of funds.

"She couldn't have profited from setting those fires," Mabley explains,
"but she wasn't able to close those deals. She always saw herself, or wanted to
see herself as upper class—a real society person. As I recall, she would have
forfeited her earnest money in both cases, and perhaps been liable for a
penalty, but primarily I think she just didn't want to be embarrassed."

Marge's support group for the arson trial included two women who had
been jurors in the Congdon murder trial. Mabley took that as an indication
of her puzzling charisma.

"I can't explain it," he says, "but it was real. She had those people wrapped
around her little finger. My wife overheard her instructing some of them in
the women's restroom during the trial. She told them to shake their heads
and frown when the state's witnesses testified, so the jurors could see their
disagreement."

Marge tried to put her spell on Mabley as well. "She came up to me one
day late in the trial and told me that I'd cost her $90. I asked how that could
be. She said that I'd worn a cardigan to court under my jacket, and she liked
it so much that she had to buy one for her son. It was kind of charming in an
odd, openly manipulative way."

Another incident during the trial could be interpreted two ways. Mabley
mentioned to a clerk that he had a headache, and Marge overheard him.

"At recess she offered me some Panadol, which she described as the main
pain reliever used in Europe," Mabley recalls. "I took the pills from her, but I
never swallowed them."

By the time Mabley finished with Marge's past he had cut the legs out from under Meshbesher's attempt to portray her as a victim. He proceeded to remind the jurors that the timing of the Cranberry House blaze was exquisite. Had it occurred before the September 1 closing, there would not have been a sale. Instead, it burned during a two-week window in which the new owners had closed and purchased insurance but had not yet moved in. It was an inside job, he stressed, and only one person besides the owners had a key.

Marge had tried unsuccessfully to get the trial postponed because of Hagen's health by claiming he had suffered a heart attack and needed constant care. When it came time for him to testify, she said he was too ill to come to court. The judge allowed him to testify on videotape.

Mabley elicited some straightforward answers when he asked if Hagen knew where Marge had gone the morning of the fire. "He gave Marjorie his complete and absolute support," says Mabley. "No doubt about that, but he accidentally gave some very good evidence for the state. I think that really angered her, even though I'm sure that he didn't intentionally harm her case. He just told the truth as he knew it—on that point at least."

Meshbesher argued that it was Marge's notoriety rather than any real clue that made the investigators suspect arson. He said that the evidence indicating use of an accelerant was inconclusive. It didn't work. The jury found her guilty of both charges.

Marge remained free on appeal, but the Hagens' lifestyle was testimony to their reduced circumstances. Marge had always gone to great lengths to demonstrate that she was to the manor born. One of her signature affectations was the bestowing of names on the properties she purchased—"Cranberry House," "Homestead"—but the home she and Hagen lived in while they waited for the court of appeals to rule was named by the company that built it—Airstream. They parked it at a suburban trailer court.

In February 1983 her appeal was denied, and she began serving a thirty-month sentence in Shakopee prison. She served less than two years before she was released, and the couple headed for Arizona, where she would go on her next arson spree.

Marge was unable to make bail after her 1990 arrest in Ajo. She made repeated pleas to get her bail lowered, based on the assertion that her husband needed her care. One reason they fell on deaf ears was because Hagen seemed to be doing all right without her. His pallor disappeared. He gained weight. He stated taking short trips around Arizona with the family dog.

Marge was initially charged with the attempted arson of her neighbor Mark Indivik's home, but after she had spent more than a year in jail, a grand jury handed down another ten-count indictment, based on the arson at the Del Sur yard, in which her vehicle and three others were destroyed.

"We had good solid evidence on that case as well," says sheriff's investigator Alan. "Marge had an account at a hardware store in town, and we discovered that a couple weeks before the arson she had charged a pair of fence pliers. We found the tool at her home and sent it to our lab along with the section of fence that was cut to gain entry to the yard. The tech told us the cut marks matched perfectly."

Marge's attorney did about as well as he could, considering he had a client who had been caught red-handed trying to set a law officer's house on fire. In his opening statement he talked about the care Marge had been giving her eighty-three-year-old husband, who was fighting cancer. He told of her frequent trips to Mexico in search of the drugs she had decided he needed to survive.

"I guess the dramatic high point of the trial came when her husband arrived outside the courthouse in an ambulance," says Pima County Attorney John W. Dickinson, who prosecuted her. "They rolled him in on a gurney to testify."

Hagen told his story from a prone position. He said he couldn't rise because he suffered from bad disks and a tumor in his back. He had been operated on for cancer of the stomach a year earlier, he said, and he credited his wife, "a registered nurse," with keeping him alive.

"His testimony didn't have quite the impact it might have," says Alan, "because the jurors were being dropped off at the courthouse about the time he arrived, and they saw him walk over to the gurney and lie down."

Ajo residents were astonished that Hagen was flat on his back again, according to Gabrielle David, editor of the town's newspaper, the *Ajo Copper News*. She says he had made a remarkable recovery in Marge's absence. "For a man who was supposedly dying, he became very active while his wife was in jail," says David. "Everybody noticed. You'd see him driving around, eating out at restaurants. It was when she was at home that he seemed ill."

"It was pretty amazing," says Alan. "Up until then he was this little old man that Marge pushed around in a wheelchair. Now, all of a sudden, he's up on his feet and showing signs of what I'd call vim and vigor."

Hagen had been a sneak womanizer in his younger days. His flagging id revived while Marge was in the pokey, and he wasn't the least bit surreptitious about it.

"He was quite a flirt with the waitresses, and some of the other women," says David. "I never actually witnessed him pinching a lady's behind, but I heard he did. Would I ever stand up in court and swear that something his wife had been doing harmed the man? No, but it sure looked that way. Probably the first thing she ever told me when they arrived in town is that they'd moved here because he was dying of cancer, so we just assumed it was true."

A Tempe, Arizona, doctor who described himself as Hagen's "attending physician from 1988 through April of 1990" credited Marge with pinpointing her husband's illnesses. "I must say that Wallace's wife Marjorie C. Hagen served an important role in the identification of acute problems," he wrote the court in August 1991. "It is of benefit to Wallace to have Marjorie attentive and readily available."

Marge testified in her own behalf. Her attorney asked her why they had moved to Ajo. She told him they needed to be near Mexico so she could obtain experimental drugs for her husband. She said Hagen had endured four major cancer surgeries, numerous strokes, and suffered from an aneurysm. She denied setting fire to Indivik's house and said she had been in the yard to clean up the mess he left there, which she considered unsightly.

The jury found Marge guilty, and on June 11, 1993, she was sentenced to fifteen years in prison. Her attorney asked the judge to grant her twenty-four hours of freedom so she could make arrangements for her ailing husband. Surprisingly, he acquiesced.

"We thought she might make a run for the border," says Alan, "so there were officers posted outside her home that night."

The night passed uneventfully, but the next morning an off-duty officer rode by on a bicycle and smelled gas around the Hagens' home. He knocked on the door and told Marge about it. She explained that she had inadvertently left a burner on.

"She said everything's fine now, thank you very much, good-bye," says Alan.

Around noon, not long before Marge was due to surrender, Alan's office received a call. Hagen's son was on the line from Minnesota. He said that Marge had phoned him and told him his father was dead. He was certain Marge had murdered Hagen and asked them to enter the premises and investigate.

The officers found Hagen dead in his bed. Marge handed over a suicide note. It indicated that the two of them had decided to take their own lives together. According to Alan, Marge began babbling an explanation immediately. She claimed Hagen had been distraught at their imminent separation and wanted to die. She had promised to die with him but changed her mind.

Outside the house the officers found a piece of hose about the right length to convey gas from the tubing behind the stove to the bedroom. Marge was placed under arrest. According to Alan, she was very calm during the two-hour ride to Tucson.

"The sheriff's department sent detectives over to Ajo to investigate the death," says county attorney Dickinson. "I went over there with them. I remember that the suicide note said Wally wanted his dog buried with him, other than that it's a little hazy now. I do know that an autopsy revealed that he died of an overdose of drugs. We had no way to prove that his wife administered the drugs. That was our problem. There was a suicide note and no way to prove she did anything. I could surmise, even now, but I'm not going to."

Queried whether the autopsy revealed that Hagen had suffered from cancer, Dickinson said he would have to review the report to answer that question, and he didn't have much interest in doing so. Others including Marge's biographer and townspeople from Ajo are adamant that the autopsy showed that Wally was cancer free.

Thus, the legend of Marge the murderess thrives in Arizona, just as it does in Minnesota. Out West she is reputed to have at least two and possibly three notches on her gun.

But the doctor who treated Hagen has a different story to tell. "Mr. Hagen suffered from gastric carcinoma," he says. "One of the best oncological surgeons in this area operated on him. He tried to excise it, but he discovered that it had spread to the lymph nodes. He took out what he could, and we told Mr. Hagen there was nothing more to be done."

According to him, a large incision was required, and in the course of the operation the surgeon observed that another one of Marge's claims about her husband, that he suffered from an aneurysm, was true as well. "It didn't appear to be extremely serious," says the doctor. "There would have been few if any symptoms, and the chances of it causing him any trouble before he died of cancer were slim.

"When I first met Wallace in 1988, I thought of him as a Viking from Minnesota," the doctor says. "He was tall and good looking, but by the time we decided to operate, he had just wasted away. After the operation we advised him to get on with his life. We told him he had about six months. He took it very well. He said he was really itching to get on the road and hoped he could regain enough strength to drive again. Apparently he did. I remember getting postcards from him."

So the resurrection of Hagen had nothing to do with his wife's incarceration. The timing was simply coincidental. He recovered better and lasted longer than either his doctor or his surgeon thought he would, and made the most of it.

"I once remarked about that to the surgeon," says the doctor. "We agreed that we talk to patients about their prognosis as if they're statistics, but they aren't. They're people, with their own unique chemistry, and their own will to live, or not to live. So who the hell knows?"

He said he had always found Marge to be knowledgeable about her husband's condition, and about illness in general. "She may well have been giving him alternative medicines of some kind from Mexico," he says. "That's not unusual around here. From what I saw of Mrs. Hagen, she was like thousands of other people from Minnesota that we see in Arizona. Kind of stolid and matter-of-fact. I thought she was trying to get away from the snow, that's all."

Once county attorney Dickinson and his staff decided not to prosecute Marge for murder, they offered her a deal. She pleaded guilty to all charges stemming from the arson at the Del Sur yard and received no additional time. She was released from the Arizona Prison for Women in January 2004, at the age of seventy-two, having spent a total of thirteen years behind bars, in two states. She is said to be living in the Tucson area. No one who is privy to her affairs was willing to discuss her financial situation, but she will probably be just fine. She's an heiress.

A Note on Sources and Previous Publication

Two stories, "The Difference" and "Portrait of an Heiress at the End of Her Career," were written for this book. The others were previously published as noted but have been updated and substantially revised for publication here.

"The Family That Couldn't Sleep at Night"

This story was serialized in *Sweet Potato*, a Twin Cities weekly, in 1981.

I interviewed William C. Rieman, a retired Minneapolis police detective who worked on the case. He was clearly torn between his desire to talk about it and his reluctance to help publicize the complicated circumstances surrounding the lives of the O'Kasicks and what he still considered to be the worst crime he ever investigated. Jerry Roy remembered James O'Kasick from his Franklin Avenue days. Sheila Hegna, who grew up near the family, said the O'Kasick brothers' father, Mike, was a mean drunk who had his kids boosting car parts and selling them at the Washington Avenue junkyards before they were in the fourth grade. James Crawford, former head of the Minnesota Highway Patrol, still had a vivid recollection of the day he gunned down Roger and Ronald O'Kasick. Richard O'Kasick kindly gave me copies of two unpublished manuscripts for reference, "The Birth of James O'Kasick" and "Behind the Red Flats," his memoir of his family.

Minneapolis police records and Anoka County court transcripts were helpful, as were newspaper articles in the *Minneapolis Star, Minneapolis Tribune, St. Paul Pioneer Press,* and *St. Paul Dispatch*. To clarify, the friend of the O'Kasick family quoted in a *St. Paul Dispatch* article misstated the year of Mrs. O'Kasick's death.

"Happenstance"

This story was serialized in *Pulse*, a Twin Cities weekly, in February 2000.

I interviewed Frank Mendoza in Oak Park Heights Prison. I have seen bigger guys, but they were a long way off and wearing football uniforms. Judith Sims remembers her encounter with Mendoza, Jackson, and company quite well. It happened so fast she didn't have time to be afraid. I also talked to Ben Richards, the off-duty policeman who rescued her; Howard Brandby, the father of one of the victims; Randy Nordling, who knew them both; and Robert Streitz, who prosecuted Mendoza and Jackson for Hennepin County.

The story contains facts gleaned from transcripts of police interviews with Robert Jackson and other court documents, including a March 1989 complaint from Oklahoma charging Mendoza with assault with intent to kill Eugene Watson.

"Miss Abyss"

Earlier versions of this story were printed in *Twin Cities Magazine* in September 1988 and the *Minnesota Law Journal* in March 1989.

Ed Wittkopp's parents, Nadine Wittkopp and Dr. Thomas Wittkopp, agreed to be interviewed for this story although they were obviously pained to do so. My thanks to them. Attorney Thomas Bauer was very forthcoming about his former client Anna Vanderford. Attorney Ron Meshbesher, who represented her on appeal, had less to say. Prosecutor Stephen Redding and Ed's friends Paul Teien, Jeff Wyman, and Tod Sigler provided important information. Vanderford spoke to me briefly, and several of her ex-lovers spoke at length (but didn't want their names to appear).

"The Courtship of Linda Winbush"

This story was originally published in *Minnesota Journal of Law and Politics* in May 1991.

I interviewed Dick Oakes and two other lawyers who knew both Leonard Richards and R. T. Stratton, the attorney Richards murdered. I also relied on district court documents connected with Richards's trials and appeals, several of which were written by Richards, and Minneapolis police reports concerning the murders of May Wilson and R. T. Stratton.

"A Marriage of Convenience"

This story was published in *Minnesota Monthly* magazine in July 2001.

My interview with Michael Gianakos was revealing. I have rarely interviewed a prisoner who said he was guilty, but some are more convincing than others. Michael struck me as a person who might be easily led, but the prosecution's case rests on the assumption that he planned, organized, and executed a cold-blooded murder in plain view of his own children. Baloney. Michael's sister Tracy Lowrance provided some interesting documents, including Jamie Dennis-Gianakos's writings. The prose is good, but the picture that emerges of the author is not very flattering. Diane Mellis, Jamie's aunt, and Troy Hackett, a former boyfriend, portrayed her as a sociopath. Attorney Rick Henderson was helpful. Investigator Dave Bjerga was not. The story contains information from Jamie Dennis-Gianakos's notebooks and journals, *Fargo Forum* newspaper articles, and court records.

"The Orchid Murder"

This story was published in the *Minnesota Journal of Law and Politics* in May 1990.

I interviewed Betty Nachtscheim at length. She believes she knows who killed her husband, but she wishes her beliefs could be validated in court, which will never happen. Her daughter Teri Peters was especially enlightening about Russ Krueger. Norman Wartnick says he is not guilty. If he is, then he is a bold intrepid killer—and he doesn't look the part. Ron Meshbesher succinctly described the legal machinations surrounding the several civil cases stemming from the murder, and Inspector Sherman Otto of the Minneapolis police was blunt and matter-of-fact about a less than sterling investigation.

I also consulted Minneapolis police reports found in court documents from the civil trial of Wartnick and the malpractice case against his attorney Phil Gainsley, plus the records of those cases. The Minneapolis police file is closed because the case is technically open. That is a maddening legalism because it is not and never will be investigated, but no big loss, because Russ Krueger "lost" most of it anyway.

"Danny's Boat"

This story was serialized in *City Pages* in 1986.

I had many conversations over the years with the following people and used what they told me liberally: Danny Seymour, Paco Grande, Steve Arhelger, Jay Hines, Chris Hamley, Phyllis Cooney, Roland Flint, and James Wright. Others who were interviewed specifically for this story include George Gardner (brief), Steve Kaplan, Ted Hartwell, and Kate Moore. Kaplan was particularly helpful.

Entire pages of the FBI file *Daniel Seymour and Robert Breckenridge—Crime on the High Seas* are blacked out, but plenty of information was still there. The reasons cited for many of the redactions was that they would jeopardize a U.S. intelligence operation, which the search for Danny was not—or was it? Clearly there is a thin line when the former CEO of United Fruit is involved. The *Report of the U.S. Senate's Select Committee on Assassinations* (citations 118–26) was enlightening regarding Richard Cain.

I have copies in my possession of Isabella Gardner's letters to Kate Moore and the letter from "Rico" dated August 23, 1973.

The following articles were useful: "Yacht Hijacking: The Deep Six Connection," by Howard Kohn and Clark Norton, *Rolling Stone,* January 1976; "Richard Cain and the Castro Plots," by Michael Cain, *Back Channels,* September 1994; articles in the *Chicago Tribune* and the *Chicago Sun-Times* about the murder of Richard Cain in December 1973, and a *Time* magazine story about Cain's murder dated January 7, 1974; "The Ripe Problems of United Fruit," by Herbert Solow, *Fortune,* March 1959.

Finally, I consulted three books: *A Loud Song,* by Daniel Seymour; *The Fish Is Red: The Story of the Secret War against Castro,* by Warren Hinckle and William Turner; and *An American Company,* by Thomas McCann (a history of United Fruit).

"The Difference"

Lieutenant Arlen Holland, a police detective for the city of Minnetonka, was helpful. Something that didn't get into the story was his remark that he wished he had gotten to know Russell Lund Jr. because he seemed like an interesting person. Hennepin County Sheriff's Detective Charles Kelly was concise and to the point about the obstruction of justice investigation that was aborted when Lund committed suicide. He stands by the record, and the record speaks for itself. Richard Setter, former chief of the Minnetonka police, is a private investigator who handles sensitive issues for wealthy clients, which leaves him neither the time nor the inclination to discuss things with writers. Attorneys David Rosten, Joe Friedberg, and Peter Watson gave someone their word that they wouldn't tell what they knew about Lund's whereabouts and activities after the murders. I don't know how they'd stand up to torture, but they stood up admirably to me.

The Minnetonka police file on the murders of Barbara Lund and E. Kevin Kelly is six hundred pages long and full of useful information. *Minneapolis Star Tribune* articles about the murders and the Flight Transportation Corp. affair were helpful, as was the videotape of a speech by FBI counsel Coleen Rowley in January 2003 at the Hamline University Law School.

"A Prayer for Uncle Charlie"

This story was published in *Twin Cities Magazine*, October 1985.

I had short interviews with Yvette Ward, Charlie Ward's widow, and Richard Rupp, who worked for Ward and knew him personally. Willis Miller, editor of the Hudson, Wisconsin, *Observer,* talked about Ward. He remembered Ward's excellent horsemanship and recalled Ward's habit of going to bars in Hudson, buying people drinks, and getting them to talk about what was going on around town.

I used information from articles in Twin Cities newspapers; "The Third Party Gets a Rich Uncle," by Jack Alexander, an article in the *Saturday Evening Post* in September 1938; and "The Last Tycoon," by John D. Thornton, an article in *The Counselor,* a specialty advertising trade magazine, in January 1983. I consulted histories of the Mexican revolution and of the states of Nevada and Arizona, as well as two books: *Stopping the Presses,* by Marda Liggett Woodbury; and *The Gonif,* by Morris "Red" Rudensky and Don Riley.

"Portrait of an Heiress at the End of Her Career"

Attorney Ron Meshbesher, who represented Marge in two trials, was the only person who had anything good to say about his client. David Alan of the Pima County, Arizona, sheriff's department provided interesting insights about the investigation of the arsons in Ajo, Arizona, and how they affected that community, as did Gabrielle David, editor of the *Ajo Copper News.* Howard Caldwell, Roger Caldwell's brother, sounded like a man who wanted to believe the best about his brother. Dan Mabley, who prosecuted Marge in Hennepin County, Minnesota, was kind enough to correspond with me by e-mail from Kosovo, where he was involved in war crimes trials. Pima County Attorney John W. Dickinson, who prosecuted Marge in Arizona, stuck to the facts. He indicated, without saying so directly, that he had taken some heat for not prosecuting Marge for the murder of Wally Hagen. Hagen's Arizona physician, the author of several documents that are part of the court record, spoke with me on condition that his name not be used. In my opinion what he told me proves conclusively that if Marge killed Hagen, she did it as an act of mercy.

The investigators' reports from Minnesota and Arizona were helpful. So was *Glensheen's Daughter: The Marjorie Congdon Story,* by Sharon Darby Hendry.

Bruce Rubenstein is a writer who specializes in true crime and legal stories. His work has appeared in many publications, including *City Pages, Minnesota Journal of Law and Politics, Mpls St. Paul Magazine,* and *Chicago Magazine.* He has received several prizes, including the Chicago Bar Association's Herman Kogan Media Award.